Criminal Justice Through The Ages

From divine judgement to modern German legislation

D1239436

Published and distributed by: Mittelalterliches Kriminalmuseum
Burggasse 3, D 8803 Rothenburg o.d.T.
Federal Republic of Germany
Telephone: 09861/5359

„ERLASSEN ABER SIND DIE GE-
SETZE, DAMIT AUS FURCHT VOR
IHNEN DIE MENSCHLICHE BOS-
HEIT IM ZAUME GEHALTEN UND
DIE UNSCHULD UNTER DEN EHR-
BAREN GESICHERT, DAGEGEN
UNTER DEN BÖSWILLIGEN DURCH
DIE FURCHT VOR DER STRAFE
DIE GELEGENHEIT SCHADEN ZU
STIFTEN, EINGEDÄMMT WERDEN"

LEX BAIUVARIORUM UM 740

Translation
But the laws are promulgated so that out of fear of them human wickedness may
be held in check and purity among the upright may be safeguarded, whereas
among the wicked fear of punishment may restrain their disposition to cause harm
or injury.

Criminal Justice
Through The Ages

From divine judgement to modern German legislation

Translated by John Fosberry

Du solt nit falsche zeügknüß geben
Als lieb dir sey das ewig leben.

Court Session, Bamberg Halsgerichtsordnung, 1508

(Scroll text:) Thou shalt not give false witness as eternal
life is dear to thee.

Volume IV
of the publications of the
Mediaeval Crime Museum, Rothenburg ob der Tauber

(C)1981 by Mittelalterliches Kriminalmuseum, Rothenburg o.d.T.
Printed by Druckerei Schulist, Heilsbronn

Printed in W. Germany

Contents

Note: Except where otherwise specifically stated, the pictures, documents and exhibits reproduced in this book are in the possession of the Crime Museum in Rothenburg o. T.

A bibliography has been omitted intentionally, as the relevant literature is exclusively German. Readers interested in the literature should refer to the German edition.

Foreword

This volume is the English edition of the German book „Strafjustiz in alter Zeit", one of the publications of the „Mittelalterliches Kriminalmuseum" in Rothenburg ob der Tauber, West Germany. The crime museum in Rothenburg is the only historical law museum in the Federal Republic of Germany and collects and preserves antique objects relating to the law of the 12th to 19th century from the European and especially the German-speaking area. The function of the museum would be only incompletely fulfilled, however, if it were to limit itself to making the museum exhibits accessible to the public. Only the scientific evaluation of the vast amount of material and publication in a book that everybody can understand can enable museum visitors and those who have not yet seen it to grasp the history, that is, the development of the law.

The development of German law, an important, integral part of European legal history, must not be regarded as being restricted solely to Germany. The early epoch of European law, a period in which there were as yet no states, was characterized by the various bodies of tribal law. Though the latter were not uniform, they were similar in many respects. They differed only in the allowances made for the natural conditions in the area of settlement (e.g. at the sea coast different conditions prevailed than in the mountains) and for the specific characteristics of the tribe. The law of the Anglo-Saxons (present-day England) differed therefore only slightly from that of the Alemanni (present-day Switzerland). In the vast empire of Emperor Charles the Great (768-814), which extended from the Ebro (Spain) in the west to the Oder (Poland) in the east, and from the North Sea down to Rome, thus embracing the heart of Europe, there was already a fundamentally uniform European law in the shape of the Capitularies and, in particular, the courts everywhere had a similar make-up (courts with lay assessors). In the late Middle Ages, when Europe was already divided into territorial states, the national bodies of law evolved under the marked influence of Roman law. In their turn, these national laws gave new impetus to each other, that is, new findings in the one system were taken over by the others. The European states' policy of conquest (colonial policy) exported European law to the overseas possessions (Spain to South America, England and France to North America, etc.), where the later independent, new states took it over into their own legislation.

It is the object of this book to present an outline of this development as exemplified by the legal history of the German-speaking territories. Naturally, it reflects specifically German legal conditions, but in many respects what is recounted here is applicable also to the legal history of the other European countries.

This book was published in German in spring 1980. Its good reception and the large numbers of museum visitors from English-speaking countries have persuaded us to bring out an English version. We trust that it will be as well received as the German original.

In conclusion, I would like to express my sincere thanks to all, especially the translator and the institutions, whose co-operation made this book possible.

Rothenburg o.d.T., in spring 1981

The Editor
Christoph Hinckeldey

etching by H. Rosemann

The Building of the Former Commandery of the Order of the Hospital of St. John of Jerusalem in Rothenburg ob der Tauber

The Order of the Hospital of St. John is the oldest religious order of knights and was founded in the 12th century. The object of the order was and still is the care of the sick. In about 1200, the knights of St. John moved into the rural area of Rothenburg, and in the 14th century into the town itself. Between 1393 and 1410, the building of the commandery and the adjacent St. John's church were built. In 1718, the commandery building received its present form (baroque). Following the secularization of 1803, i.e., the dissolution of the religious territories and priories, it passed into the possession of the Bavarian state and served as an administration building. In the course of an administrative reform in 1973, the building became vacant. Extensive restoration work converted the building, which is a protected monument, for museum purposes. Since 1977, it has been the home of the Mittelalterliches Kriminalmuseum. Thus, in the mediaeval town of Rothenburg ob der Tauber with its abundance of architectural monuments, a historic building has been put to a use in keeping with its importance.

6

History of German Lawmaking

by
Prof. Dr. Dr. Friedrich Merzbacher

In the Germanic epoch of our legal history and development, the law as a public peace code was essentially unwritten customary law. Rules of law were developed in the course of legal practice and mainly handed down by word of mouth. The bulk of Germanic law was manifestly pure tribal law rather than statute law. Our knowledge of legal conditions in the Germanic domain is derived not so much from statutory norms, but rather from observations of Roman writers like Caesar and Tacitus.

The entry of the Germanic tribes into world politics as state-forming peoples from the 5th century onwards went hand in hand with codification of their laws (leges germanorum). But for those codifications they, too, used Latin, the universal language of the Middle Ages, although the language of the courts was not Latin but Germanic. The most important recordings of late Germanic law are found in the Frankish sources, the so-called "folk" or tribal laws, the leges barbarorum. The earliest codification of Frankish, and hence German, law is the Lex Salica*. At the same time, it is the most famous of all tribal laws. The oldest version of the Lex Salica that has come down to us is the 65-chapter text, which reflects kingship as it existed in France (1) up to the death of Clovis* in 511. Since it also touches upon the Frankish dominion south of the Loire, which was set up after the West Gothic war of 507, the oldest version of the Lex Salica must have been compiled between 507 and 511. Frankish legal terms were inserted in the Lex Salica in the form of the Malberg glosses (2). The Lex Ripuaria, i.e., the law of the riparian Franks, was probably compiled during the reign of Pippin III in the period from 743 to 751. However, it seems that this source of law was

(1) The area of settlement and sovereignty of the west Germanic Franks. At the time of Clovis I it covered: present-day Belgium, Luxembourg, France (with the exception of Burgundy, the Provence and Gascogne), both sides of the Rhine from Basle to the German-Dutch frontier and both sides of the Main almost to the Czech frontier.

(2) The Malberg glosses comprised explanatory interpolations in the Latin text of the Lex Salica, which contained technical terms customarily used before Frankish courts. Malberg = court hill, court locale.

not developed uniformly, but from heterogeneous elements. Some researchers therefore place the origin of the Lex Ripuaria in the 7th century. But also the other tribes of the great Frankish empire compiled codifications of their laws. In addition to that of the Rhenish Franks, i.e. the Salians and Ripuarians, the Alemanni, Saxons, Friesians and Thuringians, the Bavarian law that has been handed down is by no means the least important. The Lex Baiuvariorum numbers among those laws of which abundant records have come down to us. The research work of Konrad Beyerle indicates that the Benedictine monastery at Niederaltaich on the Danube played an important part in the drafting of this lex. Decisive impetus for the drafting of the law was probably given by Eberwind, the first abbot of the monastery, which was established in 741. It seems highly probable that the Lex Baiuvariorum was compiled between 730 and 744, that is, presumably under the rule of the Bavarian duke Odilo. On the surface, this lex seems to be the product of the then prevailing political "balance of power". No less a person than the already mentioned German law expert, Konrad Beyerle, has rightly emphasized that its language is "not the language of a ruler, but the phraseology of a moralizing writer". Although the then duchy of Bavaria was regarded as part of the Frankish empire, no strong political pressure on the tribal duchy is perceptible.

It was not without good reason that this people under Frankish rule was to be governed by a law in keeping with its customs. In this instance, however, the ecclesiasical influence on the wording of the lex seems to be remarkably strong. The law itself is subdivided into three sections: church matters - ducal matters - people's matters, though the king, being the Frankish law-giver, was of pre-eminent importance.

Apart from the tribal or "folk" laws, the most important sources of law in the Frankish empire were, above all, the capitularies promulgated from the Carolingian* epoch onwards. In principle, they constituted territorial law; they had unlimited territorial and temporal validity. These law sources were named capitularies because they were divided into capitula (chapters), although designations such as edict, decree, precept and constitution were quite customary. Roughly speaking, the capitularies constituted the king's law as distinct from the people's law. In the capitulary legislation, royal interdictory power was able to take effect in the law-making sector. Depending on their content, a distinction is drawn between secular capitularies (capitularia mundana) and ecclesiastical capitularies (capitularia ecclesiastica). The secular capitularies are classified in three groups: besides additions to tribal law, there were independent royal decrees conflicting with tribal law, which were supple-

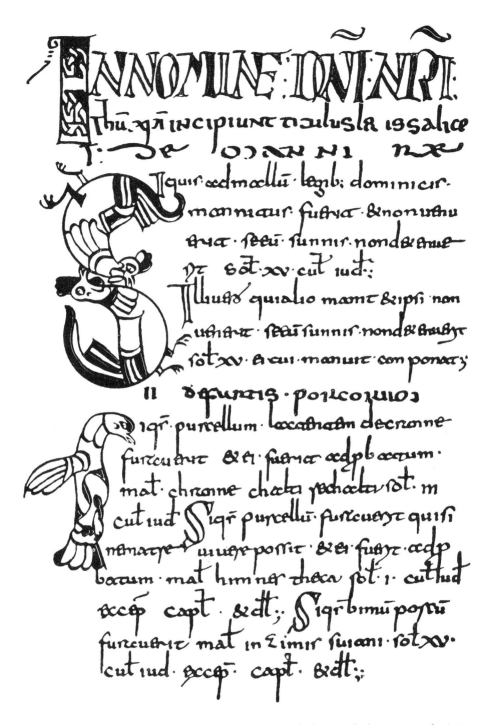

Lex Salica, the law promulgated by the founder of the Frankish empire, Clovis I (481 - 511). First page of a St. Gallen manuscript dating from 793, Stiftsbibliothek St. Gallen.

mented by a third category, namely instructions to the Frankish king's emissaries, i.e. the holders of royal powers in France. Within the framework of capitulary legislation, the king collaborated closely with the people. The capitularies supplementing tribal law applied exclusively to those subject to the tribal law concerned. Numerous capitularies were promulgated at the Frankish imperial diets after previous consultation with the magnates of the empire. The researchers have not succeeded in finding authentic copies of the capitularies. With the mention of a written law, the capitularies deliberately made reference to tribal law recorded in writing. It is remarkable, however, that the Frankish imperial chancellery possessed no well-ordered official collection of the capitularies. This explains why more or less official authority was soon gained by a private work, the collection of capitularies of Ansegisus of Fontanelle, abbot of St. Wandrille in the bishopric of Rouen, which dates from 827.

In the history of German law-making, by no means the least of the sources deserving special consideration are the so-called "law books". Law books comprise, not official enactments, but rather original private studies to which, however, legal practice and court usage have to a great extent accorded statute-like authority and evidentiary capacity. Since all-embracing codifications* of law were lacking, particularly these private treatments of law, the law books, assumed an important role in the history of German law-making, especially since they provided a clear picture of customary law in major realms of law. The law books were widely distributed and on account of their authoritative nature often formed the basis for judgments once they had taken over the role of the former, oral recitation of the law. On no account must it be forgotten that precisely the regional common law (Landrecht*) that was of such great importance later on was almost completely lacking. Consequently, for the bodies of regional common law special significance attaches to what was far and away the most important German law book in the 13th century, the Sachsenspiegel (Saxon mirror) compiled about 1225.

The Sachsenspiegel was the earliest major prose work written in German. In essence, it was a purely private compilation which contained the common law and feudal law, and later became statutory law and the source of Saxon common law*. In contrast to many mediaeval works, the name of the author of the Sachsenspiegel has come down to us. He was the East Saxon knight Eike von Repgow, born about 1180 and vassal of the steward of Quedlinburg abbey, Count Hoyer von Falkenstein, at whose request the compiler reluctantly translated his original Latin text, which is no longer extant, into German. The Sachsenspiegel text includes in its common law not only private and penal law, but also procedural and

Es hilligen geiſtes myn ne dei ſterke myne ſynne dat ik recht vñ vnrecht der ſaſſen beſcheyde na godes huldē vnde der werlde vromē Des en kan yck allene nicht vullēbrēgē Dar vine ſo bid— de ick to hulpe alle gude lude de ſchtes begert Oſſ eymant de rede bey egēde de myne dū— me ſyne vmdede dar dit boek nicht aff enſpreke·dat ſei dat beſchedē woldē na orē ſynnen ſo ſe dat ſchtes wettē· wente ſcht en ſal neymant wiſen na leyff noch leit to hebbē ·noch tozn noch giffte· wēte got ys ſuluē dat ſcht· dar vine is em dat ſcht laiff Hir vine ſcy ſey to deme geſchte dē dat vā go des wegen beuolen is· dat ſcy alſo richtē dat godes geſchte vñ tozn ouer ſe genetlikē gaē mote·:· Artioul? ·ꝑm? Got de dar is ey begȳ vnde ende aller gudē dige de dar erſten ma kede hēmel vñ erdē· dē miſchē in ertrike vñ ſatte ene in dat padijs· welker brak dē horſa vnſ allen to ſchaden dar vine

The Sachsenspiegel by Eike von Repgow, the tribal law of the Saxons (settlement area: the region surrounding present-day Hannover), compiled ca. 1225, lower German edition, Cologne, Bartholomäus Unkel, 1480.

public law. It has come down to us from numerous sources and was widely disseminated, from the Netherlands to Poland and Russia, where it was used by councillors and judges as a basis for decisions. Illustrated manuscripts have provided us knowledge of legal proceedings, legal figures, legal behaviour and legal conditions in the Middle Ages. The chief examples are the Heidelberg Illuminated Manuscript written prior to 1315 and the Dresden Illuminated Manuscript which was drawn up in the vicinity of Meissen, Saxony, between 1350 and 1370. In southern Germany, the counterpart of the Sachsenspiegel was the Schwabenspiegel (Swabian Mirror), which was authored about 1275 by an Augsburg minorite and, like its north German prototype, contains common and feudal law. The name Schwabenspiegel is indicative of the provincial character of this law book. For all its more superficial content, the Schwabenspiegel cannot deny its derivation from the more thorough Sachsenspiegel. Moreover, in the field of common law, great importance was attained by the Upper Bavarian common law promulgated by Emperor Louis IV the Bavarian in 1346, one of the early codifications of southern German private law. It was not until 1481, however, that is was printed officially for the first time. Occasion may frequently have been given for codification of the law prevailing in certain cities by non-resident merchants and visitors who sought justice before the city courts. Only by laying down the city statutes in writing was it possible to ensure certainty of the law for persons attending the market and strangers staying in the city. Not without good reason, Hans Patze recently pointed out that also "the distrust of the various social groups into which the towns became split up in the 13th and 14th century" lent impetus to codification of local city law. City law itself derived partly from "Willküren"*, partly from personal prerogatives and partly from passages in the received common law books. In the course of the reception of Roman law, that is foreign law, the common law and city laws were revised and romanized, impregnated with borrowed elements of Roman law. For example, the Nuremberg Reformation of 1479* set out to harmonize the content of Roman law with German legal terminology and, as Wolfgang Kunkel puts it, to clothe "the foreign terminology in purely German style".After mature consideration by learned doctors and the review of the written common law, the Nuremberg Reformation itself was compared with the customs and usages of the imperial city of Nuremberg and then promulgated. Above all, it formed the basis for decisions of the secular judges and courts.

The mediaeval legislation based legal jurisdiction on the status of the German king as successor to the Roman imperators. According to mediaeval ideology, the emperor, being the living incarnation of law, the animate law so to speak, personified the high authority of imperial law.

Dis buch ſaget ſummarie von kunglichē
vñ keyſerlichē dazzu landt vñ lehen rechtē

Err gott hymeliſcher vatter durch
dein milte güte geſchliffeſtt du den
menſchen mit treſualtiger wirdig=
keyt, Die erſt dz er nach dir ge
bildet iſt dz iſt eyn alſo hohe wirde
der dir alles mēſchlich knye ymer
dancken ſol· wann des haben wir
michel recht. Vil lieber herr hyme=
liſchez vattez ſeid du vns zu deinez
hohen gothept alſo wirdigktlich ge
adelt haſt Die andern wirdigkeyt da du herr almäch
tiger ſchöpffer den menſchen zu geſchaffen haſt dz iſt die
das du alle diſe welt die ſunnen vnd den mon die ſteren
vnd die vier element feur waſſer lufft vnd erdtreich vñ
die vogel in den lüfften·die viſch in dem wage·die tier in
dem walde die würm in der erde·gold vnd edels geſteyn
der edlen würtz ſüſſen geſchmack·der blümē liechte farb
der baumen früchten vnd alle creatur. Das haſt du herr
alles dem menſchen zu dienſt vnnd zu nutz geſchaffen
durch die trew vnd miñe die du zu dem menſchen heteſt
Die dzit wirdigkeyt das iſt die das du herr den men
ſchen da mit gewirdet vnnd geadelt haſt das der menſch
die wirde vnd die ere die freud vnd wunne die du ſelbez
biſt ymmer ewigktlicheu mit dir nieſſen ſol,Der welt zu
dienſt vnd zu nutz haſtu herr dem menſchen vmb ſunſt
gegeben zu eyner manung vnd zu eynem worbild· ſeidt
des ſo vil iſt das du herr dem menſchē vmb ſunſt gegebē
haſt, Darnach ſol d mēſch trachtē wie gar noch vnmäſ=
ſig vil güthept ſeyē die du dē menſchē vmb dienſt geben
wilt, Vnd darumb ſol eyn yegktlich menſch gott dienen
mit rechtem ernſt vnd mit gantzen trewen· wañ der lon
iſt als vbermäſſigktlichen groß das nie hertz noch ſinn be
trachten mocht noch nie menſchē mund geſprechē kund
noch augen geſehē kund es nie beleuchten noch oze nye
gehözen das wir gott der hohē wirdigkeyt gedanckē vñ
den groſſē lon verdienē·des helff vns der almächtig got,

a 2

Schwabenspiegel, compiled about 1275 in Augsburg. The tribal law of the Swabians (settlement area: southern Germany, alpine foreland region); no data on printer, place and year, possibly Johann Zainer, Ulm, ca. 1479.

The emperor himself was not bound by human law, but rather dissociated from traditional law, so that on the basis of the Roman Digest * (a collection of Roman laws) he was glorified as the princeps legibus solutus (the originator - prince - of free law). According to the lapidary assertion of Ulpian, one of the great Roman classic authors, all that was the emperor's will and pleasure attained the force of law. The emperor as source and centre of the law also fitted in with conceptions of the late Hohenstaufen epoch (13th century). Furthermore, the emperor was held even by the Sachsenspiegel to be every man's supreme judge. Therefore he could also apply the norms he had previously laid down. The emperor alone could construe and interpret unclear law correctly and lend it authenticity. The imperial legislation under the later Hohenstaufens was of decisive importance for the development of national sovereignty in Germany. It was the "emperor by virtue of the law", Friedrich II (1212 - 1250), who energetically paved the way for the development of the constitution and the law. With the Frankfurt enactment on regal privileges of April 26, 1220, the imperial monarch waived the right of "spoil" (the right to confiscate the personal estate of deceased Catholic priests in favour of the sovereign) and regalian rights (rights reserved to the king - emperor - such as right of coinage, right to levy duties, market rights, etc.) in favour of the princes of the church. Since the secular sword was wielded in support of the spiritual sword, and the secular powers therefore had to support the church, proscription by the church, i.e. excommunication, was to be followed automatically within eight weeks by imperial proscription *. The sovereign further laid down that no buildings, castles or towns were permitted to be set up on church ground, either to serve the purposes of any governor or on any other pretext. With this law the emperor made very substantial concessions to the princes of the church within the empire, especially the German prince bishops, which were to have an impact on constitutional law. The statute of Emperor Frederick II in favour of the princes, which was issued in May 1232 near Cividale de Friuli in Venetia, Italy, prohibited the building of castles or the establishment of towns to the prejudice of princes. Furthermore, this imperial enactment, which is attributable to the influence of Würzburg, ordained that the centgraves * should receive their hundreds * from the local sovereign. In the public peace law of Mainz of August 15./ 21, 1235, Frederick II ordered that all princes and all vested with court jurisdiction by the king should administer justice impartially. The sovereign further commanded that the use of the highways be permitted and that on them violence should be done to no man. The imperial public peace law of Mainz additionally protected the freedoms of the churches and prescribed that proctors (Vogt) should be in charge of all houses of God. At the same time, the emperor appointed his own court judge, who

Arolus der fierde mitt gunste

götlicher miltikeit Römiſcher keiſer·Alletzpt merer
des rpchs·vnd künig zů Beheim·Des vmges zů ewi
gem gedencken·Em pegclich rpch das jn ſichſelber
geteilt iſt/das würt zerſtört·Wann ſpn fürſte ſint
worden der diebe geſellen Darum̃ hat got mitten vn
der ſp gemiſchet einen ſchwindelgeiſt/das ſp ſich ſtoſſent an dem mit
tentage/als jn dem fünſteren·Vnd hat ir kertzſtal bewegt·von ſiner
ſtat·vnd ſint blind·vnd fürer der blinden·Vnd wer jn dem finſteren
geet der ſtoſſet ſich·Vnd mit blinden gedencken begeend ſp vil miſſe
tat/die jn der teilunge geſchehent·Sage du hochfart wie mechteſtu
an lucifer geherſchet han/hetteſtu zertrennunge nit zůhulff geban·
Sage du npdiger tüffel/wie heteſtu adam vſʒ dem paradiſe geworf
fen/hetteſtu jn nit von gehorſame geſcheiden·Sage du vnkůſcheite/
wie mechteſtu Troy han zerſtöret/hetteſtu die frawen Ibelenam nitt
von irem manne geſcheiden·Sage zorn/wie kündeſtu das römiſch ge
meine güt zerſtöret han/hetteſtu nit von der zweiunge Pompii vnnd
a ij

The Golden Bull of Emperor Charles IV, (see caption of illus., p.124), 1356; printed
by Joh. Prüss, Strassbourg, 1485.

had to be a free man. This judge of the royal court was to employ a special clerk to keep records of the proscriptions and the "bloody", or criminal, judgments. This clerk had to be a layman, since matters connected with criminal court preceedings could not be handled by the clergy. On the other hand, interpretations of law in the Imperial Diet (Reichsweistümer — opinions and explanations relating to the prevailing law which were originally handed down orally and from the late Middle Ages onwards were also recorded in writing.) did not, as a rule, take general effect, unlike the rulings in individual cases in which the imperial German supreme court formally established rights which subsequently attained general validity. Recently, however, Bernhard Diestelkamp rightly stated that there is no group of such interpretations which "on the strength of their abstract formulation should and could have had a general impact". The "Reichsweistümer", therefore, cannot be regarded as normative sources in the true sense of the word.

One law was to attain the highest constitutional relevance for centuries. I refer to the Aurea Bulla, the so-called Golden Bull of Emperor Charles IV, dating from 1356.

This Golden Bull was quite certainly not the outcome of oppositional currents, but the result of the emperor's will with the consent of the German electors (seven principalities of the Holy Roman Empire were electoral principalities, i. e., their sovereigns (electors) had the exclusive right to elect the new emperor (king). Two electors together ruled the empire in times in which there was no emperor, e. g. from the death of one up to the election of the new emperor), whose position was decisively strengthened by this basic law. It has long been known that the initiative for the promulgation of the Golden Bull came from the emperor who, as Karl Zeumer once emphasized perfectly accurately, must be "regarded as the law-giver in the truest and fullest sense". The Object of the imperial monarch was to promote the general welfare of the empire by legal safeguards for the election of the king, by bringing about unity in the electoral college (the consultative assembly of the seven electors entitled to elect the king) and, not least, by safeguarding peace and order in the empire. The pre-eminent object of the Golden Bull of 1356 was to set up rules for the election of the German king. One of the chief intentions of the law-giver, however, was to strengthen the electoral principalities. The main aim of the entire legislation was to ensure the unanimous, conflict-free election of the imperial monarch. In their electoral oath, the electors, i. e., those princes entitled to vote, had to promise to give the nation a secular sovereign. The law made no provision for an election during the lifetime of the emperor. The electors had to swear an oath that they would

Inclyta pontificum legitans decreta sacrorum:
Ocia nunc felix dulcia lector habes.
Hellespontiacis mei gi deberet in vndis:
Vsus tam nitidum carpere liuor opus.
Qil facit ad terfos cumulata pecunia libros.
Nulla tenet similes bibliotheca notas.
Eximum totua si spectes fronte volumen:
Secula per cuncta viuito lucis egens.

Cecas sub latebras que sunt vitiata recõdens:
Huc oculos iuuenis porrige docte tuos.
Anceps/aut trücü nihil ista volumina geftant.
Deligno credas lingula digna ftilo.
Quualido Thelmäne sagar munimine fultus:
Imbo peregrina conteret arma tuus.
Iamq videbūtur tectis pendentia summis:
Sumpta tua nuper clara trophea manu.

Corpus Iuris Canonici, collective term for the unified collections of canon law from the period from about 1140 up to the end of the 15th century.
The woodcut shows the title page of "Decretales domini pape Gregorii noni". Paris 1518.

elect the successor as sovereign of the empire at their own free discretion without any previous compacts or agreements. Incidentally, this basic law was named after the golden seal that was affixed to the original. On one side it bears a picture of the emperor on a throne with crown, sceptre and orb, on the other the emperor's shield with the eagle and lion and the Aurea Roma as a stylized twin-turreted citadel. The Golden Bull numbered among the fundamental laws of the Holy Roman Empire, which the emperor had to promise to observe in his electoral capitulation (the assurances given under seal by the candidate to the electors for the event of his election). The first 23 chapters of this law went into force in Nuremberg, the remainder being added in the same year, 1356, in Metz.

The reform legislation of Emperor Maximilian I at the Diet of Worms in 1495 was also of great significance for the legislative of the old empire. On August 7, 1495, the monarch proclaimed the so-called "perpetual peace". From the time of the proclamation of perpetual peace onwards, no one was to carry on feuds or war against others, or rob or take them captive or besiege them, or take towns, markets, fortifications, villages, farms and hamlets by force or sack them. Any person wishing to assert a claim against another was to do so exclusively through the courts. Those guilty of contraventions were subject to imperial proscription (expulsion from the law-protected, "peace" community as a punishment for criminals. The proscribed person was outlawed, i. e. anybody could kill him with impunity). The accommodation and sheltering of those who broke the peace was likewise forbidden. On the same day, the law on the Imperial Chamber (Reichskammergericht — the Imperial Chamber's jurisdiction embraced breaches of the peace, imperial proscription, and tax law; at the same time it was the court of last resort for appeals from all regional and town courts, except where the local sovereign had the privilege of handing down non-appealable judgments) was promulgated; it was the most effective instrument for keeping the peace. The emperor set up the Imperial Chamber, appointing a presiding judge, who had to have the rank of prince, count or baron, and 16 other judges from the Holy Roman Empire. Of the judges, half had to be versed in the law, while the other half had to have at least the rank of knights.

A consideration of mediaeval legislation, the so-called common law (gemeines Recht; the law common to all citizens of a given state), would be incomplete without some mention of that part of canon law which also constituted a source of the common law. However, it was not until July 1, 1580, that Pope Gregory XIII officially gave the collections of canon law, from the so-called Decretum Gratiani (a manual of canon law that

Justinian, Institutiones Imperiales; Guilbert de Villiers, Lyon, 1516
Justinian was from 527 - 565 emperor of the Eastern Roman Empire. The collection of Roman law sources and the codification of Roman law which he ordered bears his name and lent strong impetus to the development of European law right up to modern times.

appeared about 1140) to the collections of „extravagantes" (following the conclusion of the decretals of Pope Gregory IX, collections of decretals of the popes John XXII and from Boniface VIII to Sixtus IV, extending up to 1502), the designation Corpus iuris canonici, the name by which it was later generally cited and customarily known. From the Gregorian pontificate onwards, this expression was used increasingly for publications of collections of canon law. The Decretum Gratiani itself is a textbook of canon law compiled by scholastic methods (in the Middle Ages, the scholastics, or Schoolmen, devised a method to resolve theological and philosophical problems deductively, i. e., by deriving particular knowledge from general knowledge by reasoning). It is the work of a Camaldolite monk, magister Gratian, who gave it the title Concordantia discordantium canonum in keeping with the aims of Scholasticism, which culminated in the harmonization of religious and secular thought. In this manual, around 1140, Gratian set up general tenets (distinctiones), presented fictitious legal cases (causae) and discussed legal problems (quaestiones). The second part of the later Corpus iuris canonici comprised the papal decretals. In 1230, Pope Gregory IX commissioned the penitentiary Raimund von Penafort to consolidate the law contained in the so-called Compilationes antiquae and augment it with his own decretals. This collection was published in 1234 under the title Liber Extra. These five books of the decretals of Gregory IX were later supplemented by the Liber Sextus of Pope Boniface VIII, which was published in 1298. Pope Clement V had the Canones of the council of Vienne (1311/12) and his own decretals compiled in a collection of his own (Clementinae), which he published in 1314. The collections of „Extravagantes" mentioned above date from the 15th century. Towards the end of the 15th century, Jean Chappuis, a licentiate of law, compiled his own collection, including 20 Extravagantes of Pope John XXII and, as Extravagantes communes, the papal decretals from Boniface VIII onwards. These private works did not attain the authority of similar law books, but were placed on a par with them by their inclusion in the Corpus iuris canonici.

From the late Middle Ages onwards, it was primarily the Halsgerichtsordnungen (these were the first codifications of criminal law, which were applicable only in limited regions) which played the decisive role in criminal law. They also took over Italian legal ideas. The most important examples of this group of sources of law and legislation, apart from the Halsgerichtsordnungen promulgated under Emperor Maximilian I for Tyrol in 1499 and Radolfzell in 1506, are the Bambergensis (Constutio Criminalis Bambergensis = CCB), and the Carolina (Constitutio Criminalis Carolina =CCC). Both cover criminal law and the law of criminal pro-

"Reformacion der Kayserlichen Stat Nuremberg", statute book of the city of Nuremberg, 1479, edition of 1503.

21

cedure and took due account of the reception of Roman law in German legislation; moreover, they directed the administration of criminal law into more modern channels. The Bambergensis, or "Peinliche Halsgerichtsordnung" of the bishop of Bamberg (north Bavaria) is attributable to the steward of the Bamberg court, Johann Baron Schwarzenberg. Fundamentally, the Bambergensis had its roots in the idea of justice and the common weal. Not without good reason, its author emphasized that he wrote his work in praise of God. Schwarzenberg aspired to realization of the Christian conception of justice. In keeping with the principles of a Christian way of life, he demanded just retribution for crimes. Although Schwarzenberg could certainly count on helpers from his official surroundings, the uniform make-up of the Bambergensis and the language, which is likewise homogeneous, show that this penal law reformer authored his work himself. The Bambergensis became the model for the important Constitutio Criminalis Carolina (CCC) or "Peinliche Halsgerichtsordnung" of Emperor Charles V which was promulgated at the imperial diet of Regensburg of 1532 (the imperial diet was the deliberative assembly of the estates of the empire and consisted of three colleges: the electors, the imperial princes, and the representatives of the towns. For the passing of legislation, corresponding resolutions by all three colleges and the approval (ratification) of the emperor were required). When opposing, particularistic standpoints (aspirations of members of a community of states to the greatest possible independence) threatened to obstruct this penal legislation, its failure was avoided by the so-called clausula salvatoria. It provided that old common law could remain in force. The saving clause provided that the law of the particular area prevailed and that the CCC, as imperial law, found only subsidiary application (it could be applied only if existing local common law contained no rules relating to the case concerned) provided that, as compared with the "Peinliche Halsgerichtsordnung" of Emperor Charles V, the older statutes proved to be "duly handed down, just and equitable". Nevertheless, it cannot be denied that the CCC took a fairly long time to gain general acceptance. For all that, as a "code of the empire" it numbers among the imperial laws, and this could not be changed by the addition of the saving clause.

A further vital concern of imperial legislation was the organization and reformation of a good police force and hence the promulgation of the imperial police codes. The imperial police codes of 1530, 1548 and 1577 attained special importance because they took on the character of models for territorial legislation. It should be appreciated that particularly in the 16th century the term police was used in the broadest sense of the word. The rules of law and order and the police tried to control blasphemy, excessive drinking, exaggerated dressiness, and to curb luxury.

Bambergensis. Die Peinliche Halsgerichts-Ordnung of the bishop of Bamberg (north Bavaria) of 1507. Edition of 1580.

For example, they prohibited the wearing of velvet, damask, satin and silk coats by merchants and traders in the town, and laid restraints on superfluous bridle equipment for horses and worldly clothing for the clergy. They combatted usury, and gypsies as Turkish spies, just as they did importuning by buffons, monopolies, begging and idleness. In addition, they regulated the legal questions of apothecaries, goldsmiths and craftsmen. The ius politiae embodied in the imperial police codes likewise had its impact on the local sovereigns, all of whom considered themselves empowered to manage the police in their territory and interpret the police concept very broadly.

With the widespread reception of the classical natural law in the 17th and 18th century, reorientation especially of the legislation of territorial sovereigns set in. Reforms of the Landrecht (term used for territorial statute books, which were essentially codifications of common law) were now undertaken. For example, Duke Maximilian I promulgated for Upper and Lower Bavaria his famous Landrecht of 1616, which embraced not only the police code, but also that for the courts and criminal courts. The real breakthrough of natural law in Bavaria, however, occurred only with the codification by its outstanding legislator Baron von Kreittmayr. He elaborated the Codex juris Bavarici criminalis published in 1751, which reformed Bavarian criminal law. This was followed in 1753 by the Codex juris Bavarici judiciarii (judicature code). Kreittmayr himself stressed that although the ius criminalis needed reforming most urgently, the reform of procedural law also proved indispensable. The chief concern of the procedural reform was the conception that in a well-ordered state no one should be permitted to bypass the authorities and high-handedly take the law into his own hands, but must be required to resort to the courts. Lastly, there followed in Bavaria the Bavarian Landrecht of 1756, the Codex Maximilaneus Bavaricus Civilis, which was likewise authored by Kreittmayr and came into force for the entire electorate of Bavaria, including the Upper Palatinate (north-eastern part of the state of Bavaria abutting the Czechoslovakian frontier; seat of government: Regensburg). Its object was to collect and concentrate systematically the widely dispersed and fragmentary rules of law in the state. In addition, it set out to enable authentic decisions in contentious issues and to resolve them in line with public opinion. Kreittmayr himself resolved interpretation problems by presenting authentic interpretations in his own commentaries in the notes attached to the Codex.

In Brandenburg-Prussia, the criminal law was reformed in 1620, 1685 and 1721, while in Austria it was primarily the Constitutio criminalis Theresiana of 1768 which brought about the standardization of criminal law in the Hapsburg monarchy.

24

CHRISTO AVSPICE.
PLVS VLTRA.

Des aller Durchleuchtichsten
Großmächtichsten/vnüberwindlichsten Key-
ser Carols des fünfften/vnd des heyligen Rö-
mischen Reichs Peinliche Gerichts
Ordnung.

Von Richtern/Vrtheylern/vnd Ge-
richts Personen.

ERstlich setzen : Ordnen vnnd wöllen wir / daß alle Peinliche Gericht mit Richtern / Vrtheylern vnnd Gerichtschreibern / versehen vnd besetzt werden sollen/von frommen / erbarn/verstendigen vnd erfarnen Personen/ so tugentlichst vnd best/ dieselbigen nach gelegenheyt jedes orts gehabt vnnd zubekommen sein. Darzu auch Edle vnnd Gelehrte gebraucht

A

Carolina. Peinliche Gerichtsordnung of Emperor Charles V, of 1532.
Edition of 1559, Frankfurt.

The Kingdom of Prussia presented its reform legislation in the shape of the Prussian General Landrecht or, more accurately, the "General Landrecht for the Prussian States" of 1794. Regrettably, this "statute book of compromises" was already obsolete by the time it came into force, if we compare it with the great French legal revolution of 1789. Nevertheless it popularized the legislation in Prussia and freed it from the obscure mysticism of earlier bodies of law. It contained, as a general statute book, the rules by which rights and obligations of the citizens had to be assessed. In so far as the customary law of the various provinces was to remain in force, it had to be incorporated in the provincial statute books. In the view of this legislation, general human rights were based on the natural freedom of man "to be able to seek and further his own wellbeing without injuring the rights of others." Particularly French law in the form which it assumed during the revolutionary period and under the Napoleonic empire unmistakably exerted its influence in a great variety of ways in large areas of Western Germany, especially in the Rhineland, in the Bavarian Rhine Palatinate and in Rhine-Hessen. It must not be forgotten that a decree of 1790 proclaimed the equality of all men before the law, and the Code penal of 1791 divided punishable acts into three classes: felonies, misdemeanours and contraventions. In Austria, the legislation under Emperor Joseph II (1765−1790) in the late 18th century endeavoured to preserve the authority of the legislative. The compass-bearing legal ideas initiated by the great French revolution also made their mark on the modern codifications in the 19th century. In Bavaria, progressive development was evident especially in the penal code of 1813, which was drafted by the great penal legislator and pioneer of modern German penal law doctrine, Paul Johann Anselm von Feuerbach (1775–1833), and served as a model for German penal legislation in the 19th century. It made the tenor of the prevailing law binding, not least on the judge, was based on the tenet "nulla peona sine lege" (no punishment without law), and saw the object of criminal law in preventive deterrence of prospective offenders.

The renewed longing of the people for a unified empire and law, which had already been incorporated as the goals of the liberal-nationals in the constitution formulated by the Frankfurt national assembly in 1848, pressed for national codification on a grand scale following Bismarck's establishment of the empire in 1871. Probably the most important event in the creation of a German national code of law, an exhaustive and exclusive body of legislation, was the codification of the Civil Code of 1896, which came into force on the eve of the 20th century and with which this overview is to be concluded. On looking back over the history of German law-making from its beginnings up to the 20th cen-

CONSTITUTIO CRIMINALIS
THERESIANA,

oder der

Römisch-Kaiserl. zu Hungarn und Böheim ꝛc. ꝛc. Königl. Apost.

Majestät

Mariä Theresiä

Erzherzogin zu Oesterreich, ꝛc. ꝛc.

peinliche

Gerichtsordnung.

WIEN,

gedruckt bey Johann Thomas Edlen von Trattnern,
kaiserl. königl. Hofbuchdruckern und Buchhändlern.

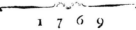

1769

Title page of the Peinliche Gerichtsordnung of the Austrian Empress Maria Theresia of 1768, edition of 1769.

Despite the criminal law reforms which began in the age of Enlightenment, the Theresiana was still based on old, traditional German criminal law. However, it did bring standardization of the criminal law in Austria and its hereditary possessions (Hungary, Czechoslovakia, upper Italy).

tury, we find that in the past centuries there was compartmentization and fragmentation of the bodies of law, particularly since the principle that imperial law prevails over regional common law could not be put into effect until the 19th century, while previously the law of a small area, i. e. the law of a minor district, could prevail over the law of a larger area and hence even over regional and imperial law. The diversity of German law is equalled by the variety of ways in which it has come down to us. Authentic law gazettes are of relatively recent date and first appeared under the constitutional monarchies, while in earlier times the original single copy of a legislative act was kept in the archives.

Declaration of the Landesfreiheit in Upper and Lower Bavaria, renewed 1553.

The Landesfreiheiten laid down the rights of the various estates (knights, towns, etc.) to participate in important state matters, e. g. taxation, declarations of war, dispositions relating to parts of the state.

Allgemeines Gesetzbuch für die Preussischen Staaten

Erster Theil.

Berlin, 1792.
bey Joachim Pauli.

The legal code already begun in 1749 under King Frederick II (the Great) aimed at creating a uniform body of law for the far-flung parts of the Prussian state. Although published in 1792, it never came into force and it was only after a number of amendments that it went into effect in 1794 under the new title "Allgemeines Landrecht für die Preussischen Staaten" (General Landrecht for the Prussian States).

Penal Law as a Phenomenon
of the History of Ideas

by
Prof. Dr. Wolfgang Schild

Present-day criminal law and the law of criminal procedure and execution of punishment is perceived by us as government rule by way of statutory norms: A person may be prosecuted only for behaviour which is already precisely described in the criminal code; he must be considered innocent until duly proved guilty, for which reason he must be given a fair trial before the eyes of the general public and without physical and mental coercion. The judge and prosecutor in the proceedings are different persons, and even the public prosecutor's office is required to take account of all circumstances that speak for the accused. The prime object of the execution of punishment is to remedy defective socialization of the offender and to lay down for him the foundation (vocation, but also mental attitude) for living a non-criminal life. In most cases the state is content to pronounce a guilty verdict and a sentence without executing the punishment, if it can be expected that the convicted person will not commit further misdeeds. In the case of juveniles, generally speaking an attempt is made to make up for the deficiencies in the socialization process of education and upbringing.

Although to some extent this is (as yet) more programme than reality, the conception and mental attitude behind this present-day approach to penal law is humane and social; offence and offender on the one hand and the state, law and society on the other are human phenomena for which all bear responsibility and which can be coped with only by all pulling together.

But on considering the Middle Ages, and even the 18th century, we are confronted with a completely different, distressing picture: We find cruelty and pitilessness on a scale that shakes our faith in the humanity of those times. Executions combined with fantastic tortures were real public fetes and there were even towns prepared to pay for such a "diversion", that is, to buy such an execution. In a secret trial before a judge who was simultaneously the prosecutor, or in earlier days acting purely arbitrarily without any legal authority at all, the main emphasis was on torture, which brought what we now consider the senseless consequence of self-indictment by the innocent under the duress of inhuman torment, and also unbridled accusation of others. On reading the documents that have been preserved, we are aghast, and now and again we are overcome not only with sympathy for the victims but also with vehement rage at the persecutors.

For us, in our present age, it is not hard to condemn those times and brand those chiefly responsible (above all the church). With the modern methods of science we work out the social structures underlying that penal law and perceive the social conflicts which an upper class tried to resolve with every means at its disposal in order to establish its leadership firmly. Social psychology reveals to us the repression mechanisms behind such excesses. These findings, moreover, are often expanded one-sidedly into guidelines for political action in the future, or at least into general condemnations of the past, taking advantage of the interest shown in such brutal phenomena by us in the present day. Or, in benevolent superiority, people look down on those "dark Middle Ages" and smile at the primitive, childish views of the people of bygone days, who were full of irrationality and, for example, burnt people as witches. Maybe we pity them also for their fear of ghosts and their wretched situation, the plagues and their medical helplessness in the face of them, the bondage of some of them and their serf-like exploitation, and the simply non-existent education of the majority. We need only transfer ourselves in our thoughts back to those times, times without electric power, hospitals and trained physicians, properly built roads, and also without schools, newspapers, pamphlets and television. We then collect and preserve what remains in museums, and gain self-esteem by dissociating ourselves from the exhibits. But there are some who feel regret that those old methods of combatting crime are no longer used today: how many social problems could be solved with them; though those concerned never see themselves as potential victims.

All these attitudes and modes of behaviour with respect to our past have one thing in common. They do not bring understanding of life in former centuries. All access to such understanding is barred by the fact that we try to see the past with our eyes and use our modern concepts and categories to comprehend it. The only way to reach understanding of those phenomena is to apprehend them from within, so to speak, from the standpoint and in the spirit of those times.

The period up to the Enlightenment can be understood only if we take account of the spiritual powers which impressed their stamp on cultural and on political life: the church (as an institution) and Christianity (as the essential, decisive force); and even the Enlightenment with its demands for liberty, equality and fraternity cannot deny that it had its roots in Christianity. Nor must the beginnings of the play of those forces be underestimated. Even the Germanic kings in the period of the Great Migrations established connections to the Christian church and the pope. When Charles the Great (768 - 814) set up his empire, he resorted to the clergy, who were then the sole pillars of education and the intelligentsia; Otto the Great (936 - 973), in fact, made the bishops the mainstays of his government. This illustrates clearly the great extent to which the Germanic peoples took recourse to Roman thought – for the church lived under Roman law and in Roman style, since it had become the state religion under Gratian and Theodosius – or christianized their traditional conceptions (and in other respects, too, the church was involved in a continual assimilation process with Germanic conceptions). People often overlook this and speak of a Germanic and Frankish period. From the standpoint of the history of ideas, the Germanic empires on the soil of the former Roman empire can be comprehended only as a unit comprising old (tribal) and Christian-Roman conceptions. Undoubtedly the traditional customs predominated among the people; christianization was for the most part of a more superficial nature, for which reason it could be overcome – as in the case of the Saxons – by the sword and blood, while those at the head of the Reich, such as the king and those of rank, including many bishops, were clearly oriented to the church, which survived with astonishing stability after the fall of the Roman empire. The "leges" (tribal laws) codified following the Great Migrations clearly demonstrate the aspirations of the rulers in that direction, indeed it is evident from the mere fact that the idea of such legislation was "received". Charles the Great was influenced by the imperial idea as it actually existed in the East Roman (Byzantine) empire, where the secular sovereign was the head of the church, assigning himself at least the rank of an apostle, if not going so far as to venture a comparison with Christ. This unity of the secular-profane and the spiritual-sacral is manifest in the term "Holy Roman Empire" applied to the empire from Otto III onwards and well into the 19th century, in the imperial insignia, which were venerated like sacred objects, and in the long-prevailing view that the anointment and coronation of the emperor gave him ecclesiastical dignity and rank. And far into the Middle Ages, the emperor was believed to have the holy power of healing the sick.

Hence it is understandable that Charles the Great and many of his powerful successors also promulgated purely ecclesiastical regulations and even claimed authority in matters of faith. A further reinforcing factor was the idea of royal supremacy, i.e., the conception that the lord over the land (the king of the whole country) was also lord over the churches built on the land (the king thus being lord over the national church) and empowered to appoint and divest the clergy at his own pleasure. It can likewise be appreciated that a church which was gathering strength could not accept such a state of affairs. The well-known controversy on the investiture of the bishops ended in effect with the defeat of the papacy as a political power and of the emperor; the empire being thereafter only a symbolic unit and spiritual power, while the formation of states in the present sense of the word took place in various parts of the empire ruled by territorial sovereigns.

From the standpoint of the history of ideas, these events of political history must nevertheless be considered as a uniform whole, for underlying all of them was the Christian church's conception of the world. The social life of mankind was always seen within the framework of the divine order, for which reason a profane, temporal society could never emerge - the measure of communal life was the church. This unity of the "realm of the church" found its living manifestation in the already mentioned idea of the Christian king or emperor. True, with the strife over investiture in the 11th century that unity broke apart, but the Christian church remained as a benchmark. Society (and the incipient state) was now a thing apart from, but not severed from the church; it remained oriented to the church and charged with its defence. This order of things within the divine creation as a whole meant that the social, communal life of mankind was still directly foreordained by God and therefore that the divine laws could be found directly. A classical example of this conception is found in the Sachsenspiegel (printed ca. 1225): "God Himself is right, wherefore right is dear to him," and "Whosoever swerveth from the doctrine of the Sachsenspiegel, speaketh lightly to his own dishonour and sinneth against God; for he who perverteth the law breaketh the commandment of the covenant. God himself teacheth us to practice righteousness and not to suffer unrighteousness."

The pictures of justice often found in court rooms, with their combination of temporal judges and Christ, the Judge of mankind at the Last Judgment, also demonstrate this linking of the law with the order of God. When this conception of order was destroyed by nominalism and the reformation, the status of the sovereign (provincial prince) was preserved from the Christian viewpoint and, indeed, was strengthened as far as his powers were concerned. The prince was assigned the function of establishing the order pleasing to God and of fighting the sinfulness of man. The emerging state and the law it decreed were to be taken as part of the order of divine salvation.

The law of this period can be comprehended only against the background of a conception of the world in which this unity of the temporal and the sacral was still real and was experienced as reality at least on special occasions and on feast days — of which the Middle Ages had many more than we do — that stood out from the daily round of toil and trouble. We can gain an insight into the phenomena of the old penal law, which we now find so revolting and appalling, only if we appreciate that in the view of the people at that time it was not just a matter of prosecuting and punishing violations of the law (as we see penal law today); on the contrary, everthing was at stake in the fullest sense of the term. The evildoer was a loathsome sinner who had violated the divine order and, in the battle between God and Satan in the arena of human society and history, had gone over to the side of evil. The extermination of the criminal was a victory for the good and was therefore the fervent duty of all Christians; it was a "ceremony" in the true sense of the word, a triumph of the good, and at the same time it was occasion for a joyful feast, also because in this way God, who was thought to be outraged by the sinful misdeed, could be appeased and his retributive penalties such as plagues, poor harvests and famine could be averted. The victory of the good was even more splendid, if the evildoer himself was successfully freed from the claws of Satan, i.e., if he made a confession, because in doing so he had disavowed the devil and returned to the fold of the church. The penal law sought also to save his soul. For this reason, a convicted person who confessed could be given absolution and could also be ministered to by a priest at his execution. At the same time, it becomes understandable why every possible means was used to obtain a confession and why torture was resorted to. What was physical suffering, if its infliction could save the evildoer's soul. In the case of certain criminals, in fact, the torture was not without danger for the torturers. Sorcerers, witches and heretics of both sexes had opened themselves to Satan and the proceedings were therefore a direct battle with the devil himself. The pain of the torture was intended (at least among other things) to drive out the devil, the agony, assisted by prayer and holy objects, was supposed to have a purging effect. The tortured person was surrounded by incense, consecrated crosses were laid under the criminal's body, his direct gaze was avoided for fear of becoming possessed oneself. For the same reason, the interrogators had to be members of the clergy, because they alone had a chance in this battle. And how great was the relief after the confession, how different the attitude to the convicted evildoer. He was then called the "poor sinner" or simply the "poor man", his wickedness was destroyed, but he himself had to be executed, and that as soon as possible and definitely in his own interest. For he had already once succumbed to the temptation of evil and even after his confession he was in danger of being deprived of salvation. His execution in a condition of repentance and expiation, provided with the consolation of the holy sacrament, therefore meant his rescue from eternal purgatory. Only if this is appreciated can it be understood why many condemned persons went to their execution with such incredible composure and, for instance, kneeled calmly before the fatal sword; it is even reported that some went joyfully to their death and called on the executioner to cause them even more suffering, and also directed enlightening words to the assembled crowd, telling them to live a Christian life and - above all - to protect the children from the influence of evil.

At least this revelation of the spiritual background will enable it to be understood why penal law has always moved and stirred mankind as a whole, and especially why an execution was a real festive occasion to which the people thronged from near and far; undoubtedly out of sensationalism, but also out of desire to experience the carnal proof of the divine order, which was the guiding reference framework for their own lives, and out of joy at the triumph of good, from which they could draw renewed strength for their own wretched existence. This religious background certainly became manifest in the case of genuine religious offences such as heresy, witchcraft, incest and sodomy; but the Middle Ages did not exhibit perfect uniformity, and definitely had their spiritual ups and downs. However, it must be appreciated that - quite unequivocally in the central Middle Ages - in the last analysis all crimes were violations of God's divine order. Even the mass criminality and poverty-induced crime in the late Middle Ages, the gangs of robbers, thieves and murderers - the "villainous" - constituted an exception only if considered superficially. That criminality was a threat, not only to the bodies, lives and property of the people, but, above all and most important, a threat to the God-given order, which included the protection of body, life and property. Only complete misunderstanding of the vital fundamentals of life in those days can lead to a comparison with the mass criminality in modern industrial societies. On the same grounds, the cruelties were certainly also reactions, expressions of hate and bitterness at the scoundrels who, on account of the weakness of the authorities, kept the people in a continuous state of fear and terror; but always against the background of the conviction that the divine order and the true Christian way of life was under attack and that by these means evil sought to triumph. A persons's own existence, and the existence of the evildoer, was comparatively of secondary importance; in the olden days, the individual hardly counted.

Similarly, the often described excessive reactions and contradictoriness of the Middle Ages can be comprehended only against this general background. What was at stake was always more than mere everyday things. Incidentally, the evil deeds themselves were of extraordinary cruelty, went to negative extremes and knew no bounds. A mere reference to the primitiveness of the people in those days says but little about them.

This does not mean, of course, that the people in earlier times did not think logically and rationally. What is said below on torture, for example, demonstrates a precise and definitely consistent line of thought, though proceeding from different basic arguments than those we recognize today. It can be demonstrated, for instance, that the notorious "Hexenhammer" (witches' hammer) was an extremely shrewd book and an attempt at rational comprehension of the world in those times so that people could live in peace and place their trust in God; for attributing accidents, all misfortunes and evil to Satan brought understanding, and the exact elaboration of methods to make his allies harmless gave security and preserved faith. Similarly, the laws of the Middle Ages always tried to prevent misdeeds and deter people from committing them, and so the execution of punishment was designed on the basis of perfectly rational considerations. It would be entirely wrong, however, to speak of "utilitarian penal law" simply on those grounds, except in the sense that the purpose of penal law consisted in preserving the divine order, in protecting the country from the anger of God and in saving the evildoer from the torment of hell.   Even the imperial police codes (e.g. of 1530, 1548 and 1577), which dealt with the minor details of everyday life (right down to clothing regulations), can be understood only in the light of their basic function, that is, to compel people to live a godly life and abstain from sinfulness.

This characterization of the conception of the world does not preclude the existence of individuals who were well ahead of their times, who certainly recognised the beliefs of their fellowmen as superstitions, exploiting them for their own purposes. But in order to grasp the overall picture of former times, we must take recourse to the typical, basic, mental and spiritual traits of the people living in those days. In short: there were probably few judges of heretics who were irreverent.

This is not the right place to describe the reasons why and the manner in which this Christian conception of the world found its end and how our present conception (which might be termed a humane, social world) evolved from it. We might note in passing, however, that in this process great importance attached to the towns, that it was in them that the real

„bourgeois" conception was born and finally won out. The way in which the townspeople carried on economic activities—referred to as precapitalism— led up to the true modern rational principles. It must be remarked in this context, however, that at least for a long time the then urban economy could exist only within the framework of the Christian conception of the world and, above all, by virtue of the deep Christian respect for work (as opposed to the conceptions of antiquity and Germanic times), which was furthered by many religious orders and to an extreme extent by Calvanism. It was not coincidence that the first, really important forms of penal confinement originated in the Calvinistic Netherlands and were then taken over in the German Hanseatic cities in the characteristic form of workhouses. "Good work as a guarantee of a godly life" was their watchword; and the religious background even of this modern type of punishment cannot be illustrated more clearly.

It is not our purpose, however, to describe developments in the past few centuries; on the other hand, it is necessary to go back in history beyond the Christian church's conception of the world, which was formed above all by the Middle Ages. The term "Christian church" is intended here only to bring out the significance which the church and Christianity had for the penal law of those times. From the viewpoint of our present Christian faith, and incidentally also in the judgment of individual, and permanently isolated, theologians of those days (e.g. with respect to the mania for relics or the worship of saints), there were manifest forms of Christian superstition. They exhibited in many instances a type of popular piety which undeniably had its roots in early heathen notions. As already mentioned, through missionary activities Christianity destroyed much that was heathen, but on the other hand took over a great deal. The veneration of saints and the relic cult can be cited in this respect, but also church buildings were set up, for instance, at old heathen sanctuaries and certain ceremonies of worship were clothed in Christian garb. Moreover, the christianization of many Germanic tribes took place in a rather superficial manner: Together with the king —who himself was often not exactly a staunch Christian— the whole tribe allowed itself to be baptized. The salvation of the king (which was linked up with his new god) was decisive for the fortune or misfortune of the tribe, so faith was a matter affecting all.

Whatever the case, pre-Christian beliefs continued to be of importance for many spheres of life. In this respect, allowances must be made for education and communication facilities at that time. Very few people could read and write, there were no newspapers or pamphlets; the sole source of information was verbal tradition. All their —mostly very short—

life, most people never went beyond the villages in which they were born, and some were not even allowed to leave their plot of land. It must be remembered that the Germanic peoples (like the Romans) kept slaves, whose numbers, in fact, far exceeded those of the freemen. (Even the church originally had an extremely large army of slaves and emphatically defended the practice. For example, in 517 the council of Epao forbade the abbots to release monastery slaves, though it must be noted that, in contradiction to that order, the church otherwise, and later on quite generally, declared the freeing of prisoners and slaves to be an act of godliness and described it in many holy legends with the result that the Christian view gradually brought about the prohibition of slavery.) In the light of these social conditions it is understandable that the old pre-Christian faith was able to hold its ground for a long time, although the church tried to combat it as heathen superstition, especially when we consider that most people worked on the land and the peasants' way of life, being dependent on the soil, the weather and the sequence of the seasons, generally inclines them to a conservative attitude and a magic-sacral notion of nature, which can be divined even today from the wealth of peasant customs. It was in the towns and their commerce – as already mentioned – that the first awakening of modern rationality gradually took place.

At all events, for the sphere of penal law, which, apart from the person of the king, has always proved most fascinating for the people, superstition in a great variety of forms   must be taken into account, especially as far as the rural population is concerned, who for a long time stuck to their belief in demons and magic practices, long after the townspeople had recognized them as nonsense. At the same time, these manifestations of superstition reveal an earlier, more primitive world which is even more incomprehensible to us in our modern world and of which we can gain a rough idea only by drawing comparisons with still existing "primitive" peoples. Our concepts of state, law, crime and punishment prove entirely unsuitable for comprehending the world of the Germanic peoples prior to their christianization. Our studies take us into a completely alien world, as will be demonstrated in a few respects in the following.

The primitive-Germanic notion of reality can probably best be characterized as a demonic-magic conception of the world. The Germanic peoples experienced the significant and vital things in their environment (such as soil, springs, animals and plants, but also fire, hearth, house and weapons), at least in the case of extraordinary events or special occasions, as holy forces or spirits, as demonic entities depicted in a multitude of divers forms. Many of these ideas have been preserved in later sagas and fairy tales: The tree suffers when its bark is removed; the spring speaks warnings; the hero is victorious in battle, not because of his bravery, but because he wields a special sword, and many similar things. It was therefore dangerous to deal with such things, unless one also possessed certain holy powers that made it possible to master them by way of magic-sacral ceremony. Some people were particularly proficient in such matters and were esteemed, respected and probably even more feared as sorcerers or "priests" (in a primitive sense). But every freeborn Teuton saw in himself and his body, and even in his various limbs, a holy source of power derived from his mythical forbear (who was often regarded as demonically holy) and renewed ever and again by cult ceremonies, the common descendants often forming a clan. Since it was founded by the forbear, the clan was, in fact, the true vehicle of that holy power that was possessed by the individual (male) members. The power could vary and this led to the formation of noble clans and the "king's clan" (which was the bearer of the king's grace and fortunately able to pass it on to the subjects, failing which – in the event of misfortunes and defeats – the king at least had to be deposed, since his grace was no longer strong enough). It is completely wrong, however, to think in terms of blood relationship in the present-day sense. The clan was a cult community and even more: it was a brotherhood of demonic-magic power to which the young men were admitted by mysterious initiation rites, which they had to undergo in order to communicate with the dead ancestor. It was therefore in communion with the dead and ultimately with the ancestor, from whom it had not only its name, but its very identity. This unity of the living and the dead was celebrated in cult feasts and ceremonial drinking bouts – the true forms of Germanic "sacrifice" – at which the dead were assumed to be present, in order to renew or strengthen the holy power by these communal ceremonies. On such occasions, animals were slaughtered, and even human beings (in later times mainly slaves and prisoners of war), in order to absorb their strength and simultaneously to emphasize the clan's own social repute. For social life in its entirety was built up on magic-sacral foundations. Even after the old clan system fell apart, there were still men's societies which continued this cult of the dead in connection with the initiation of novices, and even in the ceremonial banquets of mediaeval guilds this sacral element was preserved; in fact, traces of it are still to be found right up to the present in some students' corporations.

Certain dead persons were regarded as "living corpses", especially if they had been outstanding during their life (like the old ancestors) or had in some way died an extraordinary death. They were ascribed a demonic character, which resulted in an ambivalent attitude towards them: they could be venerated and their holy power absorbed in the cult, or at least the aid of the "helping dead" could be entreated; on the other hand, however – and this belief persisted much longer, in superstitions probably right up to the present – they could be feared as no longer human "spectres" who could find no peace in the grave and were repeatedly a danger to the living. It was therefore necessary to perform certain magic acts to prevent their haunting the earth. Many corpses found in bogs have provided evidence that they were thrown into bogs, weighed down by stones; or their heads were cut off, they were pinned to the ground with magic stakes or a stake was driven through their body, and thorns were laid over them. They could also be burnt and their ashes scattered or thrown into rivers, or one could let their bodies be carried away by water, etc.

Even the emergence of certain deities brought no essential changes in this demonic-magic conception of the world. There is much that indicates that in the course of history three different religious systems followed one after the other, and in each case various elements of the older faith were taken over and worked into the new, with the result that (in the "round dance of the gods") various groups stood side by side. We find gods conceived in animal form (e.g. Ullr, Skadi), who date back to the hunting and fishing cultures, along with earthbound gods of fertility (e.g. Nerthus, Tuisto, Frey and Freyia, and the Vanir as a whole) who, with their veneration of the dead, ritual annual feasts and the "matronae cult" date back to the late Stone Age and the beginnings of agriculture. Superimposed on these beliefs in the late Stone Age were the heavenly "Aesir", the deities of the pastoral, warlike peoples, who brought with them also ancestral worship coupled with the rule of the god of the dead and war (Woden/Odin). A common trait of all Germanic gods was a downright demonic character, which is also true of the Aesir, e.g. of Woden/Odin as the god of the dead, of war, of poets, of magic and ecstasy, but also the god of thieves, and this likewise applies to Loki and Thor, the chief Aesir. They were unpredictable, of primitive ferocity; personal relationships to them (such as loyalty and love in matters of faith) was inconceivable, on the contrary they themselves were described as artful and cunning, and mostly downright inconsistent. They aroused more fear than trust, and often the sole reaction was to attempt to influence them by magic, which was the task of the "priests", who were not really a class of their own, but rather particularly outstanding people who, by virtue of their magic holiness, could venture to enter into relations with the deities. Under no circumstances must the Germanic gods be conceived as personifications of abstract principles of any kind (possibly of an ethical nature) as found in polytheistic high religions. They were, rather, mighty and powerful, like persons of high standing, for which reason, though regarded as creators of the world, they were never considered the founders of a divine order. A god of law, too, was unknown to the Germanic peoples. Consequently, the ethics of the gods could not be disobeyed so there could be no necessity for "purging" and "penance". The order of the world was rather the conflict and interplay of demonic forces in accordance with magic laws. Only under the influence of Christianity (or possibly of Roman polytheism, with which the Germanic peoples were confronted at an early date) were some of the deities depicted in exhalted form, especially the shining Baldur to whom was assigned, after the twilight of the gods, the task of putting a new ethical world in order.

In addition to the Germanic deities, sometimes regarded as identical with them and sometimes as their attendants, there was a host of dwarfs, giants and demons who haunted the dark forests, bogs, crossroads and other ominous places. Of great importance – probably in connection with the men's societies and worship of the dead – was the "rabid horde" (the "wild chase") in which on stormy nights the dead, led by Woden (who was not described as god of the dead, of war and storm for nothing), prowled through the forests accompanied by wolves, which were regarded as sinister demons. Many of these conceptions have remained alive right up to the present in popular customs, although they have lost their former deeper significance.

All these briefly described elements of the early Germanic conception of the world had their consequences for "Germanic penal law", to use a popular, but highly misleading expression. Some of them are cited in the following.

First of all, the background becomes clear of what was called the "family (blood) feud" in later times. In this connection, people habitually speak of a furious reaction or primitive urge for vengeance in the Germanic peoples; but they overlook the fact that a precondition for that is respect for the individual and development of the individual personality, something that was non-existent in those days. In fact, the passionate rage that led to vengeance, above all of the death of a member of the family, was attributable to three reasons: First, the holy power of the family had been weakened and that loss had to be offset, so to speak, by killing another person, since in that way new holy power was gained. This makes it understandable why the vengeance was not aimed at the actual perpetrator, but at any member of his family (preferably its best man), why the act of vengeance once again led to a blood feud, which might be carried on up to the point of mutual extermination of the two families, and why no vengeance was taken when the killer slayed one of his own family.

41

Secondly, the opinion was held that toleration of the deed would entail a further loss of power, because the family would be proved cowardly and weak. In this connection, people often speak of the "honour" of the Germanic peoples, which led to vendettas; but entirely without justification, if what is meant is the ethical quality of a person, for that notion is specifically Christian. The Germanic peoples definitely possessed – like Arminius, for instance – a natural wiliness. But what was involved was the magic power embodied in the people who formed the family. This also makes it understandable why it was by no means necessary for the member of the family to have been killed wilfully or culpably. The mere causing of his death was sufficient, because that resulted in a loss of holy power. Thirdly, there was the danger that if no vengeance was taken, the dead person might return as a ghost to take the matter into his own hands and, being an unpredictable demon, might inflict punishment on the members of his own family for not fulfilling their holy duty.

If the family feud is appreciated as a cult rite, it becomes clear that this reaction followed only serious encroachment on the well-being of the family; above all, when a member of the family was killed and also after every action affecting the self-esteem of the family in such a way that it could not be tolerated. At this juncture it should be noted that neither the slaves nor strangers belonged to a family kinship unit so that their death as such was no reason for vengeance, unless, for example, the master of the slaves felt he had suffered injury to his property. Even insults led to vendettas; not on account of a loss of honour, but because of the resulting loss of holy power, which simultaneously meant abasement in the cult organization. To speak merely of social prestige is to ignore the vital fundamentals.

The community of the people (clan or tribe) extending beyond the individual family was not affected by such vengeance or the resulting strife between families. On the contrary, ever and again it was necessary to reorganize the magic-sacral modus vivendi among the various families endowed with holy power.

Similarly, the folk (or tribal) society saw no reason to intervene in matters within the family itself. If anybody weakened the power of his own family in an intolerable manner, e.g. by killing a relative, the family could kill him or banish him, which in those times also deprived him of any chance of survival. They bothered even less about the closer relationships within house communities. The house, too, was a cult community, the cult rites devolving upon the house father, who also exercised authority over his wife, the children he had taken in and the free servants, his powers extending to expulsion, selling and killing. He had an even greater degree of authority over the slaves, who were not even recognized as persons. On the other hand, it must be appreciated that those people were regarded as equivalent to his tools or weapons and their actions were therefore deemed to be his actions; if, for instance, a slave killed a free-man of another family, it was likewise grounds for a blood feud.

There was one sphere, however, in which a joint reaction of all the families was essential, that is, when the holy foundations of the entire tribe or people were attacked. This was the case when places of worship were desecrated, when the sexual rules of the families were violated (this included homosexuality), and when the military strength of the people was diminished, e.g. by desertion or cowardice. In such cases a solemn ceremony was held. The people, that is, the free, arms-bearing men, assembled at a place of worship, at the grave-mounds of important ancestors, at mighty rocks, at holy springs or under certain trees, and pronounced in ritual form the necessity of the killing, the sentence probably being executed immediately afterwards in concert. The finds of corpses in bogs indicate that the miscreant was battered or stabbed to death and sunk in a bog. It can be assumed that – possibly along the lines of the sacral initiation rites, which also included symbolic killing by hanging (like Wodan who, according to the myth, was hanged on a tree) – in some cases offenders were hung on certain trees. Stoning to death was also known. Under certain circumstances, desecrators of places of workship were slain at the site of their crime, or thrown into the sea from cliffs in order to ensure or improve fertility, an effect which could be intensified by castration. Whatever the case, in these ways the corpse was prevented from returning as a ghost.

Karl von Amira interpreted these killings as sacrifices for the insulted gods, probably wrongly because, as already mentioned, the Germanic peoples did not have any corresponding conception of the gods, or at most only in much later times influenced by the Roman example. Nor can there be any question of "atonement" for the disturbed divine order, for that implies guilt and trangression, which were still unknown to the Germanic peoples. Also the treatment of the corpses found in bogs argues against the sacrifice theory and more for the modern version developed primarily by Bernhard Rehfeldt, which sees these killings either as reparation magic or purging magic or as forms of the initiation rites. This latter theory corresponds most closely to the world-conception of the Germanic peoples, but the subdivision into several forms of magic seems artificial and the idea of purging (as atonement) appears – as already mentioned – inappropriate to those times. I would like to bring to the fore as a uniform principle the idea which is most clearly evident from the treatment of the corpse: the person slain in this sacral-magic manner was considered a public enemy who, through his negative force, diminished the holy power of the people and thus proved himself a demonic creature who had to be destroyed, which not only called for his being killed, but required the final destruction of the negative force of the living corpse.

This conception of the "criminal" as a demonic creature is also supported by phenomena that can still be found in the superstitions of the Middle Ages. In some cases the evildoer was regarded as a "wolf": the great variety of tales about the "werewolf" (i.e. man wolf) are practically common knowledge. In earlier times, the wolf was a definitely demonic animal: he lived in the forest, in those days the primeval forest that was the haunt of all demons, and—according to the ancient reports—devoured corpses, for which reason he often prowled around cemeteries, and he took part in the chases of the "rabid horde", in short: he embodied demonic power, just as a person who had committed such terrible misdeeds as murder of his parents or incest demonstrated that he was a demonic creature who had to be driven out, stoned or killed in some other way, and the corpse then subjected to further "treatment". Such "treatments" as impalement, cutting off the head, etc., are still found in modern times, also in connection with the belief in vampires. Reports have come down to us of werewolf trials in Dole in 1573, in Cologne in 1589 and 1590, in Angers in 1598, and as late as 1717 in Salzburg and 1720 in Tamsweg. Klaus Völker has collected a great deal of material on this subject. All this casts a clarifying light also on many notions in connection with witch trials when we consider that Satan, seen as the ruler over many demons, was thought to be able to seize power over witches and warlocks not only in sexual intercourse, but quite generally. The idea that execution of the evildoer had the purpose of "cleansing" and "expurgating" the land appears in an entirely lew light. Without doubt, as already mentioned, it presupposes the Christian idea of culpable transgression; but the notion that such a transgression could "besmirch" and must therefore be eliminated is based on ancient, magic conceptions of a purging magician.

On the other hand, until far into the Middle Ages it was believed that the demon could be destroyed even in the wolf or in some other animal's body; reports have come down to us of animals being brought to trial and of such "offenders" being executed in the traditional manner by the executioner. Right up to modern times, animals that were sexual partners in cases of bestiality were burnt with the offenders, and here the motive of purification by fire undoubtedly played a part.

44

Even objects were sentenced in judicial or quasi-judicial proceedings. In the case of the goods of a werewolf this is easily explained by the danger of infection. But the burning down of a house in which a woman was raped can probably only be attributed to the above-mentioned idea of magic defilement.

A demonic creature was not destroyed by death alone. Here again, reports have come down to us from the Middle Ages of trials of dead persons which culminated in a sentence to execute the corpses. Similarly, the bodies of sucides were not buried but, for instance, placed in barrels and thrown into the river so that they would be carried off. The general rule that the bodies of persons who had been hanged or broken on the wheel should not be taken down and buried, but left to decompose was, in fact, likewise punishment of the corpse.

The superstitious belief in the demonic power of the criminal was also evident in a large number of ceremonies at the execution, which will be recounted in the section on executioners, and in the notion of a special holy power of the parts of an executed person's body, etc.

At all events, these examples show how necessary it is to go back to the religious beliefs of the people in those times and to the remains of old superstitions in order to understand penal procedure even in the Middle Ages and early modern times (especially with respect to capital punishments, but also to a lesser degree with respect to all other types of punishment).

In the foregoing, we have touched upon at least a few of the fundamental factors affecting the history of penal proceedings, the development of punishments and their execution. They make it evident that that history presents an evolution process in which at least three successive conceptions of the world can be traced out,   though they have ill-defined limits, sometimes merge with each other and sometimes overlap (as faith and superstition), but can nevertheless be distinguished from each other as demonic-magic, Christian-ecclesiastical and human-social conceptions which make up our world; it becomes evident, too, that that history signifies the development of all penal law in the direction of humaneness: from the demon to the sinner and then to the criminal who, as one of our fellowmen, contravenes the penal law promulgated by us; from magic-sacral destruction to killing for the sake of the divine order and the salvation of his soul, and then on to punishment intended to enable him to live a socially blameless life.

History of Criminal Law and Procedure

after Prof. Dr. Wolfgang Schild

Before embarking on a summary of the history of German criminal law, a few preliminary remarks are called for. Up to the present, the views advanced by scientists on developments in the olden days have varied substantially. The almost complete lack of authentic sources resulted in historians having to rely frequently on conjectures, which were naturally coloured by the authors' individual inclinations or even by their political intentions. The source most frequently resorted to by the legal historians is the "Germania" written in 98 A. D. by Tacitus, the Roman historian. Though his interpretation of conditions and events may often have been coloured by his personal views - and is therefore hardly acceptable without reservations - the facts which he reported can usually be accepted as reliable.

In the early Germanic age, there was no such thing as a state in the present sense, and hence no prosecution by the state. The family, i.e., the consanguine family based on common descent, performed the functions later assumed by the state. It was the mainstay of the cult, of material existence and legal order and had magical-sacral significance. The family exercised penal jurisdiction over its members and protected them against harm from outsiders. Every injury to the honour, the property and life of a family weakened the family and thus endangered its continued existence. Being aware that the family had to restore its hallowed order itself, in self-defence it took vengeance on the offender and his family. Endless family wars were the result. They ended ultimately in the weakening, if not the complete extermination, of the families concerned. As they became more settled and tribes (peoples) developed, i.e., unions of many families, it became necessary to demarcate the area occupied by a tribe. For the families united in the tribe, this gave rise to the obligation to protect that area against attack from outside. The curbing of the endless family conflicts was now imperative, because they also entailed the weakening of the military strength of the entire tribe. This introduced a new development of the law, the institution of the fine. Under this procedure, the offender's family surrendered part of their livestock or weapons after the opening of the feud, and in later times also beforehand.

46

The victim's family accepted the gift and refrained from further acts of vengeance. The agreement was substantiated by ceremonial oaths on both sides. It would be completely wrong, however, to regard such a transfer of goods as the price of averting vengeance. The material value of the livestock and weapons was of subsidiary importance. They, just like the unharmed body of the family member, were rather an integral part of the man's personality and hence part of the family's integrity. If the family's integrity had been injured or diminished by a crime, it was remedied or restored to its former condition by giving livestock or weapons in restitution. One fact illustrates this particularly clearly: under certain circumstances it was possible for an offender to enter the family of a slain man as his substitute and to take up his position in the family.

The bargaining on the reparations and the waiver of a family feud took place out of court and in ceremonial form. The significance of the accompanying oath which had to be sworn by both parties had little in common with present-day oaths. It was a conditional self-damnation for the event of non-observance and was sworn in ritual from and involved touching holy objects. Whoever broke the oath exposed himself to the independent magical forces of the objects on which the oath was sworn, for instance, those of his own sword. At a very early date, in such negotiations the help was sought of particularly respected men who could mediate without themselves being drawn into the controversies. The location of the negotiations was mostly some holy place.

From this method of avoiding family wars, which in the beginning was certainly not general custom, the "fine" procedure was further developed. The offender's family first approached a mediator, who laid down the time and place for the bargaining and summoned both parties to attend. A precondition for the proper conduct of the proceedings was the affirmation under oath by the participants that they would refrain from all war-like action for the duration of the negotiations and would respect the authority of the mediator.

With the growing importance of the tribal or national community and the consequent emergence of a "public" authority, the affected families were granted the opportunity of appealing in such cases to the "Thing-versammlung", i.e., an assembly of the people at a holy place. In such instances, it was necessary to observe particularly strict ritual formalities in view of the cause, i.e., the killing of a person, and the objective, i.e., prevention of interfamily war. A high-ranking member of the tribe, who subsequently presided over the assembly, staked out the place of assembly with holy twigs or pegs, thus forming a "sanctuary". The magical-

Lex Baiuvariorum

(Chap. VIII) On Women and their Legal Causes that often occur

1. Should any man lie with another's wife, who is a free woman, and be caught in the act, he shall make atonement to the husband with the "wergeld"* of the said wife. And should he be slain in bed together with the wife, he shall lie dead in infamy unrevenged instead of the fine he would have had to pay to the husband. And should he have placed one foot in the bed but, being hindered by the wife, have done no more, he shall pay a fine of 15 schillings for having wrongfully set foot in another's marriage-bed.

2. Should a bondsman do such a deed and be slain together with the free woman in the marriage-bed of another, in consideration of the harm suffered by the former the "wergeld of the wife shall be reduced by 20 schillings; all else, however, shall be paid by his master until the sum of the fine is paid in full. But should the bondsman escape and not be slain, but be found guilty of the crime, his master shall surrender him for 20 schillings to the man whose wife he violated; the remainder of the fine, however, shall be paid by the master in full, since he placed too little restraint on his bondsman.

3. Should any man lay hand on a free woman out of evil lust, whether she be a virgin or the wife of another, which the Bavarians call "indecent groping", he shall pay a fine of 6 schillings.

4. Should he raise her clothing above the knee, which they call "pulling up clothes", he shall pay a fine of 12 schillings.

5. But should he tear her head-covering from her head, which they call "Walcwurf" (bonnet-snatching) or should he tear hair from the head of a virgin out of wanton lust, he shall pay a fine of 12 schillings.

6. Should he abduct a virgin against her will and that of her relatives, he shall pay a fine of 40 schillings and a further 40 schillings to the public treasury.

7. But should he abduct a widow who, out of necessity, leaves her house for the sake of her orphans and out of her own neediness, he shall pay a fine of 80 schillings and a further 40 schillings to the public treasury because such presumption deserves to be forbidden and the protection of widows must be founded on God, on the duke and the judges.

8. Should any man commit fornication with a free woman with her consent, but have no intent to take her to wife, he shall pay for the deed a fine of only 12 schillings because she was not yet betrothed nor married by her relatives to a man, but allowed herself to be violated of her own free will.

9. Should any bondsman commit fornication with a free woman and it be proved, the master of the bondsman shall deliver him up to the relatives of the violated woman to receive the deserved punishment or to be slain, but shall otherwise pay nothing; for such presumption awakes enmity among the people.

10. Should any man lie with an emancipated woman, whom they call "freed", and who has a husband, he shall pay a fine of 40 schillings to her relatives or to her master or to her husband.

sacral power of this sanctuary was intended to prevent the two families from commencing hostilities. At the assembly itself, apart from the assembly president and the members of the two families, also those men who had gained experience as mediators in previous "fine" proceedings had an important function, for they contributed that experience to the proceedings, especially with respect to the amount of the fines. They, above all, were able to pass judgment by virtue of their expert knowledge and experience. Since at that time, however, there was no fixed legal code with norms from which a solution of conflicts and thus a judgment could be derived, the activity of these men cannot be regarded as "finding" a judgment. They rather attempted to reach a decision which could be recognized by both families, that is, they tried to mediate.

The prime objective of such proceedings was to curb the senseless and harmful family wars. This was possible only when the magical-sacral relationship between the two families and hence the holy order of the tribe (people) was restored. The culpability of the offender or contributory culpability of the victim was not the subject matter of the proceedings and had no significance whatever. Hence it is understandable that there was no equality of participants. The holy power of a noble family, for example, ranked incomparably higher than that of a more lowly family. If the victim had belonged to a low-ranking family, under certain circumstances the judgment might call for a low fine.

Subsequent development strengthened this procedure up to a point where fixed fines gradually crystallized out for certain acts and their consequences. The bodies of common law like the Lex Salica (ca. 500 AD), Lex Baiuvariorum (8th century) and others, which were originally handed down orally and later codified, contained their own lists of pecuniary penalties, laying down the fines payable for specific offences. It would be entirely wrong, however, to regard them as catalogues listing the "cost" of an offence. For a long time, even after christianization, restoration of the holy integrity (or power) of the injured family was the fundamental idea of this procedure. Only later, with the spreading of trade and thus also of money, did this significance recede into the background, giving way to a more commercial conception. These lists of fines also changed the role of the "assessors". Their chief function from then on was no longer mediation between the families, but assessment of the facts of the case. Then all that was necessary was to pronounce the extent of the fine laid down in the catalogue. The remainder of the proceedings also underwent a fundamental change. The initiative was no longer taken by the offender's family offering atonement, but by the victim's family, who demanded atonement. From now on, a clear distinc-

11. Should any man lie with a freed virgin, he shall pay a fine of 8 schillings to the relatives or to her master.

12. Should any man lie with the bondmaid of another and she be married, he shall pay a fine of 20 schillings to her master.

13. Should any man lie with a bondmaid who is still a virgin, he shall pay a fine of 4 schillings.

14. Should a freeman cast out his free wife out of aversion though she has no shortcomings, he shall pay her relatives a fine of 48 schillings; but to the wife he shall pay her dower in keeping with her descent. And all that she brought in of her father's goods shall be returned to the wife.

15. Should a freeman, having fairly become betrothed to the free daughter of another as the law demands, desert his betrothed and, in contravention of the law, take another woman into his house, he shall pay a fine of 24 schillings to the relatives and shall swear with 12 oath-helpers from among his family, who shall be named to him, that it was not out of hate for her relatives nor on account of any crime, but out of love for the other that he married the other; and (the matter) shall thus be settled among them and thereafter he (the father) may give his daughter to whom he will.

16. Should any man abduct the betrothed of another and by persuasion take her to wife, he shall return her and atone for the deed with a fine of 80 schillings.

17. Should any man seduce a free woman as if he intended to marry her, but then leave her by the wayside, which the Bavarians call "Truglüge" (falsity), he shall pay a fine of 12 schillings.

18. Should a woman drink a potion to procure a miscarriage, if she be a bondmaid she shall receive 200 lashes; but if she be a freewoman she shall lose her freedom and become the bondmaid of him whom the duke names.

19. Should any man deal a woman a blow, causing premature birth so that the woman dies thereof, he shall answer for manslaughter; but if only the foetus be destroyed and it was not yet living, he shall pay a fine of 20 schillings; but if it was already living he shall pay the "wergeld".

20. Whosoever causes an abortion shall initially pay 12 schillings and thereafter he and his issue shall pay one schilling every year in autumn down to the seventh generation, from father to son. And should they fail to pay in any year, they shall again pay 12 schillings and so forth in the aforementioned order until the reckoning is fully paid.

21. Our forbears and judges have decreed such prolonged atonement, ever since the religion of Christianity has taken root in the world, because the soul, having taken on flesh, could nonetheless not attain to the light of birth and must suffer longlasting punishment, for by abortion it has been delivered into hell without the sacrament of rebirth.

22. But should a bondmaid be mistreated by any man so that she has a premature birth, if the latter (the child) was not yet living, a fine of 4 schillings shall be paid.

23. But if it is already living, he shall pay a fine of 10 schillings to the mistress of the bondmaid.

tion could be drawn between plaintiff and defendant. The complaint was entered orally with ceremonial phrases and ended with a challenge to the defendant to answer the complaint. The defendant could then either admit the justification of the complaint or deny it word for word, likewise in ceremonial form. Before the court, strict attention was paid to observance of the prescribed forms. Any contravention of those forms by the parties, such as a mere slip of the tongue, a wrong formulation or an occasional stutter could bring an unexpected and undesired turn in the proceedings, or even result in losing the case. Later on, this resulted in each party retaining the services of an "advocate" experienced in such matters. His words carried weight only if publicly acknowledged by the person he represented. If the advocate made mistakes, the person he represented could reject the advocate's words and undertake a new, proper presentation. If the defendant had admitted the justification of the complaint, the (final) judgment was passed immediately, laying down the fine payable by the defendant. If he had denied the charge, a judgment was likewise passed immediately. On the one hand it laid down which of the parties had to bring evidence (Beweisurteil = order for evidence), and on the other, however, it was simultaneously a conditional final judgment, laying down the fine payable in the event that the defendant was the loser. The formal stringency of the court is also demonstrated by the proceedings for reaching and pronouncing the judgment. The parties brought their complaint and answer in the form of judicial questions. Each of these questions had to be answered with a judgment, which the judge called upon an "assessor" to find. Once he had found it, the judge asked those assembled whether the judgment was fair and just and whether they would comply with it, vulborden" it, that is, give it their approval. If the answer was in the affirmative, the judge ordered the judgment to be carried out. If any person refused the "vulborden", the assessor was instructed by the judge to find a different judgment, on which the majority of the assessors then decided. The most rigourous form of objection (demurrer) was the "Urteilsschelte" (censure of judgment), which was not only a rejection, but also a charge of having found an unjust judgment. The censurer had to be the equal of the judgment-finder and to present the censure while standing:

Lex Salica

On the Touching of the Hand of a Woman

1. Should a free man touch the finger or hand of a free woman - legally defined as "pressing" - he shall be sentenced to pay (600 pfennigs, which make) 15 schillings.

2. Should he touch - legally "press" - her arm, he shall be sentenced to pay (1200 pfennigs, which make) 30 schillings.

3. Should he lay his hand on her elbow - legally "pressing the upper arm" - he shall be sentenced to pay (1400 pfennigs, which make) 35 schillings.

4. Should any man touch a woman's breast - legally "by the breast" - he shall be sentenced to pay (1800 pfennigs, which make) 45 schillings.

Note: "Wergeld" in the early Germanic era and the Middle Ages (as under old Anglo-Saxon law) was the expiatory payment or "man-price" which, in the event of a killing, had to be paid by the killer and his family to the family of the slain person to avoid a blood feud (vendetta).

Charles the Great introduced silver currency. The system remained in force up to 1000 A.D.

1 pound of silver = 20 soldi = 240 pfennigs

Some examples of the purchasing power of money (according to the Lex Ripuaria):

1 schilling	=	one horned, standing, healthy cow
2 schillings	=	one ox
12 schillings	=	one horse
3 schillings	=	one sword without scabbard
7 schillings	=	one sword with scabbard
6 schillings	=	one ornamented helmet
12 schillings	=	one coat of mail
3 schillings	=	one untamed falcon
12 schillings	=	one trained falcon
1 pfennig	=	24 pounds of bread

"stende sal man orteil schelden sitzende sal manz vinden".
(Standing shall the judgment be censured, seated it shall be found)

The Sachsenspiegel required the censure of a judgment to be in the following words:

> "daz orteil daz der man gevunden hat
> daz ist unrecht, daz schelde ich unde
> zie michz da ich mirz zu rechte zin sal."
> (The judgment that the man has found
> is unjust, that I censure, and I claim the
> justice that is my right.)

The chief issue of the entire proceedings was whether the two parties should be permitted to present evidence. Basically, only one party was conceded the right to present evidence, without granting the opponent the right to present counter-evidence. In these early trials, the main thing was not the plaintiff's right to substantiate his complaint, but as a matter of principle, the culpability of the defendant. It was assumed that the defendant had better knowledge of his own actions, for which reason it was usual to concede him the right to give evidence. The party obliged to adduce evidence had to vow to the other party that he would provide the evidence. Over and above that, the defendant had to vow that, if his evidence was rejected, he would pay the fine laid down in the conditional judgment. And with that the trial was already at an end. The evidence was presented outside the court and without the court's participation, possibly before witnesses called in for that specific purpose. So there was no assessment of evidence by the court; that was left to the opposing party to the action. It is important to note that evidence was not the proving of facts, as it is nowadays, but merely purely formal evidence. Consequently, a final judgment was generally not necessary, for the logical conclusion as to who had won and who had lost could be drawn from the "Beweisurteil" by the parties themselves.

An important and much-used form of evidence was the oath. The accused could acquit himself of the charge made in the complaint by swearing an oath of innocence. He could make the oath more convincing evidence by having himself supported by oath-helpers. The latter, however, must be clearly distinguished from the witnesses known to modern law, for they did not need to know the facts or give testimony concerning them. Oath-helpers merely swore that the oath of the accused was pure and he should therefore be believed. In most cases, the oath-helpers were members of the accused's family, but in later times they might also be nominated partly by the plaintiff. When swearing oaths, strict formalities were observed. The slightest slip of the tongue and any contravention of the formalities made the oath invalid. But once the oath had been sworn in due and proper form, it was regarded as proof. The plaintiff could then resort to the "oath-censure", that is, a charge of perjury. This then led to a duel with the accussed and possibly with each individual oathhelper, in which victory was deemed a manifestation of the truth. A duel could also be demanded by the plaintiff in cases in which there were no oath-helpers, e. g. where strangers were involved.

However, the duel really belongs to the next group of means of proof, i. e., the forms of divine judgment (ordalia). – For the olden days, when man did not as yet venerate an omniscient and just God, this term is certainly not very fitting, but up to the present we have no better expression. – In the distant past, man ascribed magical powers to certain (holy) objects such as swords, twigs, etc., and was swayed by belief in the elements. So what could be more obvious than to leave the decision on guilt and innocence to those powers. And so divine judgment was resorted to in order to find the truth. A distinction must be made between two types of divine judgment in the olden days, the "ascertainment ordeals"– demanded by the accusing side – and "defence ordeals" – used by the accused to avert prosecution. The first type included the "lot ordeal": applying magic rituals, small sticks were cut from twigs, marked with symbols and ceremoniously thrown into the air. Guilt or innocence was construed from the way they then lay on the ground. This ordeal, however, should really be termed an oracle, for its message was not a direct one, but had first to be interpreted and was thus dependent on the arbitrary findings of the interpreter. The cold water ordeal was also an ascertainment ordeal. The accused was laid with bound limbs on the water surface; if he went under, he was innocent; if he floated, he was considered guilty, for the water, a clean element, had not received him.

The defence ordeals included the ordeal by fire (or fiery trial). The person seeking to prove his innocence held a piece of glowing hot iron in his hand and carried it nine steps, or walked barefoot over 9 glowing hot ploughshares (Empress Kunigunde). The so-called "caldron-dip" was also one of the fiery ordeals. The bare hand had to be dipped in a caldron of boiling water and a stone or ring taken out. Once the trial was over, the injured limb was bandaged in ritual manner. If, after a few days, the wounds showed signs of healing, without suppuration, etc., the trial was deemed to have been passed and the person concerned to be innocent.

When these ordeals originated is a matter of dispute. Their basically magical character speaks for a very old age. They are found in all human cultures and at all cultural stages. For all that, it can be assumed that their practice began at a relatively late date, when oath-swearers could not be believed unreservedly. The ordeals became more frequent when bondsmen and slaves were also included in such proceedings, for they were not eligible to swear an oath. The divine judgments used later on in the Christian age will be dealt with elswhere.

Whereas so far we have dealt with evidence, means of proof, which had to be brought in accordance with an order for evidence issued by a court, we must now turn to another and completely different type of evidence, namely that of "in flagrante delicto". If a person was caught in the act (in flagrante), which included the capture of the fleeing offender, the person whose rights had been violated could kill the offender immediately. Normally, this sort of action, which also included self-defence, would have resulted in a blood feud started by the offender's family. But a deed of such manifest nature, though it weakened the holy power of the offender's family, demonstrated the negative power of the offender himself, as a result of which the killing of an offender caught in the act had to be tolerated by his family. A precondition for this, however, was the overtness and hence the incontestability of the deed. Since there were only rarely witnesses of the deed, for one's own slaves were unable to swear an oath, the man who had killed the miscreant had to establish the overtness. This was done by raising a "hue and cry" and presenting the facts to the neighbours who flocked to the scene and as far as possible also to members of other families. If the family of the killed offender was not convinced of the course of events, the oath of the neighbours protected the killer from vengeance. This later developed into a special form of proceedings. A court was quickly convened and the body was brought before it. A complaint "against the dead man" was then brought by the man who had killed him and his guilt was proved by the oaths of the plaintiff and the neighbours. This ceremonial act was known as "clarification", There were also other methods of clarification. The corpse was laid on a scaffold, or he could be laid out publicly at a crossroads, hanged on a tree, or have his head cut off and impaled on a stake. The choice of the crossroads was important, for it was considered the abode of demons and the dead. A person who placed the corpse there and survived the act had spoken the truth. The Lex Ripuaria, Chap. 77, prescribed: the man who had killed the offender caught red-handed must place the body "before witnesses at the crossroads on a bier and keep watch over it for 40 or 14 nights and then swear before the judge at the court that he had killed him because his life was forfeit. Should he fail to do this, he shall be condemned for manslaughter." In the course of time, this procedure underwent a change. A person who had been caught could not be cut down immediately, but had to be captured and bound. Together with the neighbours who had gathered in response to the hue and cry, the plaintiff brought the offender, with pieces of evidence, such as torn or bloody clothes or his stolen booty, tied to his back, before a quickly convened court, sometimes directly at the scene of the crime, and laid a charge against him. In such proceedings, it was impossible for the defendant to avert the complaint by an oath of innocence. Owing to the overwhelming evidence, the judgment was perfectly clear. When the neighbours had sworn their oath, the offender was handed over to the plaintiff, who could then deal with him at his own discretion. He was allowed to kill him, in which case originally the "clarification" of the corpse was necessary, or keep him as a slave. If the plaintiff decided to kill the offender, these proceedings ensured that the latter's family could not take vengeance on the plaintiff and that the plaintiff was not required to pay a fine.

While the capture of a fleeing offender was recognized at an early date as "in flagrante delicto", as already mentioned, this concept was later extended to the search for the offender, mostly a thief, including the following up of clues and house-search. In a house-search, however, strict formalities had to be observed on account of the great importance attached to the domestic peace. This extension of the concept "in flagrante delicto" also modified the importance of the oath-swearing neighbours. They had to inform the court about the pursuit and capture of the offender, and gradually they became witnesses in the sense of modern law.

A further development in proceedings was that the master was no longer held responsible for the actions of his slaves. By surrendering the slave concerned to the injured family he could avert their vengeance; originally together with an expiatory payment which, however, was small. Gradually this procedure was adopted also for crimes committed by freemen. The family was given the opportunity to disown the offender by ceremonial "repudiation", probably often performed before a court, and to hand him over to the family of the injured party, thereby avoiding vengeance. These developments make it clear that the magical-sacral power of the family receded ever farther into the background, giving way to ever warmer kinship relations. As a result, vengeance took on a different significance; it was now only a reaction to injuries suffered and developed into armed conflict (feud). From then on, there was not only killing, but also ravaging, i. e., material damage was done. Those feuds that were carried on became more brutal. Divested of their sacral nature, they became purely human strife. Although this development might well be termed regression, it contributed to the ending of feuds, because now they could be morally condemned and effectively combatted by creating an authority which developed the necessary norms. All this was initiated by the spreading of Christianity, for from this point onwards the further evolution of German criminal law was subjected to its influence. Belief in magical-demonic powers was replaced by belief in an omniscient and just God. From then on, nature was considered God's creation. The Christian-ecclesiastical conception of the world became the leitmotif for human co-existence. The priest-emperor notion deriving from the last epoch of the Holy Roman Empire (Byzantine/East Roman) was taken over by the Germanic peoples as the "Christian king" principle, in which they incorporated their own traditions. The distinction between emperor and king will not be discussed in this context, as they were of equal importance in early Christian times; even the Sachsenspiegel (1225) still used both terms side by side.

In the case of the Germanic peoples, the family with the greatest holy power, which was hence the most respected, provided the leader of the tribe. The new spirit of Christianity caused the importance of the family to fade and the king became a personal ruler. He no longer derived his power from that of his family, but was deemed to have been installed in his office by God, as whose representative he exercised authority. The anointment and consecration by the church were an expression of the king's "holiness". The kings and — from Charles the Great onwards — emperors ruled "by the grace of God" or "in the name of our Lord Jesus Christ", they considered themselves "crowned by divine dispensation". The king was the holder of sovereign and judical power, which found expression in the building up of an administration, in the promulgation of his own laws and the gradual recognition of his exclusive judicial authority. This also involved an oath of loyalty to the king which had to be sworn by the people and placed them in a position approximating that of subjects. However, the oath of loyalty must be seen only as a component of a feudal system that was dependent on personal relationships. There were no institutional government authorities, but only the personal ties to the sovereign which, in the final analysis, were similar to the king's ties to God. The task of the Christian king was to make the Christian order of life into a comprehensive secular order and bring about a theocracy. The preservation of peace and concord; justice; the protection of Christendom; dissemination of the faith; care, consolation and help for the poor; protection for widows and orphans were the guidelines of the "government programme". A decisive factor for the further development of law was the idea of justice and peace. Peace, however, was understood in this context as the state of law and order prevailing within a commun-

Transcription and Translation of the Facsimile of a St. Gallen Manuscript of the "Lex Salica" dating from 793 A. D.

St. Gallen, abbey library

The Latin text of the beginning of the "Lex Salica", which was written in (pre-)Carolingian minuscules (small letters) and is here transcribed and supplemented, reads:

In nomine Domini nostri Jesu Christi incipiunt titulus legis salice.

I. De mannire.

Si quis ad mallum legibus dominicis mannitus fuerit et non uenuerit, se eum sunnis non detenuerit, sol. XV, culpabilis iudicetur.

Illi uero, qui alio manit et ipsi non uenerit, se eum sunnis non detenuerit, sol. XV. ei cui manuit, conponat.

II. De furtis porcorum.

Si quis purcellum lactantem de cranne furauerit, et ei fuerit adprobatum, (malb. chranne chalti, rechalti) sol. III, culpabilis iudicetur.

Si quis purcellum furauerit, qui sine matre uiuere possit, et ei fuerit abprobatum, (malb himnes theca) sol. I. culpailis iudiceteur, excepto capitale et dilatura.

Si quis bimum porcum furauerit, (malb. in zimis suiani) sol. XV. culbapilis iudicetur, expecto capitale et dilatura.

Translation

In the name of our Lord Jesus Christ the title of the Salic Law begins.

I. On the summons.

Should any man be summoned pursuant to the royal laws to appear before a court and fail to appear, provided that no impediment (i. e. justifiable hindrance) prevented him, he shall be sentenced to pay 15 schillings.

But he who summons another and fails to appear himself, provided no impediment prevents him, shall pay him whom he summoned 15 schillings.

II. In thefts of swine.

Should any man steal a sucking pig from a sty, referred to in court as a "sty pig", and it be proved, he shall be sentenced to pay three schillings.

Should any man steal a piglet than can live without a mother, referred to in court as a "yearling", and it be proved, he shall be sentenced to pay one schilling in addition to reimbursement of the value and a "dilatory" fine.

Should any man steal a two-year-old swine, referred to in court as a "herd yearling", he shall be sentenced to pay 15 schillings in addition to reimbursement of the value and a "dilatory" fine.

Note: The terms in brackets in the Latin text are from the Malberg Glosses, i. e., interpolated legal expressions in the language of the Franks, which were used in oral proceedings before the court in the open air on the "Malberg" hill.

ties and their members. The gods of the Germanic peoples were anything but just, in fact underhandedness was imputed to them. The Christian God was entirely different; he was justice personified. The preserved pictures of justice from mediaeval law courts illustrate clearly the connection between the dispensation of justice and God's omnipotence. From now on, it was not the mighty, but the just who was intended to win, because truth in God gave him the strength to do so. The idea of a general, public peace was likewise new. It is hard to establish to what extent the idea of a unity that forged the entire people into an enduring peace community was known to the Germanic peoples. Very early reports indicate that a sort of public peace already existed. The only question is how far it extended and what spheres of life it embraced. Peace to the Germanic peoples was primarily family peace, the preservation of peace within the family combined with defence of the family against the outside world (blood feud). The peace idea of Christendom was of a completely different nature. Generally speaking it was derived from the bible and was defined in its most significant form by St. Augustine (Aurelius Augustinus) in De Civitate Dei. The notion that all dominion was a dominion of peace was common property from the 6th century onwards. In some spheres, it was possible to establish links to the Germanic conception, e. g. in the sphere of cult peace. Even among the Germanic tribes, a fugitive enjoyed asylum within the places of worship. The Lex Frisionum (802/803 A. D.) went considerably further; even when feudal vengeance was sought, it prescribed peace in one's own house, in church, on the way to and from divine service, and on the way to and from court hearings.

The chief aspiration of all public peace regulations was to curb feuds. But the rulers of the Merovingian and Carolingian periods failed to achieve any lasting success with the peace they ordained, for its implementation was always dependent on the personal power of the king and he could never rule alone, because in many respects he had to depend on the nobility and the clergy. The lists of fines laid down in the bodies of local common law, in conjunction with the royal constraint to submit to their imposition, were considerably more effective.

These bodies of common law, however, cannot be compared with our present-day statutes. They were records of the precedents and practice of the "Volksgerichte" *, on the codification of which, however, the king undoubtedly exerted his influence. The kings, being resonsible for peace and justice, attempted by means of their sovereign and judicial powers to put additional regulations (capitularies) into effect and thus to influence the development of law. For the most part, however, these endeavours were fruitless, because the kings lacked the necessary organizational instruments and in most cases also the power.

Beginning with the transformation of family vengeance into the feud, over the course of the years the fine-imposing proceedings gave way to expiatory proceedings that were permeated with Christian notions. In procedural practice, to be sure, the old customs lived on, especially with respect to evidence. From this period onwards, oaths were sworn on the Gospel or relics, in the belief that retribution for perjury was forthcoming, no longer from magical-sacral powers, but from the Holy Spirit. The divine judgments were likewise christianized. They were determined in the presence of one or more priests in a church or churchyard and were embellished with liturgical ceremonial. The ceremony was usually preceded by three days of fasting and prayer, the last night being passed waking in the church. The following morning a mass was read, the person submitting to the ordeal made an offering and received the sacrament. Then the priest exhorted him to make a confession, if he felt guilty. This was followed by exorcism to exclude any devilish tricks, and by the blessing of the element involved in the ordeal, calling upon God to reveal guilt or innocence. Duels were fought by professional combatants with previously consecrated weapons. In the ordeal of the "trial slice", the bread and cheese were replaced by a consecrated wafer. The divine judgments, though continually opposed by popes and kings, persisted until they lost their credibility and were finally banned in the 13th century by the pope (1215, by the Lateran council/Pope Innocence III, and 1222 Pope Honorius III), but without their disappearing immediately from legal life. The cold water ordeal, for example, was again used as a "witch's trial" in the 15th century with the approval of the church.

Expiation was also christianized in the course of time. With the disappearance of the magical-sacral background, the apology came to the fore, strongly influenced by the church's penance system. For instance, in the case of a killing, the killer had to ask slain person for forgiveness in public, either in church or in the churchyard, often wearing a penitent's hairshirt and with a candle in his hand. Forgiveness was granted him "for the sake of God"; then the oath of adherence to the truce of God was sworn and substantiated by the kiss of peace and a drinking bout. Frequently, in addition to a money payment, the offender had to bear the cost of masses for the dead, set up a cross of atonement or make a pilgrimage. The expiatory contracts which regulated all these matters were originally concluded through the mediation of a third person, often a priest. Then the court of law gradually took over the function of the mediator until finally the expiatory payment was fixed by a court judgment. A precondition for this was a functioning court organization. The king therefore decreed that a so-called "echtes Thing" (regular court of law) lasting three days should be held every six weeks, at which all freemen capable of bearing arms must appear without being specially summoned. If necessary, an additional "gebotenes Thing" (specially convened court) could be held, for which the people had to be specially summoned. The "Thing" was presided over by an elected judge, assisted by the "Rachinburgen" (assessors), of whom there were usually seven, whose function was to formulate a judgment. In the course of time they became real legal experts, a development that was furthered by the codification of common law. There was a further court set up by the king, over which he himself or his authorized representative presided. This "king's court" had no fixed location and was held as necessary in the various parts of the land. Although this king's court was of no great effect for a long time, it was nevertheless a manifestation of the king's God-given supreme jurisdiction, which the king could delegate by virtue of his judicial powers.

A further step in development was the transfer of the judicial office from the judge elected by the people to the counts. The reason for this was ostensibly the evolving enforcement proceedings. If the court had awarded the plaintiff a fine and the defendant failed to pay, the plaintiff was not permitted to satisfy his claim by forcibly seizing property, but had to resort to the count, who enforced the court decision for him. For his activity, however, the count retained part, mostly one third, of the fine as so-called "peace money" (often also known as "fractions"). For this reason, the count often took part in court proceedings until a time arrived when he, as a delegate of the king, was appointed honorary chairman and later actual chairman of the bench. In this way, the people's court, too, became an organ of royal sovereignty and the effectiveness of court proceedings was considerably enhanced, especially since the "peace money" was demanded for the proceedings themselves so that only two thirds had to be paid out. The trend of later development was to allot the judge, not just part, but the entire fine, so that he then had a personal interest in conducting the trial. On the other hand, the king's attempted to force corrupt counts who refused to administer justice to ensure the functioning of the courts on pain of punishment. The delegation of judicial functions by the counts to subordinate courts (Zentgerichte = hundreds courts) with jurisdiction over minor matters resulted in a further weakening of the position of the litigating parties. Soon the summons to the defendant was no longer issued by the plaintiff, but by the judge. Any person who failed to answer a summons or to fulfil the judgment was summoned to appear before the king. If he failed to answer this summons, too, his proscription or banishment was declared. Under the king's law of 816 A. D., banishment could also be declared by the count. Banishment or proscription meant expulsion from the community. The proscibed person thus lost the protection of the law, he was an outlaw and any one could kill him with impunity. Proscription also involved the loss of property, in some instances also the destruction (devastation) of his house and a general prohibition on providing the proscribed person shelter and food.

The building up and improvement of the court organization was one of the most important concerns of the kings. The next significant step in development was the reform of the judicature by Charles the Great. The hitherto customary "Rachinburgen"* were replaced as judgment-finder's by "Schöffen" (assessors) appointed for life, the number on the panel remaining seven. The biggest change, however, resulted from the introduction of the "Rügeverfahren" (charge-laying system). Particularly respected men, who were bound by oath, had to notify the judge of crimes and criminals known to them. The notification was equivalent to a formal charge and offenders named by such "Rügegeschworenen" (sworn charge-layers) were brought to court. The complaint of a private plaintiff was no longer necessary, because proceedings were now initiated and carried out by the authorities. Prosecution of crime had thus become a public matter (maxim of ex officio action). The trial itself proceeded in the manner customary in the "Volksgerichten" (people's courts). In the course of time it was modified only to the extent that the judge himself laid down the amount of the fine, which was payable to him. Thus the idea of compensating the injured party by an expiatory payment made by the offender lost significance in favour of a payment to the judge as the holder of the king's judicial power, which subsequently led to the "fiscalization" of the now emerging penal law. Being aware that these now enforceable expiatory proceedings could not be adequate in the long run, the king laid down real punishments at an early date. The grievous punishments prescribed in the bodies of local common law, i. e., corporal and capital punishments for slaves, were now also laid down for freemen, though their execution was not made imperative. The freeman could "ransom" himself by paying a sum of money fixed by the judge. This "right of ransome" and the later increase in the grievous punishments prescribed made the administration of justice a good business, though this was not to its detriment and, in fact, contributed to its high repute. In consequence, of course, above all in the late Middle Ages, there were also negative side-effects. The poor had to suffer the grievous punishment, while the rich could nearly always pay a ransom.

Parallel with this development, there was also a change in the site of the court. While in Germanic times the place of worship was the site of the court assembly, following Christianization it was moved to the cemeteries, in front of or in the church. The king's law of 818/819 A. D. issued by Louis the Pious contained the instruction to the counts to build houses for court assemblies so that proceedings could be held regardless of the weather. From then on, courts were held in inns, in special court porticos, halls or houses and, above all, in the town halls. The later, secret inquisitorial proceedings, which often involved torture, made it necessary for trials to be held exclusively in closed rooms.

The great variety of court sites demonstrates that in those days there was not question of uniformity in the administration of justice. Because the king, the supreme judicial power appointed by God, was unable to abolish the dominion of the land lords over their slaves and the "Grundholde" (approx. villeins; peasants under the protection of the lord), with their own courts the lords themselves or their delegated proctors administered justice in minor matters. The only possible way for the king to exert his influence was to legalize this independent judicial system by granting judicial powers, sometimes including high-court powers, to the land lords or their proctors. Also in the case of lords spiritual, where high court jurisdiction was concerned it was necessary to appoint proctors, for under prevailing church law (up to 1298) the lords spiritual were not permitted to pronounce death sentences. And as the towns became more powerful, they, too, developed a judicature of their own. A jurisdiction developed that was vested in the town judge, who was appointed by the lord of the town or by the already elected council, and renewed annually by a ceremonial civic oath. Later on, the lords of towns, and above all the king, granted the towns lower court and in some cases also high court jurisdiction over all persons living in the town and its surroundings. This fragmentation of jurisdiction is also clearly illustrated by the tribal laws, which embodied not only the penal law, but also the substantive law. As their names indicate, the Sachsenspiegel and Schwabenspiegel had no general validity. They were applicable only to members of the tribe regardless of where they were, but had no territorial validity for the tribal region. In this connection, the Sachsenspiegel (ca. 1220-1235) in particu-

Town hall with court portico, from Livy, Roman History, J. Schöffer, Mainz, 1523.

lar deserves special mention. Its author, the knight Eike von Repgau, collected Saxon tribal law and Eastphalian common law and compiled it in a so-called "mirror". Although the Sachsenspiegel was a purely private work, in northern Germany it soon attained statute-like repute and was used for the most part word for word as a model for the upper German law book, the Schwabenspiegel (1275).

Even when the tribal laws had to give way to the regional bodies of common law (Landrecht) there was still no standardization of the law, for in addition to law of local significance, there were the laws of the "estates", e. g. for knights of town citizens, or for the "Rechtskreise" (realms of law) such as royal court law, feudal law, and public service law. In the Westphalian fehmic courts, the concept of the Frankish count's court, the true king's court, endured longest of all. In contrast to most of the Landgerichte (regional courts), which in the course of the Middle Ages became courts of the land lords, they maintained the direct link to the king in the shape of the "Blutbannleihe" (grant of power over life and death). As king's courts which administered justice under royal authority in the king's name, they claimed - in addition to the usual jurisdiction of the regional courts - authority within their judicial districts to pass judgment on capital crimes committed outside their territorial jurisdiction in cases in which justice was denied or delayed by the regular judges. The fehmic court was held either as an open court for regular legal cases or as a secret court to deal with "external" cases. The fehmic court could also convene as an emergency court outside Westphalia in cases in which an offender was caught in the act. It was not until the 15th century, however, that the fehmic courts attained the zenith of their power. But since the land lords and especially the towns would not and could not tolerate the intervention of outside courts in their areas of jurisdiction, the influence of the fehmic courts was broken before the end of the 15th century and they were reduced to unimportant peasant's courts. Great importance also attached to the ecclesiastical courts, especially under Charles the Great, who also entrusted high members of the clergy with government functions. For example, the bishops' "Sendgerichte" * attained a powerful position. Originally set up to supervise ecclesiastical communities, they were now also used to administer secular justice. The proceedings took the form of the Carolingian charge-laying procedure. Everybody, laymen and clergy, men and women, free and unfree were obliged to attend. They were all called upon to present their complaints and to disclose all offences known to them against life and property, sexual offences, perjury and false witness, superstitions, but also contraventions of the ecclesiastical order. The bishop, acting as

The Sachsenspiegel

The following pages contain excerpts from illuminated manuscripts of the Sachsenspiegel. There is no systematic order of themes in the originals; here the illustrations are arranged according to subject matter in the interests of a clearer presentation. Unless otherwise indicated, the pictures are from the Heidelberg Manuscript, ca. 1330.

Emperor and Pope

Pope and emperor, "the spiritual and temporal court", seated peacably on the throne with the symbols of their power, the crosier and the sword (Common Law III 63, Art. 1, sentences 2).

King Constantine conferred on Pope Silvester the right to exact, in addition to the ecclesiastical, also the secular "peace money" of sixty schillings to make all those submissive who do not want to atone with their bodies, by compelling them through their property. In this way, the temporal and spiritual courts shall act together (Common Law III, 63, Art. l, sentence 1).

God the Father, seated on his throne, bestows on the kneeling pope the spiritual, and on the kneeling emperor the temporal sword. The two powers are of equal birth and descended direct from God and are hence of equal rank within Christendom. They rule in the name and for the honour of God and in humility before Him. The fact that, at the coronation in Rome, the emperor holds the stirrup of the pope's horse does not mean that the emperor is a liege of the pope, like a vassal before his lord. The presentation in the Sachsenspiegel, ca. 1230, indicates merely a gesture of politeness and humility. In the Schwabenspiegel of 1275 a change has taken place: God bestows both swords on the pope and of his own accord the pope hands over the temporal sword to the emperor.

From the Dresden Illuminated Manuscript of the Sachsenspiegel.

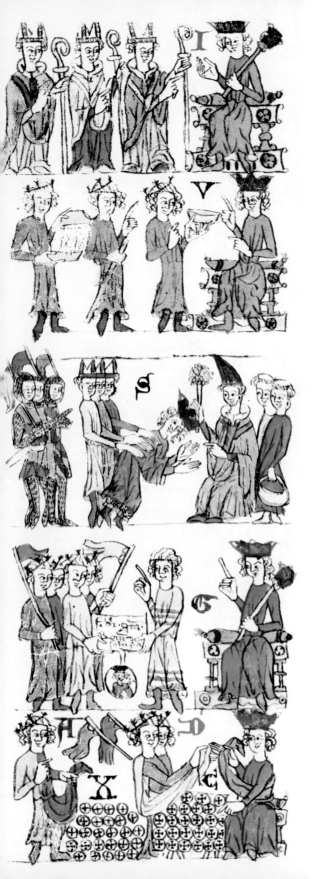

Election of the King

At the election of the emperor, the first shall be the bishop of Mainz, the second he of Trier and the third he of Cologne (Common Law III 57, Art. 2, sentence 1).

The Count Palatine of the Rhine hands the king the golden bowl; the Duke of Saxony, the marshal, bears the marshal's staff; the Margrave of Brandenburg, the imperial butler, brings the king a bowl of warm water. The cupbearer, the King of Bohemia, is absent, because Eike von Repkow denies him first-ranking electoral rights "because he is not a German" (Common Law III 57, Art. 2, sentence 2).

The king has gone to Rome to receive the royal benediction from the Pope. The six first-ranking holders of electoral rights accompany the king to testify to the pope as to the legality of the king's election (Common Law 4, Art. 2).

Levee

The king commands a "court day" or imperial levee with an imperative gesture. The messenger repeats this imperative gesture before the princes and hands over the king's letter with seal and the inscription "F(ridericus) d(ei) gr(atia) kom(anorum) semp(er) a(ugustus) .." (Common Law III, 64, Art. 1).

Before the king stand the princes who are bannered liege-lords and failed to answer the summons to the levee. From beneath their cloaks they produce the money. The king holds out his cloak to receive it. The amount is C = 100 pounds peace money. On the left, a representative of "other people", whose peace money is only 10 pounds. (Common Law III, 64, Art. 2).

The Public Peace

Sunday will be the Day of Judgment. The picture shows the divine Judge on the apocalyptic rainbow, the globe in his left hand, his right raised to bless the ressurected (Common Law II 66, Art. 2).

Priests, girls, women and Jews are at all times protected by the king's peace. The king points to the lily, symbol of peace; before the king stand a monk, a secular priest, a woman (with hood), a girl and a Jew (Common Law II 66, Art. 1).

Peaceful places: where peace always prevails: churches, ploughs, mills and (not illustrated) churchyards, villages within their moats and fences, and the king's roads on the water and on land (Common Law II 66, Art. 1).

Peaceful times: Finally there are days of peace which include the Thursday, Friday, Saturday and Sunday of each week, Thursday because, among other reasons, on that day God took Christ up into heaven and thus opened up the way there for us (Common Law II 66, Art. 2).

On Friday God created man and on Friday he died on the cross for his sake (Common Law II 22, Art. 2).

On Saturday God rested in the sepulchre after his martyrdom. On this day, too, the priests are ordained. (Common Law II 66, Art. 22).

A Jew is wounded in the arm and struck down by a Christian. The evildoer, recognizable by his coloured coat, is condemned by a court judgment; with an imperative gesture the judge orders execution. The executioner wipes the blood from the sword with the tail of his coat (Common Law III 7, Art. 3.).

With a blow of the sword the pursuer kills the fleeing breaker of the peace. He remains unpunished if, as illustrated, he can affirm with 6 oath-helpers that he wounded the evildoer in the act or in flight (Common Law II, 69).

An exile, recognizable by the sword in his neck, is sheltered in a house and given food and drink. On the right, the host avers by an oath of innocence his ignorance of the banishment, remains unpunished and need not pay the judge any peace money. (Common Law III, 23).

Excommunication harms the soul, but takes from no man his fief or right, unless followed by the imperial ban. On the right, a priest pronounces excommunication by breaking a candle over the reclining man. The man is dead, which is why his soul issues from his mouth and is received by a devil. At the left, a beheaded man lies on the ground, a banished man executed by order of the count with the sword of the executioner seen in the picture. Beside the executioner and dressed in green is the man who captured the exile. (Common Law III, 63, Art. 2).

Breach of the self-offered peace. The two similarly dressed men in the centre mutually swear peace. But by his actions (broken lily, the peace symbol) the man on the left reveals his intention to break the peace. The other points warningly at the executed man at his feet. The other men are the executioner, who is wiping the blood from his sword, and witnesses of the oath (Common Law III 9, Art. 2, sentence 2).

The imperial proscriber has a sword with crown and the proscribed man an ordinary sword in his neck. The attitude of both indicates their role as plaintiff. Their complaint is levelled against the man in the centre who, with a gesture of refusal, declines to answer them. The judge's gesture confirms the defendant's legal right not to answer the imperial proscriber and the proscribed man (Common Law III 16, Art. 3).

Feudal System

The seated king bestows on a bishop the "sceptral fief" (ecclesiastical fee) and on a secular imperial prince the "flag fief" (knight's fee) (Common Law 20, Art. 5).

The king must pass on the flag fief within "year and day". Year = (LII) 52 + (IIIIII) 6 weeks + 3 days (the disc of the sun lies below the 3rd stroke). The time symbol is behind the princes, i. e. the due date is past. With visible effort the emperor holds on to the fief flag. The two princes try to wrest it from him; they are asserting a legal claim (Common Law III 57, Art. 2).

Sitting at the left and right, two princes by birth; they are of equal rank as shown by the escutcheons. The vassal rejects the fief offered by the prince in yellow by turning his back to him, but kneels to accept the flag fief offered by the other (Common Law 20, Art. 5, sentence 2).

A priest, a merchant (with ell), a peasant (with cattle-driving stick) and a woman cannot be granted a fief. The feudal lord expresses refusal by turning aside with a gesture indicating incapacity (Common Law 2, Art. 1).

If one of them is nevertheless invested with a fief, it is not hereditary. The peasant's son in the background indicates with a gesture of regret that he has no right to inherit. (Common Law 2, Art. 2).

A priest and a woman receive imperial property as a sceptral fief, making them also eligible for a knight's fief; at the left, both grant subordinate fiefs. (Common Law 2, Art. 6)

Left: Granting of a "castellan" fief by a priest; right: handing over of a church-door key as symbol of an ecclesiastical fief. In each case the overlord is seated, while the feoffee is kneeling (Common Law 2, Art. 7).

The kneeling feoffee pays homage to his overlord, here depicted as a judge of the feudal court. Right: the man is in the house of his lord, indicated by the hand round the post of the house. As a sign of respect he lets the lord precede him. The raised oath-finger shows that this is included in his oath of homage (Common Law 3).

Right: the green fork at the neck indicates expropriation of the estate by the feudal court, the handing over of the glove the conveyance to the overlord. The loss of the contingent fief is shown by the finger pointing at the fief symbol.
Left: Termination of the fief is symbolized by the lord setting fire to the vassal's house with a torch. He also withdraws his hand, taking possession of the receipts. By offering ears of grain the vassal indicates that he wishes to retain the fief. (Common Law 20, Art. 4).

The feoffee requests renewal of the fief. The Roman numerals indicate the term of a year and a day. The man needs both hands to offer his men to the overlord, so the artist has given him a third hand with which he calls the men behind him as witnesses. (Common Law 22, Art. 1).

Due Dates

Levies and their due dates presented in the form of a peasant's calendar.

Three lambs indicate the tribute of lambs due on May 1 (St. Walpurgis's day). The date is indicated by the green tree (may-tree), which was set before the house and farmyard on that day in keeping with an old custom.

Orchard and vineyard tenth due on St. Urban's day (May 25). The date, the end of spring crop-tending, is indicated by trees and grape-bearing vines.

The meat tenth is due on St. John's day (June 24), here represented by ox, calf, goat and cock.

St. Margaret's day (July 13) is the due date for the corn tenth. According to legend, she bound up the devil; behind her lies the corn that was laid in the ditch beforehand.

Roots and herbs indicate the benediction of spices on August 15, and the geese the goose tenth.

"Sundry levies and aids" are due on St. Bartholomew's day (August 24). On a pole he is carrying the skin which, according to the legend, was stripped from him. Levies and aids are lying on the table.

The mint, vineyard and mill indicate that the levy is due on specified dates (Common Law II 58, Art. 2).

Fief renewal by the lord in favour of the heir to the estate who has attained his majority, with commendation rites. Centre: "the child" confirms by an oath the date on which he became "of full age", for on this depends his right to the fruits of the estate. If he was of full age by St. Urban's day, the fruits are his, otherwise they belong to his lord; this is symbolized by the vine (Common Law II 58, Art. 3).

The date for notice of termination between the lord and his feoffee is Candlemas (Feb. 2). The candle stands for Candlemas; the lord turns the feoffee out of the house, indicating that the notice is served in due time in accordance with the law (Common Law II 59, Art. 1).

Court Proceedings

When the king comes into the country for the first time, all unsentenced prisoners must be brought before him. The king's messenger in front of the castle cites all prisoners before the king's court with an imperative gesture. A prisoner stands before the king, pleading his case with lively gestures. His feet are manacled and his escort is holding his arm (Common Law III, 60, Art. 3).

At intervals of 18 weeks (XVIII) the count must hold his court in his court precinct; those required to attend are the mayor, seated beside him, the court beadle and four assessors (seated), recognizable by their cloaks (Common Law III, 61, Sect. 1,3).

Every man may be called to account only pursuant to his tribal law. He must appear for every trial except by duel. Claims to landed property may be asserted only in the district where the estate lies. Left: the defendant standing on the land where he was born. His back is turned to the plaintiff, who is armed for a duel, because the latter is not standing on soil on which the defendant is obliged to accept the challenge (Common Law III 33, Art. 3-5).

Where a court is held under the king's authority, neither assessors nor judges may wear caps, hats or hoods. They must wear cloaks on their shoulders and be unarmed. Here the judge and mayor have hats on, but probably only in illustration of fixed attributes. Moreover, the judge's hat lies beneath the doffed headgear (Common Law III 69, Art. 1).

The judgment-censurer grasps the arm of an assessor as a sign of censure of the judgment. The judge instructs the censured assessor to rise from the bench. The other assessors indicate that the judgment-censurer should sit in the place of the censured man (Common Law III 69, Art. 3).

No man accused of a crime may bring more than 30 men before the court and they may bear no arms apart from swords (Common Law II 67).

The adducer of evidence brings testimony with two courthelpers as oath-helpers. At the right of the picture, the alternative to the procedure at the left: the court beadle swears on the relic, deputizing for the judge. (Common Law II 22, Art. 1).

The monk adopts a sitting position to indicate that he has been found guilty by the oath of seven of his fellows. His pointing finger means that his conviction was arrived at without court testimony. (Common Law II 22, Art. 3).

Interrogation by the court, here represented by judge and court beadle. 21 persons were interrogated, of whom seven (including the adducer of evidence) are required to confirm by an oath the party's arguments. Four witnesses capable of swearing have already been found (Common Law II, Art. 4).

The opposing party, here called on to testify against himself, indicates by his sitting position that he has been defeated. Of the witnesses standing behind him, two have already testified under oath; the oath of the others is unnecessary, as the opposing party has already indicated his defeat by his own evidence (Common Law II 22, Art. 5).

Performance of the cold-water ordeal. The man undergoing the trial lies unclothed in a water-filled tub with a rope round his body, by which he can be pulled out immediately so that he will not drown. A priest, whose presence is part of the ritual, stands behind the tub. The third figure is the opposing party who has asserted a claim. Plaintiff and defendant swear that their statements are true (Common Law III 21, Art. 2).

A woman may not appear as petitioner or bring suit without a tutor. Left: A banished man begs the protection of a priest and asks him to represent him as tutor before the ecclesiasical court. The priest indicates his consent by holding his protecting stole over the man (Common Law II 63, Sect. 1,2).

A hue and cry is necessary for initiating court proceedings. Right: a woman with headgear and a girl complain of the rape committed on them, raising their hands to swear their oath in the attitude of plaintiffs. Loose, fluttering hair and torn clothing comply with the rules for a mediaeval charge of rape. Left: the plaintiff with sword produces a thief caught in the act, his hands bound behind his back. On the thief's back, his booty is tied as a "shining signal" of "physical proof". Below: with the dead man covered with wounds and lying before the judge, a criminal caught red-handed, a "complaint against a dead man" is brought. (Common Law II 63, Art. 1-3).

Left: after the commission of rape, not only the house in which the deed was done must be destroyed (devastation), but all animals that were present must be killed (Common Law III, Art. 1).

Before the judge stands the exile (with a sword in his neck) whose banishment the judge confirm by pointing to himself. The plaintiff swears that the exile is guilty. Behind him stand his oath-helpers who testify by an oath on the relic that his oath is pure (Common Law III 88, Art. 3).

Here a criminal caught in the act is "set down". The ritual of swearing differs from that in the top picture: the plaintiff sets the relic on the head of the delinquent and takes his oath on it. The witness at the left has raised his oath-fingers of the left hand to place them on the criminal's head, while the proper oath-hand lies on the reliquary (Common Law 88, Art. 4).

Standing before the judge are men to whom a breaker of the peace has been handed over. The bound peace-breaker is in the centre. The man looking over his shoulder seems to be warning the judge to deliver the offender only against surety. The two men at the left offer to stand surety by laying hand on the offender and gestures indicating a vow (Common Law II 71, Art. 5, sentence 2).

The tower watchman sounds the horn to announce the appearance of the plaintiff and the 6 messengers. The plaintiff, with bared sword as the symbol of the hue and cry, is passing through the gate. Behind him, the judge's messengers make gestures demanding entry. (Common Law II 72, Art. 2, sentence 2).

The lord of the castle leads the guilty man before the judge. The offender indicates by gestures towards the castle that he wants to evade the issue. For this reason the lord of the castle carries his sword in its scabbard, since he is presenting the true offender and need not answer for the deed himself (Common Law II 72, Art. 3).

The mentally ill cannot be held responsible. An insane man with bells on his clothes injures another man's head with a hammerlike object. His guardian is liable for the injury and is here paying damages to a knight. (Common Law III 3 Sentences 2 and 3).

The guardian is liable for harm caused by a child under age. Here he is paying the plaintiff the "wergeld" for the person killed by the child (Common Law II 65, Art. 1).

A pregnant woman tied to the whipping post may be given no more severe punishment than that to the "hide" (birching) and the hair (cutting off of hair). (Common Law II 3).

A Jew has acquired a chalice and a book (sacred Christian objects) although such action is forbidden. The man in red levels the charge as is apparent from the gesture of his left hand. The judge passes sentence. The Jew is hung blindfolded from an ancient, forked-post gallows (Common Law III 7, Art. 4, sentence 1).

A "German" is sentenced to loss of a hand for a crime. The "German" is represented here by the "Saxon", recognizable by the knife (sax) held in his hand. (Common Law III 50).

Serfdom

If a serf has renounced his lord and declared that he belongs to another, his first lord can call him before the court. If the serf is not represented by his new lord, as is lawful, the first lord can win him back by seizing the tail of the serf's coat and by the testimony of two persons who have been his serfs from birth (Common Law III 32, Art. 9).

System of Fines

The defendant pays the successful plaintiff a fine or "wergeld" and the judge the peace money. The plaintiff's finger pointing towards the judge draws attention to the situation (Common Law III 32, Art. 10).

The imperial prince is entitled to a fine of 12 (golden) pfennigs. The number XVIII at the left of the picture means 18 pounds, which is the "wergeld" of the prince. (Common Law III 45, Art. 1, sentences 1-5).

The fine due to the freeman eligible to serve as an assessor - here depicted as a lord - is 30 schillings (XXX), which is also equivalent to 12 gold pfennigs. The number XVIII (18 pounds) is his "Wergeld". (Common Law III 45, Art. 1, sentences 6-8).

Statute of Limitations

A case is statute-barred on expiry of a year and a day, i. e. (= LII weeks) + (VI weeks). It is noon on the ensuing day, as shown by the full sun. Consequently, the defendant lets the hand with which he would gesture when answering hang by his side. He does not want to answer, because he does not need to. The judge confirms this by indicating that the period is expired. Right: a pregnant woman whose husband lies dead indicates to the heir with a gesture that she cannot be turned out of the house. (Common Law III 38, Sect. 1 and 2).

Law of Succession

A child is deemed to be born living when its voice can be heard at the 4 walls of the house. It then has the right of succession even if the father has died previously, as in this picture in which the mother of the child is wearing a widow's veil (Common Law 20, Art. 1).

The inheritance is depicted here as the sum of indefinable pieces. The bearded man, the elder, divides the pieces into two heaps. The younger man stands waiting with a mien of incapability. Only after all is divided is he permitted to choose. This illustrates the principle: the elder divides, the younger chooses (Common Law III 29. Art. 2).

The law of succession gives children of the whole blood precedence over half-blooded children. The whole-blooded ("unsundered") children are depicted as a person with two heads and the half-blooded ("sundered") as two persons. Here again, the grasping of the ears of corn signifies a legal right to the inheritance (Common Law II 20, Art. 1).

Divorce

A priest separates the spouses. The child in arms is not mentioned in the text. In the other hand the woman holds shears as a symbol of the "Gerade" (wife's separate property) which she retains. She goes towards the building standing on her property (usufructuary estate). The half-shield indicates the property brought into the marriage. The man hands the woman a pouch containing what he promised her on marrying her (Common Law III 74).

Building Law

Rainwater from the roof may flow only on to one's own farmyard. The yard must be surrounded by a woven fence (Common Law II 49, Art. 1 and 2).

Pigsty, privy and baking oven must be set up at a suitable distance, three feet from the property boundary (Common Law II 51, Art. 1).

Purchase and Liability

A horse is sold for cash in the presence of two witnesses (Common Law III 4, Art. 2).

The custodian is not liable if the thing in his custody, here a horse, is destroyed fortuitously (fire). He swears on the reliquary, averring his innocence to the pledger, who with his gestures demands compensation for the death of the animal (Common Law III 5, Art. 3).

No damages had to be paid, if a pledged animal died without any fault on the part of the pledge-holder and this could be proved under oath (here "physical proof" by showing the hide) Common Law III 5, Art. 5).

A person who keeps dangerous dogs or wild animals is liable for any harm they may cause. The victim lying on the ground at the left appears with two witnesses before the judge at the right to claim damages (Common Law II 62, Art. 1)

An attacked person kills a boar and a dog in self-defence and does not have to pay damages; he swears before the judge that it was self-defence (Common Law II 62, Art. 2).

Emperor Maximilian I summons the imperial diet to convene at Worms on Nov. 1, 1508.
Lucerne Chronicles by Diebold Schilling, 1513, Bürgerbibliothek, Lucerne.

Fehmic Court
The Freigraf, or free count (centre), bears no staff, as was customary for judges in the Middle Ages, as the symbol of his judicial power, the sword, lies before him on the table. Fehmic court picture from the Soest Manuscript XXXVIII 55, 15th century, Soest city archives.

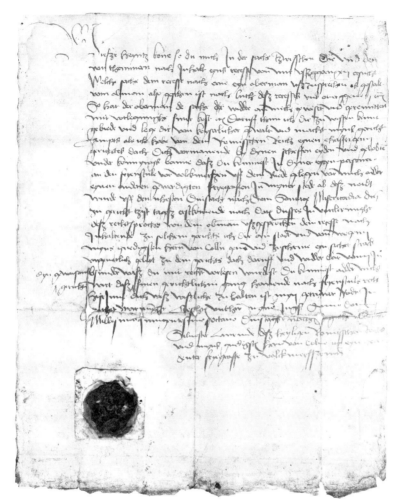

Summons to a Fehmic Court:

Take cognizance, Heinz Bone, that in the matter between you and those of Theimern, in which you besought me to have an arbiter make a decision on the basis of the agreement drawn up by me, a decision has been reached. The arbiter has returned the matter to me together with the bill of costs. By virtue of the judicial office bestowed on me by imperial authority and power, and admonishing you to keep your assessor's oath and vow and your loyalty to the king's judicial authority, I summons you to appear in person at the free count's court in Volckmerssen, situated in the Ried, before me or, in the event of my being impeded, another free count acting as my deputy. The time is set for Tuesday following Misericordia (2nd Sunday after Easter) at the usual time for the court so that as the first business the ruling of the arbiter can be pronounced in accordance with the agreement.

For and on behalf of my gracious lord, the Electoral Prince and Archbishop of Cologne, I assure you free and safe conduct to and from the court. I draw your attention to the fact that, should you fail to appear, the court will decide the matter in accordance with the law of the free count's court. I therefore give you the good advice to observe my instructions.

Done under my seal, February 8, 1508.

(Signature) Silvester Lavende (?), Free Count of Volckmerssen by the grace of the Holy Roman Empire and my gracious lord of Cologne, etc.

judge, pronounced the judgment found by the (clerical) assessors. For the execution of punishments, especially capital punishment, the secular powers were obliged to render assistance. The church on its part supported the endeavours of the king in matters relating to the law by prescribing excummunication for serious crimes, e.g. highway robbery, and inflicting it on a person proscribed by the king.

The object of all the endeavours described so far was to inhibit feuds, the biggest problem in those times. As reflected in the bodies of folk-law, the immediate killing of law-breakers had been successfully restricted to just a few cases and in all other cases in which offenders were caught red-handed it had been enforced that they must be brought before a court. On the other hand, it had not proved possible to compel such trials to be held, not before a hurriedly convened folk-court (emergency court) with immediate execution of the sentence, but before a regular court. This was due primarily to the weakness of the king and all judicial authority derived from him. The king and the lords on whom he had bestowed court powers therefore had to endeavour to restrain such uncontrollable popular justice and to get the adjudication proceedings and execution of sentences into their own hands. The "peace movement" of the 11th and 12th century can be considered the first steps in this direction; at the same time it created the conditions precedent for a new understanding of "penal law" and the "state". There were a number of reasons for this peace movement. First, it was directed against feuds, which were spreading on account of the weakness of royal executive authority. Especially for the peasants, whose access to the courts was often impeded and who were frequently completely at the mercy of an arbitrary judge, it was a sort of self-help to gain their rights. Moreover, another new form of feud had come into being, the knight's feud. This, too, was an attempt at self-help where royal administration of justice could not come into play, either out of weakness or because there were no grounds for intervention, e. g. injury to the honour of a knight. With the advent of Christendom, a new, high value was attached to the concept of personal honour. With the progressive grouping of people into estates, the finer became the differences in the honour attributed to them. The higher the estate, the greater the honour. The knights in particular had made honour — in addition to loyalty — a highly exaggerated, central attribute of their culture. As a result of this overemphasis, the slightest unconsidered statement or action was regarded by a knight as an affront to his honour, which could only be restored by a feud. Fixed rules had to be observed. The feud had to be announced by a formal challenge and certain actions had to be abstained from, e.g. the killing of an innocent person, and later on any killing whatever. The burning down of houses and devastation of the land were permitted. The knight's feud was not arbitrary violence, but was regarded as a special form of legal proceedings. For all that, it involved great insecurity on the roads, for agriculture and, above all, for the peasant population, who had to bear the most suffering. The decline of the knight's estate in the 14th and 15th century and the accompanying impoverishment resulted in the degeneration of morals and the deterioration of the feud to highway robbery (robber knights) and hence to criminal action. The followers of the ever more improverished knight ("reisige Haufen") had to be fed and kept in a good mood by fighting and taking booty.

In addition, a new form of criminality came into being, of such proportions that the traditional legal system was helpless in the face of it. The knight's feud, now deteriorated to highway robbery, the oppression of the population by exhorbitant levies, the despotism of the land lords, wars that repeatedly flared up anew and many other factors resulted in general pauperization of the lower strata of the population. The difference between poor and rich became ever greater. Economic need compelled many people to gain a living by robbery and theft. Beggars, itinerant people (jugglers, artistes, musicians, fortune-tellers), who were considered dishonest, gypsies, pilgrims, fugitive monks and nuns, escaped serfs and law-breakers expelled from society frequented the highways and became a public nuisance. The criminal elements among them often formed robber bands, who found refuge from pursuit and discovery in the then very large and dense forests. These "pernicious people" had made life insecure. By imposing grievous punishments —fines were senseless in view of the destitution of the offenders— the king and the land lords tried to combat these conditions, but with no great success. It was the second goal of the peace movement to combat this (mass) criminality successfully. The first beginnings in this respect were the "truces of God" in the 10th and 11th century. Owing to the fragmentation of government authority and the incapacity of the temporal lords to compel observation of the law, only ecclesiastical power was in a position to put a stop to the havoc. The lords spiritual and temporal exhorted the summoned Christian populace to observe the "Pax Dei", i.e. peace in churches and cemeteries and for women, children, the clergy, travellers and peasants, and the "Treuga Dei", i.e. the peace on Sundays and holy days and in certain periods of the church year, e.g. Advent. The church made it the duty of all Christians to ensure peace with all possible means and called for the overpowering and destruction of peacebreakers, not only because of breaches of the king's peace, but especially because of contravention of the divine order. It should not go unmentioned that the religious fervour of the people as a whole also

Transcription of the above feudal challenge:

Be it known to the burghermaster, council and all citizens, rich and poor, of the town of Rothenburg situated on the Tauber: On account of the debt and claim due from you to the highborn prince and lord, Friedrich Burggrave of Nuremberg, our gracious lord, whom we wish to help to the best of our ability in collecting these debts from you and your helpers, we proclaim by this document our intent to contend in peace and strife for our named gracious lord against you and your helpers and preserve hereby our honour; namely:

I, Konrad Ebe, master of the kitchen of my aforementioned gracious lord, Wernlein Pucher, Peter Hirsse, Albrecht Morsta(i)n, Starckheinz, Hanns Strawsse. — Done and sealed under the seal of the aforementioned Konrad Ebe, which we, all the aforementioned, use together with him, on the Monday preceding the day of St. Mary Magdalena in the year of our Lord 1407 (July 18, 1407).

The Rothenburg archives contain several hundred such feudal challenges dating from between 1398 and 1407. They document the controversies between the town and the burgrave of Nuremberg, the bishops of Bamberg and Würzburg and their noble vassals. The condition of the challenges permits conclusions as to the way in which they were delivered. The above challenge was delivered by a messenger, others were frayed, attached to an arrow like a feather and shot over the walls. Others have a hole because they were nailed to the city gate.

brought in its train a loss of tolerance for the Jews. Until well into the 11th century, the Jews lived in the towns without any difficulties and were separated from the indigenous population only in the sphere of the church. The persecutions of Jews which set in after the first crusade (1096 - 99) resulted in their isolation and the creation of ghettoes. It was not until the imperial public peace law of 1103 that the public peace was also extended to the Jews; this was coupled, however, with loss of the right to bear arms and compulsion to wear specific clothing (conical hat). The numerous obstacles to the pursuit of common vocations resulted in their earning their living by lending money against interest. The Christians were forbidden to do this by a church ban, by which the Jews were not bound, as they were not Christians. In consequence, large segments of the population were reduced to a state of subjection (usury), which led to ever new persecution.

The later public peace laws gradually evolved into genuine penal laws with concrete definitions of offences and their punishments. They covered not only acts in the course of feuds (arson, robbery and manslaughter), but also purely criminal offences, e.g. theft. – It should be added, however, that the tenor of the public peace laws varied so much that it is really inacurate to described them as "penal laws", since they also covered other fields such as coinage, customs duties, levies, social regulations and wage taxes for millers and craftsmen. The public peace laws will be dealt with in this article only to the extent that they were of significance for the development of penal law. This essay cannot and is not intended to give a presentation of the history of the public peace laws; that would require a special and very extensive article. – The "perpetual peace" proclaimed at the imperial diet in Worms in 1495 finally brought complete prohibition of feuds. From then onwards, this

Beggars, two woodcuts from the 15th century.

type of self-help was no longer allowed by law. It was some time, however, before the then weak government authorities were able to force acceptance of this by the nobles. The personal history of Götz von Berlichingen (1480 - 1562) gives ample information on this point. Public peace laws were promulgated, not only by the king, but also by the territorial lords, and they had varying areas of validity. Above all, as the towns gained power they had a great interest in peace and order and the security of the highways on account of their trade. And so they issued their own laws, the so-called "Stadtfrieden" (town peace laws).

The German "truces of God" contained not only ecclasiastical penalties such as excommunication, damnation, refusal of the sacrament and burial, etc., but also intentionally the old secular punishments. In this way the Lex talionis of the Old Testament (an eye for an eye, a tooth for a tooth) was incorporated into the law and this marked the point of departure for what we now consider to be the gruesome penal law of the late Middle Ages. While the proclamation of a "truce of God" was exclusively the concern of the ecclesiastical powers, very soon the kings took over the preservation of peace by promulgating the public peace laws. The early public peace laws, the first of which was the imperial peace law of Henry IV, 1103, were a sort of transition from the truces of God to the later public peace laws. On the one hand they contained an absolute ban on feuds at certain times within the truce of God, and on the other hand the penal law of the later enactments instead of the church punishments.

The most important feature of the public peace laws and the "Halsgerichtsordnungen" which followed them was that evildoers were classified according to the Ten Commandments of the Old Testament, giving rise to "genuine" penal laws. For all types of crime, not merely those in which the offender was caught in the act, they prescribed punishments and in most cases "grievous" ones. They gave expression for the first time to the principle of equal treatment of offenders, derived from the equality of all men before God. Whereas in earlier times the punishments prescribed for crimes of the unfree were far more severe than for those of the free, now the same punishment was laid down for all, and to an increasing extent capital punishment. A further step in development, though a much later one, was the pecuniary equal treatment of rich and poor by the prohibition of money payments to avoid grievous punishment. The gradual appreciation of the fact that the prosecution of crimes could no longer be left to the initiative of the person whose rights had been violated, but was in the interests of all, was likewise important.

86

Procedure also changed quite a lot. Purgative oaths were restricted and later made impossible by the probative oath of the plaintiff. The evidence of witnesses and in the towns above all documentary evidence was recognized. The testimony of two good witnesses was sufficient to bar the defendant's purgative oath and, indeed, to deprive him of the possibility of calling witnesses for his defence. The procedure for offenders caught in the act was extended to all who committed a public mischief. If proof could be brought of a public mischief, the perpetrator was sentenced as if caught in the act. This was of special importance especially in the towns which had their own judicial system. The growth of professional criminality was a grave danger for the towns, which lived predominantly from trade. They therefore set up their own organizations for the pursuit and arrest of non-resident offenders. Later on, all capital crimes were dealt with in so-called "Übersiebnungsverfahren" (seven-man

Cover:
Proclamation
of the public peace,
J. Schöffer, Mainz, 1521

oath proceedings). Seven men, who were either witnesses of the act or knew the offender's iniquitous character, swore an oath and thus proved his guilt. This procedure then developed into the more stringent "character witness procedure", in which it was not even necessary to prove a specific act by the defendant, but merely to show his social harmfulness. It was sufficient for the plaintiff to swear an oath as to the captive's evil character and have it corroborated by six oath-helpers. The role of the plaintiff was assumed by the "town complainant", a specially appointed public prosecutor. Eventually, this led to a situation in which the town council merely voted on whether and how the prisoner was to be punished. The distinction between offenders caught in the act and others was thus given up. This occured simultaneously in the "town peaces" and the "land peaces".

Subsequent developments then brought the "ex officio action"; the judge himself investigated crimes and appeared as prosecutor before the court (i.e. before the judment-finders). It was thus made the official duty of the authorities to prosecute criminals and conduct the trial (maxim of ex officio action). The trial itself was still the old complaint proceedings, but now the complainant acted by virtue of his office or was the judge himself.

This, however, did not satisfy the need for prosecution. The punishment, as retribution for the crime, should, it was felt, be inflicted on the real guilty party and, as far as possible, on all criminals. This made it necessary to investigate the true facts during the proceedings. The obligation arose for the court to inquire into the facts and circumstances of the offence and hence to determine the objective truth (maxim of instruction). This was done initially by questioning witnesses, but soon after also by interrogating the accused, who was the most accessible source of evidence. This opened up the way for the use of torture to determine the truth, a method which enabled hitherto unknown crimes to be revealed and accomplices to be found. Over and above that, by his confession (under duress) the accused took the first step towards conversion and repentance. The combination of the maxims of ex officio action and instruction became the basis for the "inquisitorial trial" (Lat. inquisitio = investigation), which was the most important outcome of the new understanding of crime. The basic idea of the inquisitorial proceedings was the combination of the roles of the prosecutor, the defender and the judge in the person of the judge. It was no longer the injured party, but the judge who entered a claim for punishment. The injured party was now no more than an informer and witness, the accused became the object of the investigation. This was a conception quite alien to the spirit of German penal law up that time and probably the most marked antithesis to the former accusation principle. Nevertheless, the old complaint procedure with a private or public complainant was theoretically preserved, but now the complainant had to bear the costs of proceedings, if he failed to prove the defendant's guilt. However, the complainant could easily evade this risk by simply laying information and setting the inquisitorial proceedings in motion. This harsh procedure also created the preconditions for bringing offenders caught in the act under the jurisdiction of the regular courts. How, apart from cases of self-defence and adultery by the wife (the latter remaining an exception for a long time), an offender caught red-handed could only be bound and delivered up to the court for the passing of sentence. The execution of the death penalty was then the task of the "Hochgerichte" (lit. high courts; courts trying capital crimes), which thus became "Blutgerichte" (lit. bloody tribunals) and gradually took over the entire proceedings. With the elimination of the old form of self-justice (killing of an offender caught in the act), the legal system had finally become the defender of the peace.

But what power was capable of translating these theoretical preconditions into action? With the end of the strife on investiture, the unity of church and state was destroyed; but not the Christian-ecclesiastical conception of the world, which now took on a new form. The church was henceforth superior to the state, and the state had become a thing apart from the church and was recognized as a secular power. Under divine law it was called upon, as a secular power, to protect the church, for which purpose it had to wield the sword. This divine law became the foundation of its own secular legal system and thus the groundwork was laid for a genuine legal system. But that newly emerged secular state was no longer the empire of the king. For he lacked the necessary power on account of the political conditions. The new form of statehood manifested itself in the sovereign territories that came into being on imperial soil. The king, too, saw himself more as a territorial sovereign, concentrating his interest increasingly on the expansion of his realm and thus on the strengthening of his own dynastic power. This development from the Christian king to individual territorial sovereigns is illustrated by the public peace laws. In 1103, the first "imperial peace" was sworn to for four years. In 1235, Frederich II proclaimed the imperial peace of Mainz, the last before the interregnum, the kingless period. During the interregnum, the initiative for the "public peaces" came from the territorial sovereigns who had also played a part in the earlier ones. Following a transitional phase in which the public peaces were brought about only by agreement with the territorial sovereigns, in the 15th century it was again possible to promulgate imperial public peace laws. The kings, however, were not in a position to ensure implementation of the regulations. With effect from the enactment of 1442, the territorial sovereigns, the land lords, bore exclusive responsibility for that. The king restricted himself to issuing a "peace act" in the form of a public peace law and threatening imperial proscription for all violations of the peace. The "Perpetual Peace" of 1495 marked the end of this development and at the same time the beginning of a new epoch: The public peace law became an imperial code resolved upon by the diet of Worms. The king had ceased to be the defender of the peace and law in the empire. He took part in establishing and preserving the public peace only by the sovereign act of legislation, while enforcement of the peace in court and execution within the territories was left to the territorial powers. From now on the regional sovereigns assumed also formal responsibility for the public peace in their territories. The imperial court and royal chamber were transformed by the imperial diet into the Reichskammergericht (imperial chamber), to which a president and associate judges were appointed. It thus lost its character of a court subordinate to the person and powers of the king.

The land lords gradually succeeded in dissolving the so-called "immunities" within their territories and in creating a uniform state territory. — Immunities were small ecclasiastical (churches, monasteries) or secular (knights, nobles) estates which were situated in the territory of a prince and enjoyed an exceptional status by royal privilege (owing fealty only to the empire). In such enclaves, court jurisdiction, police and fiscal authority were vested in a steward appointed by the "immunity sovereign" (king). Officials of the surrounding territory were forbidden to take any official action whatever within the area of the immunity. — The local sovereign, "by the grace of God" according to the notions then held, felt responsible for the wellbeing of his country and population in legal, economic and religious respects. Jurists versed in Roman law created a comprehensive code of sovereignty and government law. The regional codes provided for the protection of the traditional order, the Christian, honourable way of life, adequate supplies of commodities for the population and, first and foremost, the combatting of crime. The "Halsgerichtsordnungen" (codes of criminal law and procedure) which were then promulgated were designed to put the professional criminals, the perpetrators of public mischief, out of action. The inquisitorial procedure and the torture it made possible were suitable means to that end and were used to an ever-increasing degree. The Halsgerichtsordnungen with all their brutality were enacted because, in the opinion of the regional sovereign, punishments had formerly been too mild and too many crimes went unpunished. As time passed, the powers of the authorities were increased more and more, the right of arrest was extended, and torture was permitted to an ever greater extent; and the church gave encouragement. — The inquisitorial trials of the church, which developed almost parallel to the trend in the secular administration of justice, will not be dealt with in detail in this context. However, it should be mentioned that torture was not expressly approved by the church, although the secular courts were empowered to use it by Pope Innocence IV as far back as 1252. — Inquisitorial procedure predominated. Its chief element

Imperial Court at Rottweil, woodcut, 16th century.

was the secret preliminary session directed by a delegated judge, in which torture performed its actual evidence-producing function in the service of a very questionable determination of the truth. If the accused survived the torture without making a confession, the preliminary proceedings ended with his release, but not without previously swearing an oath of truce with which he swore to abstain from any act of vengeance on persons belonging to the court. If the preliminary proceedings ended with a confession, the formal judgment had to be pronounced in a further session, the "final day of justice"; it was a public session on the lines of customary mediaeval legal proceedings and a purely formal act, a public-spectacle trial. Since the truth determined in the inquisitorial preliminary proceedings was the basis for the judgment, they had to be repeated in the formal "final" session. To rebut a possible retraction of the confession, which only disturbed the public-spectacle trial, in the course of time the testimony of the inquisitors was admitted, who, of course, had heard the confession in the preliminary proceedings. Their statement corroborating the confession was deemed proof of the guilt of the recanting accused. Frequently, however, this show for the public was waived and the proceedings took place solely behind the closed doors of the torture chamber. Such penal justice was intolerable over the long run. On mere suspicion, possibly on account of a false accusation under torture, any one could be drawn into the trial, with little chance of coming out of it alive. When the Reichskammergericht took up its activities in 1495, so many urgent complaints about this deplorable state of affairs came in from all sides that the imperial assembly saw itself compelled to initiate a general reform of the administration of penal justice.

The new conception of the state and law made it possible to take over ideas of the Italian jurists. The latter, oriented to the inquisitorial procedure of the church and to Roman law, had elaborated the idea of the essentiality of guilt and attempted to influence the dangers of the inquisitorial trial for a truly innocent person. They also set up rules for the court's activities in order to save it from police-mindedness. The Italian jurists sought to solve the problems of torture with the "doctrine of circumstantial evidence". They worked out rules laying down of what nature and how grave a suspicion must be to justify the use of torture. Through the new class of German jurists, who had been trained in Italy, all this gradually found its way to Germany and made possible a reform of the prevailing conditions. It is chiefly due to the groundwork done by the author of the Bamberg "Halsgerichtsordnung" of 1507 (Bambergensis), Johann Baron Schwarzenberg (1465 - 1528), steward of the bishops of Bamberg, that on July 17, 1532, at the imperial diet of Regensburg the "Constitutio Criminalis Carolina", the "peinliche Gerichtsordnung" of Emperor Charles V and the Holy Roman Empire was enacted. The Carolina was the first general German criminal code and incorporated a code of criminal procedure. In addition to regulating penal procedure, it constituted the first codification of common German substantive criminal law. It formed the basis for the evolution of common German criminal law over the course of nearly three centuries.

The Carolina made it evident that the judge's activity was not to be limited merely to the performance of formal, logical functions, but was also of a creative nature and for that he must have a clear head and an inflexible character. In addition to legal ability, the judge should also have human qualities. A new feature of this code was the abrogation of the distinction between the assessors on the bench and the judge presiding over the proceedings. From now on, the judge participated, like the assessors, in finding the judgment and swore to do justice to poor and rich alike (Art. 3). The assessors, who had no legal training, thus became ever less important. The individual judge, or his learned clerk of the court, passed judgment alone in thousands of cases. It was only in more complex cases that judgement by a "college" of judges was retained, as "dubios cases" had to be placed in the hands of authorities versed in the law. A further new feature was the laying down of the judge's status under public law. What had been initiated in the era of the Electors was laid down as a principle in the Carolina: From now on the judge was an official appointed by the authorities with a fixed salary, who had to swear an oath of office and who was strictly forbidden "to take any remuneration from a plaintiff" (Art. 205). The bestowal of a judge's office as a fief, and hence its hereditary character, was finally abolished by the Carolina. In the procedural law, the ex officio and inquisitorial principle was given its definitive form. The old formal means of proof of the earlier "ordeal" proceedings were replaced by the legal theory of evidence of the Italian canonical procedure, in conjunction with which the doctrine of circumstantial evidence had been developed. The "confession trial" had already gained ground in the 15th century. This form of trial was now regulated by the Carolina right down to the last detail. The main thing in the trial was to reveal the truth to the judge by the defendant's confession. The defendant had to declare himself guilty or not guilty. The judge's function was to extract a confession by legal means and to substantiate the truth of the confession by inquiries and questions (Art. 60). Torture was also confirmed by the statute as a means of extracting confessions. Consequently the Carolina and the succeeding codes of procedure are full of provisions concerning the "painful" questions. Nowadays we find it extremely difficult to comprehend our ancestors' line of thought in this sphere. It cannot be denied, however, that despite all the torture rules, which now seem barbaric to us, the "peinliche" codes of court procedure made extraordinary efforts to limit the use of torture to what was right and proper. It was probably Schwarzenberg's most important achievement that he set up norms for its application. Torture was permitted only when there were quite specific grounds for suspicion (circumstantial evidence). Torture was to be inflicted, "according to the circumstances of the suspectfulness of the person, much, often or less, severely or mildly at the discretion of a good, reasonable judge" (Art. 58). Leading questions were not permitted and a confession made under torture was valid only if repeated voluntarily outside the torture chamber (Art. 58). A judge who tortured unjustly could be called to account and punished by the authorities (Art. 61). Such a judge was even threatened with punishment beyond the grave (Art. 150).

On account of the demand for confessions, the evidence of witnesses receded entirely into the background. The Carolina expressly permitted it and ensured that it was treated in accordance with the law (Art. 62 et seq.). It rejected oath-helpers and required witnesses to testify "of there owne trew knowledge" (Art. 65). Under the rules of evidence laid down in the Carolina, a misdeed should be provable by two or three good, credible witnesses, but a single witness was deemed to be only a half-proof (Art. 23). The main thing in the criminal trial, however, was not proof of guilt, but the confession.

In the field of substantive penal law, already known offences were given designations, others were clearly defined in understandable, popular language. This satisfied an essential precondition for uniform organization of the hitherto disordered system of "grievous" punishments, as demonstrated by the laying down of precisely specified, severe punishments for the most serious cases. In the remaining cases, however, the Carolina gave rise to the problem of punishment assessment by leaving the penalties to the discretion of the judge.

The inflexible resistance, especially on the part of the larger territorial states, during the period of its inception led to the inclusion of the so-called clausula salvatoria, which conceded the Carolina only subsidiary applicability, i.e. deviating provisions of regional or local law had precedence. Nevertheless, this did not cancel out the reformative effect and the Carolina became the model of numerous German territorial enactments. For all its endeavours to attain justice and moderation, however, it contained dangerous

Forcible presentation of an evil-doer, woodcut, 15th century.

points of departure for the later degeneration of the inquisitorial procedure: the dual role of the judge, the secret, written, preliminary proceedings and the statutory theory of evidence in conjunction with torture. One significant advance compared to the previous legal situation, however, was the provisions on the general theory of crime: liability based on guilt instead of on the outcome of a "trial", and the stricter definition of the concepts of (criminal) attempt, self-defence and complicity. The Carolina, the last great work of imperial legislation, was of extraordinary importance and introduced a new epoch in the administration of German criminal law. The inquisitorial procedure based on the Carolina endured up to the middle of the 19th century, until the stormy events of 1848 finally brought the end of this meanwhile obsolete system.

The development of the modern state, which began from the 16th century onwards, also brought many a decisive change for the administration of justice. The general decline of morals in consequence of wartime turmoil in the 16th and especially the 17th century was not without its effect on justice. The courts became corrupt and the judges bribable. It was therefore a matter of special concern to the state to remedy this intolerable situation. It therefore set out to train incorruptible and dependable judges. The training of the legal professions was regulated by the government and state examinations were prescribed for members of the judiciary. To ensure uniformity and integrity in the administration of justice, the territorial sovereigns required the lower courts to submit their judgments to themselves or the upper courts for approval.

Then, in the age of absolutism, so-called "cabinet justice", i.e. direct intervention by the land lord in judicial proceedings, exerted a strong influence on the administration of justice. Absolute monarchy was a form of government that knew no separation of powers, so the territorial sovereign possessed not only legislative, but also jurisdictional rights. His decisions, therefore, were made in the rightful exercise of his sovereign powers. Acts of sovereign, cabinet justice extended to confirmation or amendment of a court decision already handed down, assumption of jurisdiction before a court judgment was pronounced, instructions to initiate, accelerate or discontinue proceedings, to apply or abstain from using torture, to call for further evidence, or to hand down a specified judgment. From the viewpoint of the present-day, liberal state under the rule of law, the term "cabinet justice" embodies a negative, political value-judgment, for the sovereign's interventions were often in the personal interests of the prince or motivated by raisons d'etat. Particularly at the beginning of the 19th century, it was used as a political means to combat advocates of the rule of law and liberal ideas. It must be kept in mind, however, that cabinet justice was not exercised solely out of arbitrary despotism, but also in order to remedy the then usual failings of the judiciary such as lethargy, corruption, incapacity of judges, jurisdictional difficulties, etc., to ensure uniformity of rulings and to overcome the uncertainty of the law. Despite the general trenchant condemnation of cabinet justice from our current standpoint, it undoubtedly also played its part in overcoming mediaeval practices in the administration of justice.

In the middle of the 17th century, a new intellectual movement spread from England, the Enlightenment. Its self-set goal was to raise reason and human dignity to supremacy, and it also developed a new conception of the state. These aspirations also had an impact on the administration of justice. Even previously, well-known scholars such as Spee, Grevius and Oldekop had advocated humanization of criminal law and abolition of the torture used in inquisitorial procedure. They failed to achieve immediate success, but they did deliver an impetus. The decisive blow against torture was struck in 1705 by Christian Thomasius with his "Disputatio de Tortura in foris Christianorum proscribenda", in which he expressly based his ideas on the arguments of his predecessors. As a result, as early as the first half of the 18th century, bans on the use of torture in criminal proceedings were issued in various German states.

However, the resulting gap in the system was filled only in a very imperfect manner. Now, lacking a forcibly extracted confession, instead of proceeding, where there were no witnesses, to pass judgment on the basis of convincing circumstantial evidence, the courts imposed punishments for insubordination and lying and on suspicion. These penalties, mostly in the form of flogging, were as brutal, and at times even more brutal than torture, as they were not subject to such strict rules as torture.

Inquisitorial proceedings had also gained general acceptance as the predominant mode of trial in pre-revolutionary France. On account of the absolutist regime of the kings and their arbitrary intervention in the administration of justice, marked distrust of the judiciary had arisen among the people. The revolution of July 14, 1789, was the turning point. Human rights were proclaimed and the slogan was liberty, equality, fraternity. The people demanded control of the administration of justice and codetermination in certain criminal causes. The inquisitorial trial with torture, punishments for insubordination and its rules of evidence was abolished. Criminal procedure was thoroughly reformed. From then on it was based on the fundamental principle of public and oral hearings. The investigating and indicting authorities (public prosecutor's office) were completely separated from the courts. Grave crimes were tried by judge and jury, a procedure long practiced in England, but a revolutionary innovation for the continent. The Englisch and French models did not fail to have an effect in the German states. Following liberation from the Napoleonic yoke (1813), the "Deutscher Bund" was established in 1815 in Frankfurt am Main; it was a confederation of 34 states and 4 free cities, in which the sovereignty of the individual member states was preserved. For this reason it had no judicial authority in either civil or criminal cases, so organization of the judicature was left entirely to the discretion of the member states of the confederation. The liberal movements of the period from 1815 to 1848 made the reform of the criminal courts and of criminal procedure, and hence the introduction of juries, a cardinal political aspiration. Initiated by the Carlsbad decrees of 1819 (restoration), persecution of the liberals and democrats by the (cabinet) justice authorities began. This suppression of intellectual and political freedom in Germany aroused the resistance of many. A leading role in the struggle for criminal law reform was played by Paul Johann Anselm von Feuerbach (1775 - 1833). He was the founder of modern criminal jurisprudence and made a decisive contribution to the development of a liberal criminal court system. The breakthrough came fifteen years after his death in the revolution of 1848.

The Frankfurt National Assembly, the first German parliament, formulated a new constitution, which was proclaimed on March 28, 1849, including the passages:

Art. 42   Judicial powers shall be exercised by the courts independently. Cabinet and ministerial justice is not permissible. No man may be withheld from his statutory judge. There shall be no extraordinary courts.

Art. 44   Except by way of judgment and due process of law, no judge may be removed from office or have his rank and salary prejudiced. No judge may be transferred elsewhere or retired from office against his will, except by a court decision in such cases and forms as are laid down by the statutes.

With these norms the principle of the rule of law gained the ascendancy in the law of the judicature and completed a development that had commenced exactly one hundred years before with the "Esprit de lois" by the Frenchman Moutesguieus.

The new constitutions of the confederated German states then incorporated more or less similar provisions, in keeping with the constitution of the confederation. True, uniformity of the law had not yet been achieved, but pointers had been given for an organization of the system of judicature in line with constitionalism and the liberal principle of the rule of law in future imperial law. Various states and groups put up strong resistance to the impending reform of criminal law. One controversial issue was how the jury was to take part in criminal trials, i.e., in the form of a "Geschworenengericht" (with Anglo-American type jury) or of a "Schwurgericht" (with lay assessors). A further 30 years passed by before the desired uniform ruling was achieved in the meanwhile re-established German empire (1871) by the promulgation of the Judicature Act and the code of criminal procedure on October 1, 1879. The Judicature Act provided for courts with English-type juries. The jury, seated in a jury box, had to follow the trial and subsequently pass a verdict of guilty or not guilty; the sentence was passed by the professional judge.

The amended 1924 version of the Judicature Act went a step further. It transformed the "Geschworenengericht" that had jurisdiction over serious cases into a "Schwurgericht", and the lower court (Amtsgericht) with jurisdiction in minor cases into a "Schöffengericht". In this latter court, the "Schöffen" (or lay assessors) perform all judicial functions.

They are on a par with the professional judge, sit with him on the bench and take part in all decisions, including the severity of the sentence. They also have the right to question all parties during the trial.

With the coming into force of the Judicature Act and the Code of Criminal Procedure on October 1, 1879, 347 years after the promulgation of the Constitutio Criminalis Carolina, Germany once more had a uniform law in the field of the administration of criminal justice.

National Assembly in St. Pauls Church,
the first German Parliament, 18 May 1848, Frankfurt/M.

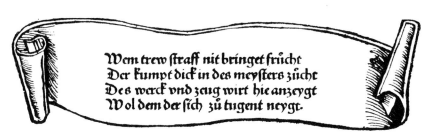

He for whom punishment bears no fruit
Shall be disciplined severely by the court.
Here the tools and implements are shown.
Happy is he who is given to virtue.

Bamberg Halsgerichtsordnung, 1508

History of Crime and Punishment

Homicide

Introduction

In earlier times, people were not exactly squeamish about imposing punishment and especially about executing a death sentence, for apart from the idea of atonement, great emphasis was placed on deterrence and putting the perpetrator out of action. How numerous killings were is uncertain; records are avialable only for certain periods and it must be reckoned with that the number of crimes that went unpunished due to primitive investigation methods was incomparably greater than at the present time, and that torture extracted confessions of offences that were never committed. Just think of the many witch trials. Figures are given at the end of the section on death penalties.

Murder

Under Germanic (1) tribal law, the killing of a person, whether wilfully or without malice aforethought, could be atoned for by payment of a "wergeld"*. From the 12th century onwards, a different conception of law and justice gained acceptance. Thereafter, deliberate slaying ranked as murder and was "painfully" punished. A slaying could be ruled to be murder only if the circumstances leading up to or related to the deed exhibited certain characteristics. Such characteristics were first and foremost secrecy of the killing, and then concealment of the corpse. Killing by night was also considered to be murder in some cases. Killing out of avarice, e. g. to gain an inheritance, murder at the incitement of others and against payment, and the slaying of defenceless and unsuspecting

(1) "Germanic" must not be confused with "German ; it is a comprehensive term covering Teutonic peoples such as Saxons, Franconians, Alemanni, etc. What is now called German (Germany) did not exist at that time.

99

persons was likewise considered to be murder. Article 137 of the Constitutio Criminalis Carolina of 1532 (penal code of Emperor Charles V) unequivocally defines murder, like the present penal code, as deliberate and wilful slaying of a human being with malice aforethought, in contrast to manslaughter in a sudden heat of passion.

The death penalty was imposed on murder. While in the days of the Franks, in the 9th century, murder could usually still be atoned for among the southern Germanic tribes by paying a multiple "wergeld"*, here and there the wheel had already appeared as a punishment. The "Landfriedensordnungen" (public peace codes) then made breaking on the wheel universally applicable as a punishment. Sentences often ordered that the murderer be dragged to the place of execution before being broken on the wheel. Murderesses were buried alive or, more rarely, sentenced to death on the gallows or by fire. The numerous variants of murder were matched by the penalties, for example, murder by burning was punished by burning under the gallows. As an act of grace, execution was often performed by the sword. In particularly grave cases or multiple offences, the sentence contained a combination of punishments such as nipping with glowing pincers on the way to execution, cutting off of the right hand at the execution site, then execution by the sword or the wheel, followed by quartering or burning. In later times (18th century), the wheel, though still used, was gradually replaced by the sword. A fugitive murderer was outlawed and proscribed.

Manslaughter

In the oldest sources of Germanic law, a distinction was made between murder and manslaughter, although the word "murder" meant nothing but death and slaying. The Middle Ages used the word "manslaughter" for every type of killing, including homicide without intent and in self-defence. There was no sharp distinction between murder and manslaughter, even though the two offences were treated differently. Under imperial law, from the 12th century onwards manslaughter was basically considered a crime deserving the death sentence. Whereas earlier it was possible to atone for this offence by paying a "wergeld", from the 12th century onwards "wergeld" was limited, if permissible at all, exclusively to unintentional homicide and homicide in self-defence. Wilful homicide was subject to capital punishment, usually by beheading and occasionally on the gallows.

If a killer pleaded self-defence, he had to surrender to the "vogt" (proctor) and swear an oath before the court that he acted in self-defence. If self-defence was recognized, the offender was free and no penalty was imposed. The law of some cities prescribed fines for manslaughter, which however were not payable to the deceased's family but to the city; i. e. they were not "wergeld", but genuine fines. This type of punishment was frequently linked with temporary banishment from the city. It seems remarkable that in times in which most brutal punishments were imposed for far less serious offences, manslaughter could often be settled by a pecuniary arrangement, though in those days it was a frequent offence. Things went so far that the death sentence was almost an exception and was passed nearly exclusively on insolvent offenders. But killers did not enjoy such mild treatment everywhere and at all times. Some cities, for instance, punished manslaughter with the sword as a matter of principle, but then the penalty was often commuted by an act of clemency to life imprisonment or military service. The offence of negligent homicide was variously punished by penal labour or flogging, depending on the rank of the slain person.

Infanticide

In the Middle Ages, the killing of a defenceless person was considered murder, and in Germanic times, too, the killing of a newly born child was called murder, no doubt because the killing was linked with concealment of the deed. Some statutes imposed only minor penalties on this offence, others prescribed the death penalty. Following the lines of Roman law, the "Schwabenspiegel" * prescribed punishment by noyade (drowning) and also the Carolina provided in the case of secret, malicious killing of a living child for the punishments of burying alive, impalement or drowning. Rending with redhot pincers was often decreed as additional punishment. In the 14th century, not much ado was made about the killing of a newborn child by its unmarried mother, because no rights of a survivor were impaired and there was therefore no cause to intervene. Among the roughly 3,000 crimes registered in this period in the "Achtbuch"(1) of the imperial city of Augsburg, only one murderess of a child is mentioned. But she was punished, not for this crime, but for being a "generally wicked person" and was chased out of town during the annual expulsion of riffraff.

1. Lit. banishment book; a penal register of all criminals expelled from the country.

While in the 14th century infanticide was committed relatively rarely (or was prosecuted less often and therefore not entered in the records?), in later centuries it is encountered considerably more frequently.

The chief motive for infanticide at that time was fear of the shame of having an illegitimate child, of being cast out of the family or employment, and the small chance of getting married. Under the then prevailing law, also concealment of pregnancy and childbirth was a punishable offence. Even premarital sexual intercourse was punished and also church penalties were imposed on such female sinners.

Originally, drowning or burying alive was the chief punishment for infanticide, but as far back as the early 17th century death by the sword became the accepted penalty.

Arson

In the bodies of law of the Middle Ages, arson was often mentioned, but its treatment varied a great deal as far as the elements of the crime and its legal consequences were concerned. A clear distinction was made between wilful arson and setting fire by negligence. This is probably due on the one hand to the fact that in Germanic "Fehdes" * incendiarism was often resorted to in order to destroy an enemy locked in a house, and on the other hand to the fact that on account of the construction of houses at that time the danger of fire was always very great. Surreptitious arson, especially by night, was regarded as an aggravated case and was termed "Mordbrand" (murderous arson). While in the tribal leges (Lex salica, lex ribuaria) * a fine was generally prescribed for arson, in the later bodies of law this offence numbered among the "inexpiable" wrongs and carried the death penalty. Under the provisions of the "Sachsenspiegel" *, simple arson was punished by beheading, but "Mordbrand" by breaking on the wheel. The Carolina, in this respect following Roman law, called for death

Beheading of the arsonist J. Kilchenmann, 1855, From a contemporary pamphlet.

by fire (matching punishment), though without differentiating between offences. The later "common"* penal law, however, adhered to the clear distinction of the older bodies of law, negligent or wilful. However, the sentences then generally passed for wilful arson varied considerably. They ranged from beheading and burning to strangling and hanging, often combined with secondary punishments such as nipping with redhot pincers. But mostly such secondary punishments were imposed because not only arson, but also other offences were involved.

Larceny and Related Offences

Theft

In Germanic premediaeval and mediaeval times, theft was the intentional, unlawful, secret taking away of things personal with the intent of appropriating them to oneself, a definition which essentially still applies today. But embezzlement and the mere use of another's property without intent to appropriate were also classified as theft.

Nearly all Germanic laws made a distinction between petit and grand larceny, depending on the value of the stolen goods. But there was no uniform limiting value. Where Frankish-German law applied, a theft up to the value of 5 schillings (later 5 florins)* was considered petit larceny, unless the deed was classified as grand larceny on account of the manner in which it was committed or the special nature of the stolen property. This latter category included theft of livestock and grain, theft by night and from churches, smithies or mills. These special types carried the death penalty, just as all types of theft had previously. Due to the influence of the church in Frankish times, the law of pecuniary fines was introduced into the administration of justice, as a result of which special importance attached to differentiation of offences according to specific criteria.

Petit larceny was punished by a fine that was a multiple of the value of the stolen goods. The "Landfriedensordnungen" (public peace codes) brought more severe penalties when they were introduced, for in place of fines they provided for punishment "to the hide and hair". Such punishments were manifold: whipping, cutting off of ears or thumbs, branding, the pillory and expulsion from the country. Often, however, they could be avoided by payment of a fine.

Under the Carolina (Art. 159), grand larceny was punished by putting out the eyes, cutting off a hand and hanging. The gallows was the traditional death for thieves. The shameful death on the gallows, however, was often commuted to a more honourable capital punishment such as beheading or drowning. While in the 14th and 15th centuries hanging was still customary, thieves in the 16th century were beheaded as an act of grace. Women guilty of capital theft were buried alive or drowned. Female thieves were not hanged, because putting women's bodies on show in public was not permitted. Pregnancy was a mitigating circumstance for women.

Qualified Cases

Regardless of whether the value of the stolen property exceeded the limit of 5 schillings or florins, the following were considered aggravating circumstances:

Breaking and entering or the use of false keys. Even the tribal laws of the Franks punished burglary more severely than simple theft. Also in later times, sentences were severe. An apprehended burglar, even if he had not yet stolen anything, was sent to the gallows.

Cutpurses were likewise punished more severely. For the theft of less than 3o pfennigs* they lost a thumb, for less than 6o pfennigs* a hand, and for second offences they went to the gallows. Theft of livestock and from churches and mills, if the estimated value of the stolen goods, after reduction by one third, amounted to 12 pfennigs*, was punished by the gallows.

In the times of the Franks and in the Middle Ages, recidivous theft was grounds for more severe penalties. The mutilating corporal punishments imposed for petit larceny served primarily to mark the thief and to facilitate proof of recidivism. Recidivous petit larceny brought capital punishment. Under the Carolina, the recidivous thief was hanged only after his third offence. But practices differed; in many cases the death sentence was imposed for the second offence.

The unlawful taking away of property of the church was a special case. Under Roman canon law this was sacrilege, "churchbreaking". In the Schwabenspiegel, the penalty laid down for this crime was the wheel. The Bambergensis*, however, limited this punishment to grand larceny from a church, e.g. theft of the monstrance, while less serious cases were punished less stringently, but always more severely than petit larceny. Lastly, the Carolina, too, prescribed that such offences be treated less leniently than secular theft.

Embezzlement

The sources of law of the German Middle Ages by no means give a uniform definition of embezzlement, nor are they unanimous with respect to its treatment under penal law. Some tribal laws regarded embezzlement of goods held in trust as theft and prescribed corresponding punishments. Other bodies of law, e.g. the "Sachsenspiegel"*, expressly emphasized that the withholding of goods held in trust was not theft and therefore not punishable. In the Carolina, Art. 170, a clear distinction was then drawn between theft and embezzlement, though for the latter the penalty prescribed was that for theft. It is often difficult to discern from old penal judgements whether the offence concerned was theft or embezzlement, for in practice embezzlement was treated as theft. That the crime involved was embezzlement can often be recognised in old judgements only from a specific formulation of the following, or similar, tenor: " ... taken away and converted to his own use". Where property of but small value was embezzled, the penalties for petit larceny were applied. In most cases, however, the value of the embezzled property-mostly public monies, taxes or guild property - exceeded the limit of 5 florins and thus entailed capital punishment, particularly since the embezzlement was mostly committed in conjunction with breach of trust.

F a l s i f i c a t i o n (and False Pretences)

There is no clear-cut definition of the term "false" in the medieval sources of law. So "false" may imply any type of deceit: first, falsification in the present sense, i.e. any alteration or replication of an object with fraudulent intent; secondly fraud, i.e. any financial injury by false pretences with the object of unjust enrichment; and thirdly, any secret, non-violent financial injury, e.g. theft. There was no uniform court practice regarding the offences of falsification (and false pretences), for which reason the punishments varied considerably from case to case.

C o i n a g e O f f e n c e s

The making of coins with a false die and minting with a genuine die but using low-grade metal were classified as counterfeiting. The latter offence, however, could only be committed by the minter at the public mint. Views on the proof required for such offences varied. Some bodies of law required proof of counterfeiting by the coiner, others considered the uttering of spurious coins to be adequate proof of counterfeiting. Under Augsburg Municipal Law in 1276, the mere possession of false money was sufficient grounds to suspect a person, unless he could bring proof of its origin and of unwitting acceptance. The quantity of counterfeit money found was of decisive importance for the meting out of punishment. An amount of 60 or more pfennigs entailed death on the gallows. Where the amount was below this limit, the offender was branded and expelled from the city; if he returned despite expulsion, he was hanged.

Older bodies of law, e.g. the Carolingian Capitularies *, prescribed the loss of a hand as punishment for counterfeiting coins; being a "matching" punishment, it was carried out on the limb that had committed the offence. Then, in the 13th century, new severe penalties were introduced, which initially supplemented and later replaced those formerly customary: boiling and burning alive. The Carolina classified the various coinage offences as counterfeiting, false marking of coins, use of nonprecious metal and "diminishing and lightening" of coins, but called for death by fire for such offences.

F o r g e r y

The making of false documents, the making and use of false seals, the wilful use of false documents and letters and the unlawful use of genuine seals by non-authorized persons were classified as forgery. These offences were widespread even in early times, as clearly demonstrated by the abundance of criminal records and judgements. In the Middle Ages, forgery was placed on a par with counterfeiting and punished accordingly. The "Schwabenspiegel" prescribes loss of a hand as punishment; from the end of the 14th century onwards, the death penalty was usual, mostly boiling or burning alive. The "Carolina", too, laid down in Article 112 that forgers should suffer corporal and capital punishment. Execution of forgers by the sword was an act of clemency due to mitigating circumstances.

F a l s e   P r e t e n c e s

Just like the concept of falsification, false pretences were not clearly defined in the old bodies of law, so there was no sharp distinction between false pretences and falsification. In the sources, false pretences are often termed "valsch, velscherei" (Eng.: falsery), expressions which also include falsification. Among the most frequently mentioned elements of the offence were the use of false weights and measures, the making of false or falsified goods, cheating at gambling and bilking, pawn swindles, abscondence of debtors and tax evasion, e.g. serving wine without paying the "Ungelt" *. In meting out punishment, false pretences were treated like theft, i.e. the penalties were graduated like those for theft, the damage caused being equated with the value of a stolen object.

R o b b e r y

Our current conception of robbery is the taking of a chattel from a person by violence or the use of threats. Since violence in medieval usage did not necessarily imply the overcoming of resistance, but any action against the will of the owner, every open, unlawful taking of chattels from another was c o n s i d e r e d   r o b b e r y. Nor did the old laws distinguish among robbery with violence, robbery at night and highway robbery. Frequently, mention was made only of highway robbery, which at that time meant predominantly robbery of ministers of religion and their servants, pilgrims and merchants. The penalties for highway robbery were severe, because this crime mostly comprised two offences, i.e. robbery and breach of the peace. There was a breach of the peace because the highways belonged to the "king's peace"*. As in the case of theft, there was a limiting value for robbery, too. The laws of some cities laid down death by hanging when the limiting value of 3 pfennigs was exceeded. In the majority of cases, a robber was executed by the sword, as prescribed by Article 126 of the Carolina. If robbery was combined with, say, arson, the penalty was burning (matching punishment).

S e x   C r i m e s

R a p e

In earlier times, an offence was deemed to constitute rape only when the raped woman "gave hue and cry" and immediately on escaping the perpetrator's grasp "complains of her distress with a broken body, with fluttering hair and torn 'gebend' " *. In the times of the Franks, rape, often combined with abduction of women, could be atoned for by freemen with a fine, only bondmen were sentenced to death. Court rulings on this offence varied in the Middle Ages. Some bodies of law recognized the deed as rape only if it was committed against a respectable woman, but not a "vagrant woman". Others, e.g. the "Schwabenspiegel", did not make this difference. Under Article 119 of the "Carolina", an offender who took the honour of a wife, widow or maiden of good repute had to be put to death by the sword like a robber. So in the Middle Ages, the usual death penalty for the crime of rape was beheading by the sword; the punishments of burying alive and impaling were probably imposed more rarely. In fact, punishment of offenders varied a great deal; while the one was sent to the pillory, birched and expelled from the country, the other lost his life.

S o d o m y

According to the chronicles of Tacitus, among the Germanic tribes sexual intercourse (paederasty) between men was punished by sinking the offenders in a bog. Bestiality, i.e. sexual abuse of animals by human beings, was placed on a par with paederasty. In Christian times, paederasty was considered a religious offence, and in the Middle Ages sodomy and bestiality were classified as heresy and punished as offences against God. The Augsburg Statute Book of 1276 provides the earliest evidence of punishment of sodomy by a secular court and clearly distinguishes between "heresy" in this sense and heresy in matters of faith. Under the Augsburg

Statute Book - Article 36 - and the "Carolina" - Article 116 - this crime was punishable by death by burning. The death penalty for sodomy was retained until far into the 18th century, though its form varied; in some cases simple burning, in others beheading by the sword and subsequent burning. Often, however, judges were lenient and the sentence was only the pillory, birching and expulsion from the country. In the case of bestiality, simultaneous burning of man and animal was usual, for the animal was also regarded as an equally guilty criminal and under the rules of the Bible (Leviticus Chap. 20, verses 15 & 16) the animal also had to be put to death.

Incest

It is doubtful whether the crime of incest, i.e. sexual intercourse between close relatives, was known to Germanic law prior to christianization.

The historical literature concludes from Germanic mythology that incest was punished by death, but up to the present this has not been proved. The Lex Salica*, too, is silent on this subject. The inclusion of the offence in the old tribal laws, for the first time under Childebert II* in 596 AD, is undoubtedly attributable to the influence of Christianity (Bible, Leviticus 20, 14 & 17). In the secular statutes of the late Middle Ages, incest was mentioned but rarely. Not until the 15th century, under the influence of Roman law, did the courts impose severe penalties on incest. The "Carolina" sanctioned this practice and left the degree of punishment to the discretion of the judges. The penalty of death by beheading already called for by the Bamberg "Halsgerichtsordnung" was later taken over by the various bodies of national and city law. While in the 16th and 17th century death by beheading, hanging, drowning and burning were the general rule, judgments in the 17th century already began to show far-reaching lenience. The pillory, flogging and banishment or long terms of imprisonment then became usual.

Bigamy

Under Germanic law in antiquity, polygamy was permissible for men, although generally they were content with one wife. The Christian church, however, declared monogamy to be the only permissible form, simultaneously giving it special importance by stressing its indissolvable nature. In Frankish times, when secular and church views clashed, there was no serious conflict because, quite apart from the size of the empire, monogamy was the customary form. So bigamy was exclusively a problem for the church. Hence it is understandable that neither the Frankish statutes nor the first big imperial enactments of the Middle Ages contained penal regulations on bigamy; nor was it mentioned in the Sachsenspiegel. Even in the 13th century, it was regarded as a misdemeanour which fell solely in the jurisdiction of the church "Sendgerichte"*. From the 13th century onwards, especially the city courts restricted the jurisdiction of the ecclesiastical courts. Bigamy could be committed relatively easily and threatened to become a social and moral danger especially in the cities. For this reason, the cities placed it under the jurisdiction of the secular courts so that for a long time bigamy was punished by both the secular and the ecclesiastical courts. The punishment imposed was predominantly beheading under the law of the Saxon cities, and drowning under that of the Frankish and Upper German cities. The Carolina - Article 121 - treated bigamy as qualified adultery, but left much unclear with respect to punishments on account of its very general formulations. This lead to introduction of the death penalty for this offence where Saxon law prevailed. This was also adhered to in the later national enactments up to the middle of the 18th century. In practice, however, the due death penalty was commuted by the courts, who often settled for the pillory, birching, branding and banishment.

Adultery

Under the old Germanic laws, only adultery by the wife was deemed punishable, i.e. a husband could commit it with impunity. The reason for this was the legal status of the wife. She was within the sphere of authority (Munt*) of her husband and her adultery was deemed violation of his rights. So the Germanic laws protected not the institution of marriage as such, but the rights of the husband. This explains why the adulterous wife was not subject to public prosecution, but exclusively to punishment by the injured husband. He was allowed to kill her or turn her out of the house in disgrace. Generally, the male party to the adultery could be killed by the injured husband or sentenced to a fine by the court following conviction only if caught in the act. In Frankish times, under the influence of the church, a change began to take place in this view. The church regarded marriage as a moral institution requiring special protection and supported the view that both man and wife could commit punishable adultery. This standpoint gradually gained acceptance in the secular sphere. But in the 13th century, the secular courts still prosecuted only adulterers caught in the act. The Sachsenspiegel, for example, mentions only adultery in flagrante delicto and completely ignores non-overt adultery. In the 14th century, the equal status of man and wife with respect to adultery gained acceptance also under secular law, first and foremost in the cities (see also Bigamy). The Carolina - Article 120 - recognizing canon law, placed adultery by the husband on a par with adultery by the wife and conceded them alone the right to file a complaint. With regard to punishment, however, the Carolina only made reference to German and imperial law. What penalty was prescribed in the individual case remained completely unclear. For this reason, the punishment of adulterers varied substantially in the various domains of law. In some areas, sentences of death by the sword or even by fire were passed, and in others only the pillory, ostracism, birching or imprisonment. In the course of time, again with regional variations, a trend towards more lenient punishment gained ground. In the middle of the 18th century, marriage was regarded as no more than a contract between two persons of different sexes and this had consequences. Bigamy was now primarily a breach of contract for which punishment under general penal law appeared unsuitable. From then on, light prison sentences were considered adequate. For example, the death penalty for bigamy was abolished in Saxony in 1783.

Religious Offences

Blasphemy

Blasphemy is one of the few offences which have retained their character as religious offences through all changes in religious conceptions. It was blasphemy to abuse, revile or defame God or the saints. Blasphemy also included profane cursing and swearing. Jurisdiction over cases of blasphemy was originally restricted to the ecclesiastical courts, but penal sanctions for blasphemy were to be found occasionally as far back as the 13th century, and then more frequently in the 14th and 15th centuries also in secular bodies of law. However varied the interpretations of the offence and the penalties imposed, all such sanctions had a common motivation: The apprehension that on account of blasphemy God might visit famine, scarcity, pestilence or other plagues upon the whole land or the city. The Carolina provided in Article 106 for punishment to be inflicted on life, limb and property according to the standing of the person and the blasphemy. Under all laws and in all jurisdictions the scale extended from fines to the pillory, immersion, temporary or lifelong banishment, birching, tearing out the tongue and on to drowning, beheading and burning. Towards the end of the 18th century, the idea of protecting God was given up and replaced by that of protecting religion. Simultaneously, punishments began to be moderated considerably.

Heresy

The name heretic was applied to persons within the church who deviated from approved orthodox doctrines and set up their own. The church of the Middle Ages had to weather many dangers emanating from heretical movements, both real and supposed, which were called heretical in order to be able to combat them. True, the church regarded heresy as a purely ecclesiastical offence, but demanded help from the state in combatting it. The secular laws of the Frankish period made no provision for the

Anneken Jans drowned in Rotterdam, 1539

Two young girls killed in the bishopric of Bamberg, 1550

Eighty Waldensians burnt in Strasbourg, 1215

William White, priest, burnt in Norwich, England, 1428.

Geleyn Cornelius, tortured and burnt, 1572

Ursel Schulmeysterin, tortured and burnt, 1570

Persecution of Heretics

from "Schau-Bühne der Märtyrer" by Joh. Luyken, ca. 1700

prosecution and punishment of heretics. Beginning in the 11th century and then on a larger scale in the 12th century, secular statutes were promulgated at the request of the church. The church demanded that the secular powers be bound by the judgements of the ecclesiastical courts and be compelled to punish heretics found guilty by them. The secular laws therefore laid down that arrested heretics were first to be handed over to the ecclesiastical courts and then, after being found guilty by those courts, to be punished by the secular powers. The usual punishment for heresy was death by burning, but sentences of lifelong imprisonment were also passed, though rarely. The persecution of heretics increased more and more in the 13th century due to the institution of the Inquisition set up by Pope Gregory IX, in fact there were literally crusades against heretics. The Waldensians and Albigenses fell victim to them in the 13th century in southern France, and the Stedingers in East Friesland. In the 15th century, the Bohemian reformer Huss was also put to death as a heretic. The Protestants, too, though themselves described as heretics by the Catholics, began to distinguish between the orthodox and the heretics and to persecute the latter. For instance, at Calvin's instigation a heretic was burnt in Geneva in 1533. The Age of Enlightenment moderated the fight against heresy. But even in the 18th century heresy was still persecuted with government assistance; Rousseau's novel "Emile", for example, was publicly burnt in Paris on account of its heretical contents, while the author evaded arrest only by fleeing.

Witchcraft

The subject of witchcraft and witch trials is covered exhaustively elsewhere in this book and is therefore dealt with only briefly at this point.

Whereas the early medieval church imposed only fines and church punishments on witchcraft, in the late Middle Ages witch hunting experienced a real boom, especially as a result of the introduction of the Inquisition. Ecclesiastic-secular trials of witches and sorcerers took place from the 15th to the 18th century, but the 17th century was the main period of witch trials. Frequently, an anonymous denunciation or an unusual physical attribute (red hair, hunchback, etc.) was sufficient grounds to be suspected of being a witch. As a general principle, interrogation was combined with torture, as it was assumed that the accused was possessed of a demon and the truth could be found only if it was forced by physical pain to leave the body temporarily. With a few exceptions, witch trials always ended with a sentence of death by burning. The tidal wave of witch trials in the 17th century is attributable above all to the fact that under torture the accused charged other persons with complicity in witch-

Charles I, the Great, Holy Roman Emperor, King of the Franks (768-814)
He lead the Frankish empire to predominance in thw occident and made
it a world power.
Painting by A. Dürer (1471—1528). Germanic Nat. Museum, Nuremberg.

Henry VII, the elected German king, being set on the altar by two spiritual Electors, 1308.

Henry VII being elected German king by three spiritual and four temporal Electors, 1308.

Henry VII being crowned German king in Aix la Chappelle, 1309.

Henry VII being crowned Holy Roman emperor by three cardinals, 1312.

Illustration of the mediaeval law derived from God. (From top to bottom:) Pope and emperor as God's bondsmen. The emperor is holding the pope's stirrup. Spiritual and secular jurisdiction: the episcopal court, the count's court, the proctor's court.
From the Dresden Illuminated Manuscript of the Sachsenspiegel, ca. 1350.

Van ordineringe der hogeste ouericheit der
Stadt hamborch

Homage. The archbishop on a golden throne, before him five men in noble robes, the first of whom offers a golden goblet, the second a hunting falcon and a pouch full of money, and the third two greyhounds.
(Soest Nequambuch, 14th cent.)

Left: Council meeting in Hamburg. All 24 councillors are assembled, in the centre the 4 burgomasters and the two "word-keepers" of the year. They wear signet rings and have the right to deal with secret or urgent matters among themselves; they can also send out letters under their own seal. The next in rank is the syndic (as a doctor of law he was equal to the knights). He is sitting on the right-hand side bench, in his hand the large document that symbolizes his status. The distribution and precedence of the seats corresponds in general to present-day custom; the council table had a green cover like that still usual now. Outside the railing near the columns, council and court servants. (Hamburg City Law of 1497).

Van schickinge unde voeberige des nedderst
gherichtes,

Court proceedings. Left, on the throne a prince and his consort. The prince raises his index finger in warning, the princess her right hand. The hovering devil shows that the two gesticulating men on the right are evildoers or false witnesses (Soest Nequambuch, 14th. cent.)

Left:
Ceremonial opening of the court in the old court house in Hamburg. In the centre, the proctor, who presides over the proceedings, on his right and left, councillors who assist him and the court clerk with quill and inkpot; at the side of the table, the judgment-finders, 12 citizens and "thingmen"; centre foreground, the beadles leading off a convicted man to his punishment, as the arms of royal authority they bear long white staffs and rank as agents of the authorities. In the foreground, several parties; on the left, citizens watching the proceedings (Hamburg City Law, 1497).

Van pynlike sake dat hogeste belangende,

Picture of a Court by Derick Baegert in the Wesel town hall, 1493. In the background, the raised judge's bench; in front of it an oath-swearer. A court servant holds out to him the relic on which he is to swear. The figures of the angel and the devil symbolize a warning against perjury. On the courtroom wall, top left, a picture of the Last Judgment.

Left:
On the left: courthouse with proctor and lords of the court, in front of them, bareheaded, the complainant, the lay advocate and the defendant. In the foreground: the "Broad Stone", in the centre the Kaak, a pillory of peculiar form – roofed cage on a high wooden post – similar to a pigeon-cote. Procurers and other wanton people were put in the Kaak; a "fallen" woman, for instance, had to cradle a straw doll in her arms and wear a straw wreath in her hair. On the Broad Stone, slanderers had to recant. An executioner's assistant is birching an old virago; the maximum penalty was nine times six strokes. Foreground: a court servant in green, with sword, is leading a man to the Kaak. The grey building with straw roof is the Büttelei (beadle's house), a degrading prison; the picture shows prisoners behind barred windows, visible from the street, to serve as a deterrent. To the left of it, a witch engaged in devilish work. Bottom right: a homicide trial; the corpse had to be present and also the proctor, lords of the court, citizens as judgment-finders and the court bailiff with sword. Outside the wall: the place of execution or "beheading hill", symbolized by gallows and wheel, and in front of them an execution (Hamburg City Law, 1497).

Pro mesura plꝰ eiꞇ plagꝫ ṙei nō bis ⁊

quadragiꞇ non excedris

Van wedde vnde bote ,

Accusation. On the left, the judge with crossed leg, one hand on his knee, the other raised with eloquent gesture. In front of him, a man with raised sword, his back to two figures of whom one apparently has his hands bound behind his back, the other has his hands crossed in front of him (Soest Nequambuch, 14th cent.)

Left:
Trial of minor crimes atoned for by a fine paid to the court or a composition paid to the injured. In the centre, the proctor and the two court stewards of the council. The complainant's hand has been injured; behind him, two witnesses. On the left near the column, the defendant and in front of him his lay advocate on whose arm he lays his hand as a sign of approval of the latter's actions. Nearby, two horseman whose gestures indicate that they caught the offender in the act and brought him to court. Far left: a fight, one man has a dagger raised. Right background: a waggon with flour sacks before the city mill. (Hamburg City Law, 1497).

The Golden Bull, 1356. This document, named after its golden seal and the most important document from the reign of Charles IV, is an extensive piece of legislation regulating, above all, the election and coronation of the German king and the duties and rights of the Electors. Proclaimed in 1356 in Nuremberg and Metz, it remained in force up to 1806.

Peace treaty of Feb. 10, 1364, Brünn: Emperor Charles IV, King Wenzel IV, King Louis I of Hungary and the dukes Rudolf IV, Albrecht III and Leopold III concluded a peace treaty. followed by a succession agreement, which was the basis of the Habsburg sovereignty up to 1918. Family, court and state archives, Vienna.

Certificate of employment (reference) as a gardner for two years, Vienna, 1724.

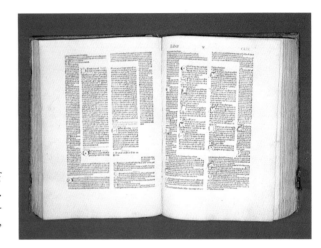

Justinian, collection of statutes and laws of the Byzantine emperor Justinian I (527-565). In the centre the text of the law and surrounding it the commentary. Incunabulum, printed 1482.

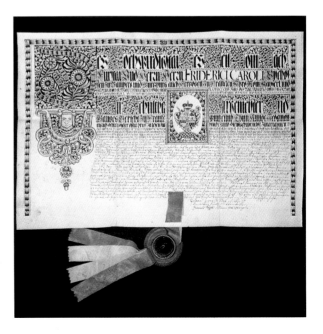

Document confirming honourable birth; Frankenwindheim, 1738. Apart from the classification of people in estates (classes), a distinction was made between "honourable" and "unhonourable". The concept "unhonourable" was derived from a person's birth (family) and the practiced vocation. Executioners, flayers, musicians, actors and itinerants were considered "unhonourable". They and their children could never attain citizen's rights and the related benefits or learn a trade. Moreover, "unhonourable birth" was a blemish that persisted up to death.

Certificate of marriage with 13 seals, 1551

Patent of nobility with the king's grand seal in a costly capsule, 19th cent.

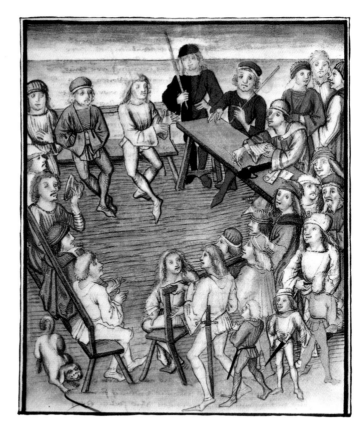

Court session
Berne Chronicles by D. Schilling,
1483, City Library, Berne.

Noble lords before the court.
Berne Chronicles by D. Schilling,
1483, City Library, Berne.

Court session, early 16th cent.
In the foreground, the criminal is brought into court; in the background,
illustrations of various punishments. Woodcut by H. Burgkmair.

Illustration of various punishments, Tengler Laienspiegel, 1509.

craft, thus initiating new trials. Towards the end of the 17th century and in the early 18th century, the authorities adopted a more reasonable attitude, under the influence particularly of publications attacking the witchcraft mania (Fr. v. Spee, Thomasius *), and gradually cut down the witch trials. The last burnings of witches in Germany took place in Würzburg (1749), Endingen at the foot of the Kaiserstuhl range (1751) and Kempten (1775). Among the people, the belief in witchcraft has endured to some extent right up to the present and even now the courts occasionally have to deal with it.

Werewolves and witches in the Principality of Jülich,
Augsburg pamphlet, 1591

Political Crimes

From ancient times, political offences have numbered among the gravest crimes a person could be accused of. In early days, however, the scope of the concept was far broader than in modern penal law and it often happened, particularly in periods of political unrest, that those in power charged opponents on empty pretexts with political crimes to get them out of the way. The most serious political crime was treason to the empire, country or city. It was always considered treason when a person played another, especially when he owed the latter loyalty, or that other person's goods into the hands of an enemy.

So treason, as understood in the Middle Ages, was not necessarily an offence against the state as a community. The penal sanctions for treason, therefore, by no means always related to political crimes. Treason was punished by death. Even in the earliest Germanic times, traitors were hung on trees. The Frankish period and the Middle Ages punished high treason by hanging, drowning, beheading, burning and breaking on the wheel, and from the 14th century onwards also with quartering. From the turn of the 15th to the 16th century, quartering became the punishment for all forms of treason, not only political treason. In Article 124, the Carolina also names quartering as the penalty for men, and drowning for women. Dragging to the execution site and tearing with pincers were also mentioned as additional punishment. Under Augsburg city law, a traitor was beheaded if he pleaded guilty, and broken on the wheel like a murderer if he pleaded not guilty. If material damage had been caused, the traitor had to pay double the loss to the injured party and 10 pounds to the bailiff. If the offender was insolvent, his life was forfeit as if he had taken the goods himself, i.e. as if he were a thief.

The concept of political crimes also includes lèse-majesty. The body, soul, honour and goods of the king or emperor were considered legal interests especially worthy of protection and a conspiracy or rebellion against king or emperor was punished as a breach of the duty of loyalty. As a general principle, this offence was punishable by death, but by way of clemency milder penalties such as mutilation, banishment or imprisonment could be imposed, but also ostracism and "Reichsexekution"* were applied, especially against the great within the empire. With the development of national sovereignty, the concept of lese-majesty was extended to cover conspiracy and rebellion against the national sovereign or, in the cities, against the council. The Carolina laid down beheading, banishment and flogging as punishments for treason. Persons who obtained knowledge of a planned rebellion and failed to report it immediately were placed on a par with the rebels and punished. In the cities the offences were manifold and the punishments varied. The political offences included, for instance, defamatory speeches against the council, tearing down of a publicly displayed regulation of the authorities, damage to the city walls, climbing over the city walls, moving away from the city without renouncing local city rights and without paying outstanding taxes, and seeking one's rights before an external court. The list of penalties extended from the pillory to imprisonment, mutilation and banishment and on to the various death penalties.

Beheading

Beheading was distinguished from hanging, burning, drowning and burying alive by the fact that the killing of the criminal was not left to the forces of nature, but was carried out by instruments made and wielded by human hands. The old death sentences demanded specifically that in beheading two pieces were to be made of the condemned person and that the two parts were to be separated from each other so

that there was a space between them, i.e. so that death actually occurred. The most frequently used instrument was the sword, and from the 16th century onwards the two-handed version. The axe was used more rarely. Execution with the sword called for the greatest dexterity on the part of the executioner. With a single stroke he had to cut between two vertebrae and sever the head from the trunk. It was so easy to miss, and then he had to strike a second time. A botched beheading was not infrequent and was taken into account by the laws, for they often emphasized the inviolability of the executioner, imposing severe penalties for contempt of him. Contemporary illustrations of executions in early times give a far better insight into the methods practiced than written descriptions that have come down to us. Most of them present the following picture: The condemned person is kneeling on the ground or a special structure, his hands bound or folded in prayer. The shirt is pulled well down from the neck, leaving it bare. This baring of the neck was not only due to the practical consideration that the cloth might reduce the impact of the stroke, but was also done for ritual reasons. Clothes were regarded as appendages that changed the personality and might falsify the true nature of a person. A striking feature in many illustrations is the completely free pose of the condemned. No bonds, no holding by the executioner's assistants. We will not go into whether this bore witness to the extraordinary willpower of the condemned or to the complete breaking of his will to live by the tortures previously suffered. After the beheading, the severed head was impaled on a stake or the city gates, as a regular practice in early times and frequently later on.

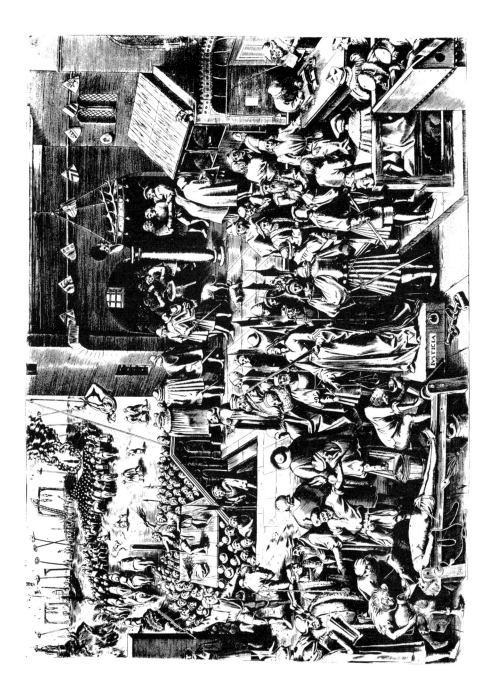

Justitia, allegorical portrayal of justice, copperplate engraving by Pieter Breughel the Elder (1525-1569). The engraving shows nearly all court procedures, from interrogation and torture to the court proceedings and the various forms of punishment.

The Place of Execution. The market place, where the city hall stood, where the court convened and degrading punishments were carried out, was originally the place for beheadings. Deterrence may have been the predominant motive for this. Even later, when the place of execution lay outside the city gates, beheadings were occasionally carried out on the market place. This was done above all in times of war or in the case of political opponents, because within the protection of the city walls the execution could proceed in greater safety and without being prevented forcibly by friends of the condemned person. Much-hated criminals convicted of capital offences were also beheaded on the market place to provide an outlet for the fury of the population. Later on, execution sites were transferred outside the city gates. Frequently, a raised, rectangular or circular, masonry platform was built. Steps led up to it either from the outside or the inside. The platform had a wooden or stone floor, the latter type often overgrown with grass. Here the execution could be performed so that onlookers had a good view, but could not hinder proceedings. The platform was large enough to accomodate not only the condemned person and the executioner, but also the public witnesses and the priest. This sort of place of execution was called a ravenstone, because the body of beheaded persons was laid on wheels and pecked and eaten by ravens. On the ravenstone only beheadings and occasionally breaking on the wheel took place. Where there was no special place of execution, beheadings were performed also under the gallows.

On October 21, 1830, in accordance with the decision of the High Court of Appeal, the double murderer Friedrich Cörper, journeyman plumber of Nuremberg, 31 years of age, was publicly put to death by the sword in Nuremberg.

Hanging

Even in olden days, hanging was a widespread form of capital punishment, for there were trees everywhere. Hanging was regarded as dishonourable and shameful, for which reason it was the most usual death penalty for thieves in the Middle Ages. To illustrate how often this sentence was passed and carried out, here is one example: When the pits below the gallows in  Augsburg were opened in 1471, 250 skulls of hanged persons were found, while at the same time another 32 (!!) thieves were still hanging on the gallows. A hemp rope, and occasionally a chain, were used for hanging. Two ladders were leaned against the gallows. The hangman fastened the noose on the gallows hook, then he and the condemned person climbed the ladders. On reaching the top, the hangman placed the noose round the condemned person's neck, descended and pushed the ladder on which the doomed man stood aside, leaving him hanging in the air. The weight of the body tightened the noose, the windpipe and blood vessels were closed off, causing death. Pulling the criminal up to the top of the gallows was more painful. The noose of a long rope was placed round the neck of the condemned person as he stood on the ground, the rope was thrown over the gallows or threaded through the gallows hook, and the delinquent was then pulled up by the hangman's assistants or a horse. With this method, death occurred more slowly than when the body plunged from the ladder. While beheaded persons were given a funeral, the hanged frequently had to be left on the gallows until they fell of their own accord, i.e. until decomposition was so far advanced that the body fell apart. Secret removal of a corpse from the gallows, e.g. by relatives, was forbidden and regarded as interference in the execution, because leaving the corpse hanging on the gallows was a part of the punishment. That was also the reason why hanging was considered dishonourable and shameful.

There were also harsher forms of hanging, e.g. hanging by the feet or with dogs. In the first of these forms, the delinquent was hung by the feet with his head down. Death occurred only after many hours and sometimes only after several days. Hanging with dogs was an additional ignominy intended to symbolize the criminal's infamous character. This punishment was mostly inflicted on Jews.

Brandenburgifche halßgerichts
ordnung

Cover of the Brandenburg Halsgerichtsordnung (code of penal law and penal procedure),
printed by Jobst Gutknecht, 1516. The woodcut shows the most usual places of execution, instruments of punishment and torture used at that time.

135

Execution of six criminals in Wohlau, Lower Silesia, 1661. Left, top and bottom, the trial on the market place in front of the town hall; right, top and bottom, the execution immediately after trial.

The Place of Execution.

In antiquity, the branch of a tree was the gallows, Where possible, dead trees without foliage were used. According to religious notions at that time, a lifeless tree was a source of life-inhibiting forces, i.e. killing forces. The tree chosen for the hanging was regarded as a sacrrificial tree, for the Nordic god Odin, god of the winds and lord over life and death, died on a tree. And the cross on which Christ died was an artificial tree. Thus an instrument of punishment became the higest religious symbol of Christianity. According to conceptions at that time, the tree or gallows absorbed all the mysterious forces of the hanged person, the holy forces of the sacrificed (Christ) and the evil forces of the criminal. This explains the fear of touching the gallows; there was the danger that one might be seized by the evil forces slumbering in it.

In the early Middle Ages, the setting up of artificial gallows was ordered by Charles the Great *. Whether the knee-type gallows now often used as a pictorial symbol was the earliest form cannot be definitely established, but this seems reasonable, since it is the nearest approach to a branch standing out from a tree trunk. In most cases, however, the gallows consisted of two upright posts with a crosspiece. Later, threelegged gallows were usual. Three vertical posts stood in a triangle and were connected by crossbeams. Often the gallows had a raised masonry base and sometimes the uprights were stone columns. There was also a form of gallows, on the crosspieces of which another gallows was erected for the more severe punishment of hanging at a greater height. When punishing a band of robbers, for instance, the leader was hung on the higher gallows and his accomplices below him.

The gallows was the symbol of penal jurisdiction. This may explain why it stood on a rise, visible from far away, and was of especially durable construction. This conspicuous location also served as a deterrent. The names of plots of land or hills (gallows meadow, gallows hill) still bear witness today of the location of the gallows.

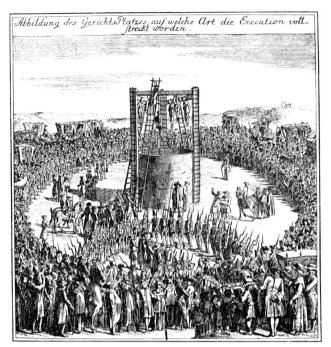

Picture of the place of execution
and the manner of execution.

Executions in Berlin,
above 1713, below 1718, contemporary copper engravings

138

The erection of the gallows was the responsibility of the authorities. Because to touch the gallows brought dishonour, craftsmen often refused to do the necessary work, since they would then be punished or expelled by their guilds. Consequently, customs arose which seem strange to us. So that nobody could be taken to task by others for helping to build the gallows, all guilds had to do their share. To the sound of music they all made their way to the place of execution. The masons and joiners did the main work, but the others, e.g. the merchants, gave symbolic help by carrying wood or stones; even the judges lent a hand. When the work was over, they went back to the town to take a meal together. So on top of the actual building costs, the cost of the meal had to be paid. Examination of the old accounts reveals that the incidental costs for the music and meal often exceeded the actual building costs.

Breaking on the Wheel

Breaking on the wheel, a punishment inflicted only on men, was customary from early Germanic times until far into the 18th century. It was regarded as the most ignominious and dishonourable punishment and was inflicted only for murder. The criminal was laid out on the ground with outstretched arms and legs, hands and feet tied to pegs, and timbers were laid under the limbs and body so that hollow spaces were left beneath him. The executioner then broke every limb and the spine with a wheel; the number of blows was laid down in the judgment. The dying, or dead, man's limbs were then threaded alternately under and over the spokes. Finally, the wheel was placed on a post or the gallows. If first the bones of the legs, then the arms, etc., were broken, death came very slowly, and often the criminal was still alive when he was threaded through the wheel. It was therefore an act of mercy to direct the first blow of the wheel at the neck. Other mitigations of punishment were hanging, beheading or stabbing in the heart before breaking the condemned man on the wheel. But this could also be done as a combination of several punishments for various different crimes (cumulation). For each execution a new wheel was used, which had to have nine or ten spokes. Death by breaking on the wheel was often combined with dragging. The condemned man was laid bound on a hide or board and dragged by a horse to the place of execution. An aggravation of punishment consisted in nipping the breast, arms or hips with redhot pincers at certain places on the way.

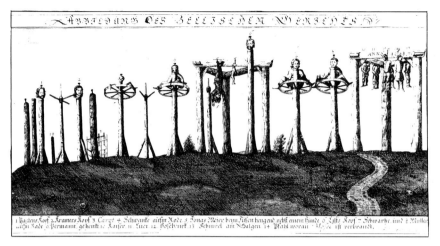

Cellisches Gericht, 1698, contemporary copperplate engraving

Drowning

Drowning was a widespread punishment in the Middle Ages. It
was mostly inflicted on female
offenders, but also on men. Usually, the hands and feet of the
condemned person were bound
prior to throwing him into the
river from a bridge. Where there
was no river, a pond or pool was
used. If the water was not deep
enough, the delinquent was
pushed under water with poles or
forks until he was dead. Frequently, a sack was also used, to

which animals were added, e.g. dogs, snakes. Large wooden tubs were also
used for drowning. The criminal was placed in a sack and the executioner
pushed the upper part of his body over the edge of the tub and held him
under water until death ensued.

Boiling

From the end of the 13th century onwards, boiling in water, wine or oil
was laid down by nearly all national and city laws as a punishment for
falsification. In particular, heretics were also sentenced to death by boiling
in water.

140

Burning

Burning was a form of capital punishment that was often used in the Middle Ages. The basic idea of this punishment was to completely wipe out criminals whose crimes were considered particularly atrocious. There

was therefore a great variety of methods of inflicting this punishment, and everything connected with it had its own special significance. Fire, one of the most elementary natural forces, had the power to purge, and devoured all evil. The smoke that arose, and with it the evil of the wrongdoer, was carried away by the wind. For this reason, witches were mostly burnt on hills where the wind could blow freely. Even the ashes of burnt criminals were considered dangerous, and so they were thrown into the flowing water of a river or stream that would carry them away. Thus fire, wind and water, the three elements, shared in exterminating the evildoer.

Execution by fire varied from place to place and from crime to crime. In the one case the delinquent was bound and laid on a pyre, in another he was tied to a stake and the fire laid around him, and in yet another he was tied to a ladder, raised and pushed with the ladder into the flaming pyre. As an act of mercy, the wrongdoer was sometimes strangled before the burning or, to end his torment more quickly, a small bag of gunpowder was tied to his neck. But old accounts also report that the executioners, who were often more humane than the people or the judges for all their gruesome calling, unobtrusively strangled the condemned or stabbed them in the heart before

Abbildung des Scheiterhaufen für den Hausdieb und Brand
Stifter Joh. Chr. Hopner Berlin datum 15 August 1706

they were burnt at the stake. Where an offender was beheaded or hanged and subsequently burnt, there were two possible reasons: it was either an act of mercy or consecutive infliction of several death penalties for several capital crimes. The increase of witch trials in the second half of the 16th century set fires ablaze all over Europe and made burning the most frequently capital punishment.

Burying Alive and Impalement

The Sachsenspiegel and the medieval imperial laws make no mention of the punishment of burying alive; the Carolina prescribes it only for infanticide. Nevertheless, this punishment was inflicted, mainly on men and women who had committed sexual offences. Exactly how this punishment was carried out cannot be established definitely from the available sources. In all probability we can assume the following: The offender was laid, alive and bound, in a pit dug near the gallows and the removed earth thrown back over him. To make any return of the condemned person more difficult, he was laid face downward like a suicide and tangled thorny bushes were placed over this grave. If the delinquent was placed on his back, a tube was put in his mouth, not to enable him to breathe, but to give the soul a chance to leave the body (soul-hole). Impalement was very closely related to burying alive. After burial, a stake was driven into the pit and through the condemned person. On the one hand, this was done out of the superstition that it would make a return of the dead more difficult, and on the other hand to bring death more quickly. Furthermore, impalement had a symbolic significance as a "matching punishment" for the rapist; the woman who had been his victim was allowed to deliver the first three blows and the executioner did the rest.

Burying alive and impalement, however, were not frequently used punishments and in early modern times fell almost completely into disuse.

Immurement

The punishment of immurement was a substitute for execution and can be considered a later form of burying alive. Especially in the case of convicted members of the higher classes, a sentence of immurement was passed as an act of grace instead of a death

"Immurement" of a criminal, copperplate engraving. 1725.

142

penalty. This was done to save the family the shame of a public execution and the convicted person the touch of the executioner. However, this punishment was also inflicted on simple people. Immurement must not be interpreted literally, i.e., that the wrongdoer was walled up in a cell and received nothing to eat or drink so that he died a harrowing death, but as life imprisonment. The prison might be a cell built on to the house of the executioner, who then had to provide for the prisoner, or, in the case of persons of higher rank, a room in their own house or that of a member of the family. The family then had to provide for him until the end of his life. No matter where this dungeon was, the prisoner had to remain in it up to his death and for his fellow-men therefore he was no longer part of this world. Very rarely, as an act of clemency by the court, previous release was allowed, but always coupled with the injunction to leave the country or city and never return on pain of death.

Quartering

A distinction must be drawn between two types of quartering. On the one hand quartering alive, on the other after execution.

The former was probably the original form. The Alemmans carried out this punishment on traitors with an axe. A better known form was that in which each arm and leg was tied to a horse's tail, the four horses were driven apart and the delinquent literally torn apart. Gregory of Tours, bishop and historian (540-594) describes this type of punishment in his

Quartering of the regicide J. Clement, Paris 1589, contemp. copper engraving

143

most important work "Gesta Francorum". He reports on the execution of Queen Brunehild, who was tied to a horse's tail and torn to pieces, and by the slaying of 200 Frankish girls in the same way by the Thuringians. But this gruesome death penalty was also inflicted in more recent times, for instance in 1757 at the execution of the unsuccessful regicide Robert Daumiens in Paris.

In the Middle Ages and more modern times, however, this punishment was inflicted nearly always after the previous killing of the delinquent. The criminal was first beheaded, hanged or strangled and only then quartered. So quartering was the final act in the execution and was regarded as aggravation of punishment or a second penalty when more than one capital crime had been committed. Contemporary illustrations show the repulsive, macabre nature of such proceedings. The four parts were then hung on a gallows or beside highways as a deterrent, e.g. in Frankfurt on Main in 1616, marking the end of the "Fettmilch revolt" (Vincenz Fettmilch, leader of a constitutional reform movement).

Cumulation of Death Penalties

If a person had committed several offences, each of which was a capital crime, the judgment contained an enumeration (cumulation) of the punishments incurred for each separate offence. This has been referred to occasionally in the preceding sections on the individual punishments. So as prescribed by the law, for each individual crime the specified death sentence was passed. It was up to the court to decree in what order they were to be carried out. Since every human being has but one life, only one of the punishments could lead to death. The gravity of the crime was probably the decisive factor in laying down the order in which sentences were executed. In the interests of a better understanding of cumulative death sentences, here is an arbitrary example: The criminal was dragged

to the place of execution, nipped on the way with redhot pincers (aggravated punishment), then broken on the wheel (for murder), laid on the wheel while still alive and hanged on a gallows standing near the wheel (for theft), and finally burnt with the wheel and gallows (for bestiality), after which the ashes were thrown in the river. The suffering this poor sinner had to bear before he eventually died is unimaginable.

Mutilating Punishments

General Remarks

The object of punishments in earlier times was to deal out retribution to the offender for his misdeeds, not to better or resocialize him. A person once punished was expelled once and for all from the community of honourable citizens. The guiding principle of old German law was that the punishment of a criminal should remain evident as long as he lived. Violators of the law had always to carry their mark of Cain. Everybody should know that they had a criminal before them. Mutilation as a legal punishment derives from this idea. In very early times, it was inflicted only on the unfree. When used on a freeman, it was an act of mercy in place of a merited death sentence, and thereafter he was one of the rightless. In the days of the Carolingians, the use of mutilation as a punishment increased. Frequently it was former capital offences such as arson or theft, but also less serious offences such as perjury and false pretences that could formerly be atoned for with fines, which were now punished by mutilation. Under Frankish law, mutilating punishments could be usually evaded by paying fines and were carried out only in cases of insolvency. The importance of this form of punishment grew in the following centuries. Whereas in the 12th century, cutting off the hand was the only mutilating punishment, in the 13th century others were introduced such as blinding, cutting off the ears, etc. In the late Middle Ages a variety of mutilating punishments were widespread on account of their deterrent effect. The Carolina (1532), Article 159, left it to the discretion of the judge to substitute mutilation for a death sentence.

Blinding

Putting out the eyes was the severest mutilation and was often inflicted instead of a death sentence. Originally a penalty applied only for breaches of the peace, it was later the punishment for a broad variety of crimes. All who threatened the person or property of others and were unable to pay a fine to the bailiff were banished from the country or city. If they returned despite banishment, their eyes were put out. The loss of one eye ranked as a milder punishment.

Executions in Augsburg as listed in the Penal Record Book exhibited in the Kriminal-museum (Crime Museum)

1545 – 1553:	Hanging	10	
	Sword	2	
1554 – 1562:	Hanging	2	
	Sword	15	
1563 – 1571:	Hanging	17	
	Sword	12	(including a case in which the limbs of the condemned man were broken and he was then laid on the wheel)
	Wheel	2	(1 case with dragging)
	Water	1	
1571 – 1576:	Hanging	6	
	Sword	5	
	Wheel	1	(dragging)
1576 – 1580:	Hanging	17	
	Sword	7	
	Wheel	1	(dragging)
	Water	3	
1581 – 1587:	Hanging	24	
	Sword	5	
	Wheel	3	
	Water	1	
1588 – 1596:	Hanging	17	
	Sword	13	
	Wheel	2	
	Water	1	
1596 – 1605:	Hanging	13	(1 case, first hanging then burning)
	Sword	8	
	Wheel	1	
1608 – 1615:	Hanging	7	
	Sword	12	
	Fire	1	
1615 – 1632:	Hanging	5	
	Sword	25	(1 case, first sword then burning)
1633 – 1653:	Hanging	2	
	Sword	6	(2 cases, first sword then burning)
1654 – 1699:	Hanging	3	
	Sword	31	(11 cases, first sword then burning)

Executions in Nuremberg:

15th century	200	In the diary of the executioner Meister
16th century	289	Frantz of Nuremberg, who plied his
17th century	282	trade from 1573 – 1615, we found that
18th cent. –1781	142	he sent 361 sinners to their death.

146

Cutting off the Hand

The most frequent mutilating penalty was the cutting off of a hand. Offences punished by the loss of a hand included breach of the peace, perjury, assault and battery causing permanent injury to the victim, damaging city fortifications, cheating at gambling, repeated use of false weights, repeated bearing of dangerous weapons. Which hand was cut off in a given case is difficult to establish. It can be assumed that generally the hand most valuable to the offender was cut off. In most cases it was probably the right hand, the reason for which, according to Jacob Grimm *, being that the right hand was the sword-hand. In most cases the hand was laid on a block and struck off with an axe. More rarely, a knife and a wooden mallet were used.

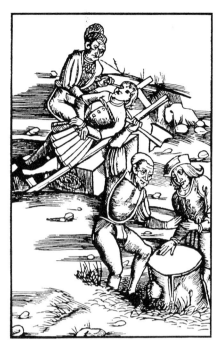

Cutting off of a hand and blinding, Tengler Layenspiegel, 1509, section.

Cutting Off of Fingers

The cutting off of fingers was undoubtedly a milder form of cutting off the hand. For similar offences, the delinquent could be sentenced to loss of his fingers for a less serious act, or to loss of the hand for graver crimes. According to Frankish sources and under some bodies of penal law, poaching, pursecutting and petit larceny led to cutting off a thumb, usually from the right hand. Perjury was punished by cutting off the oath-fingers, so a perjurer could never again swear an oath.

Cutting off the Ears

In antiquity, cutting off the ears was a punishment for serfs, because it left them completely fit for work. In the Middle Ages, cutting off of the ears was often combined with banishment. This punishment was also inflicted for blasphemy and the bearing of forbidden weapons. In most cases only one, but frequently both ears were cut off. The old court judgments indicate that this punishment was mainly inflicted on women. It was used relatively rarely for men. This may be due to the fact that men were hanged for theft. As it caused only slight physical disability, cutting off the ears was a punishment intended to serve as a warning to the wrongdoer to lead an orderly life and observe the law in future.

Cutting out the Tongue

Cutting out the tongue was a „matching" punishment, for it was the penalty imposed for crimes committed with the tongue, that is, by the spoken word. The Sachsenspiegel laid down that a court might be held only with the king's permission. So any person who ventured to hold a court without the king's authorization had to have his tongue cut out, since the judgment he had passed by word of mouth was unlawful. Offences leading to loss of the tongue were perjury, bearing false witness, blasphemy, slander, false accusations and defamation of the authorities. The condemned person's tongue, or part of it, was cut out with scissors or a knife.

Whipping, birching and cutting out the tongue, woodcut 1539

Degrading Punishments

General Remarks

At all times, a person's honour was a precious and vulnerable possession. In Germanic times, any one who fled from battle or was guilty of any dishonourable deed lost his honour. In Frankish times, dishonouring, degrading punishments were still relatively rare. Later on, when corporal punishment was used in addition to or instead of the death penalty, separate degrading punishments were developed. All punishments which wiped out the wrongdoer's personality, i.e. all forms of capital punishment, and also all corporal punishment, ostracism and proscription were, of course, simultaneously degrading punishments. At many an execution, however, special consideration was given to the honour of the condemned person, for instance the execution chair was covered with velvet or the like. Degrading punishments in the narrower sense were those which publicly defamed in a humiliating manner, mortified or completely dishonoured. The Carolina expressly associated certain punishments with dishonour. Similarly, all punishments executed by the hangman brought dishonour. Particularly in the Middle Ages, a great deal of inventiveness was demonstrated in devising degrading punishments. It should be noted, however, that degrading punishments were by no means restricted to the Middle Ages, but were also applied in more modern times and even in the 19th century.

In the following, the most important degrading punishments will be dealt with, though no claim to completeness can be made, above all on account of local differences.

Censure

The mildest form of degrading punishment was the censure. A person who had committed a slight offence against the community was punished with public censure. This was an urgent warning not to repeat such an offence.

Recantation and Apology

If a person had spread untrue, defamatory allegations concerning another or accused him of a punishable offence without being able to bring proof, he was forced to recant and apologize. The offender had to stand in a public place, and in some cases even kneel, to declare his recantation and apology in a loud voice, and to strike his mouth with his flat hand as a visible sign of his misdeed.

Wearing Degrading Garments

The symbolic significance of clothing is as old as clothing itself. It demonstrates the rank and status of the wearer. So what was more obvious than to make persons who placed themselves beyond the pale of the community by their actions, their peculiar origin or their vocation recognizable to all by special clothing.

The appearance, and in the broadest sense the dress, of a person includes the hair. The hair-style, open or tied, long or short, permitted conclusions to be drawn with regard to a person's legal status. Only the freeman wore long hair, while the bondsman's was cut short. Consequently, cutting off the hair of the head was a degrading punishment from time immemorial. Men and women who had committed sexual offences had their hair cut off, a degrading punishment still inflicted in our times by moblaw.

Shortening of a woman's dress was a customary degrading punishment. The mothers of illegitimate children and female adulterers had a broad strip cut off the bottom of their dress in public. Clothing served primarily as protection from inclement weather and the shortening of the dress meant exposure, deprival of protection and disgrace.

Like the reduction or shortening of clothing, compulsion to wear certain garments was likewise a degrading punishment or at least the mark of those considered dishonest. Insolvent debtors were therefore required to wear a yellow hat and incompetent farmers a white hat (Schaumburg-Lippe, 18th century). The sharp distinction between Christians and Jews demanded by the Catholic church resulted in Jews having to wear a pointed hat and a yellow patch on their breast as identification. To enable better supervision of prostitution, which though tolerated was viewed with suspicion by the authorities, prostitutes were ordered to wear conspicuous clothing characteristic of their calling. Executioners, too, were required to wear different clothing than the normal citizen.

The clothing regulations issued in the 14th and 15th century, above all in the cities, made breaches of them practically inevitable. Contraventions of the clothing regulations were punished mainly by fines, but in some cities the tipstaffs had orders to remove on the open street too opulent clothing not in keeping with a person's rank.

Roof Stripping
The symbolic significance of the roof as protection has been handed down to us from the distant past. If a man allowed himself to be beaten by his wife and this was confirmed by witnesses, the roof over his head could be stripped, for the common view was that he was no longer

worthy of that protection. However, this symbolic punishment was applied not only to persons, but also to communities. Where towns had contravened the regulations of the empire, the roofs were removed from the city towers and the gates were unhinged. Milan is an historical example. In the struggle of the pope against Emperor Frederick I, Barbarossa *, the city sided with the pope and was conquered by Frederick I in 1162. As punishment, the emperor did not enter the city through a gate, but through a breach specially broken through the wall. In this way he demonstrated that the city was no longer worthy of the protection of a wall.

Symbolic Procession

The symbolic procession was a punishment often decreed in place of merited, more severe penalties, in most cases corporal punishment. Bondsmen, who ought to have been hanged, had to walk barefoot through the streets with a rope round their necks. Freemen bore the sword on such occasions, instead of being beheaded. The carrying of candles derives from ecclesiastical penitential law and secular sanctions. Originally a voluntary expiatory sacrifice, from the late Middle Ages onwards the carrying of candles was a church-imposed penance for persons found guilty of witchcraft and adultery. It was then taken over into the secular law of atonement as a special form of expiation. Wrongdoers whose offences called for birching had to carry the birch. The punishment for those guilty of disloyalty to their masters was to carry a dog, for from time immemorial the dog has been considered man's most faithful companion. Saddles or ploughs were also carried in symbolic processions.

From a church penance of obscure origin, the punishment of stone-carrying in public developed in the cities. The name of the stone varied regionally: Bagstein (bicker-stone); Schandstein (shame-stone); Lasterstein (slander-stone); Klapperstein (chatter-stone); Krötenstein (toad-stone), the spoken words were as venomous as a toad; Flasche (flask), Prangerstein (pillory-stone), Kakstein (pillory stone). The offences for which this punishment was imposed were many and various: quarreling, impious swearing, blasphemy, adultery, pandering, receiving stolen goods, concealing found property, theft and false pretences. Stone-carrying was widespread far beyond the frontiers of Germany and was mostly inflicted on women, more rarely on men. Where a woman committed an offence for which normally a fine was payable, the woman had to carry the stone so that her husband's property remained unharmed. The stone was hung round the neck of the miscreant by the bailiff, and thus „burdened" he or she had to walk a prescribed distance. If the stone were set down on the way, an additional fine had to be paid. The weight of the stone varied considerably, ranging from 12.5 to 90 kilogrammes, for which reason the judgments referred to small or large stones. The stones had a great variety of shapes and could also be of wood. They often bore inscriptions, e.g. in Saxony-Anhalt: "He who hath strife and discord sown, must carry this all through the town." Preceded by the town piper or drummer, the procession moved off. The route·was always lined by crowds of onlookers who gave vent to their satisfaction and malicious glee with catcalls and abuse. Even assault, for instance by throwing eggs, was allowed, for during the execution of their punishment the wrong-doers were not protected by the public peace. To end on a curious note, in Sübersdorf the judges even supplied the eggs.

From the end of the 15th century onwards, the punishment of stone-carrying was imposed ever less frequently; it was replaced by the "fiddle-yoke" or "neck-violin", which in the cities satisfied the need for a symbolic manifestation of punishment better than the stone.

Wheelbarrow pushing was the punishment for lovers guilty of unchaste conduct. In Rothenburg ob der Tauber, for example, such conduct en-tailed an additional church penance; the "permissive" maiden had to stand in front of the church door wearing straw plaits (see colour plates) and the seducer had to come to service on three successive Sundays wear-ing a straw coat. Furthermore, the seducer had to push his beloved through the streets of the town in a wheelbarrow and the onlookers were allowed to throw garbage at them. Then, accompanied by the jeers of the watchers, they had to plough a certain area of farmland. The mantles of infamy (see colour plates) were a popular means of taking to task the in-veterate bibbers who squandered house and farm on drink. This mantle of infamy in the form of a barrel, often decorated with derisive illustra-tions, was placed on their shoulders, and thus branded they had to walk through the streets of the town. The "iron maiden" (see colour plates) may well be called a curiosity of legal history. Because of the long spikes inside it, it was regarded for a long time as an instrument of execution and hence as proof of the cruelty of medieval penal practices. Admittedly,the famous legal historian Karl von Amira (1848-1930) also proceeded from the assumption that the iron maiden was an executioner's tool. He ad-vanced the opinion, however, that it was never used as such, but served only the purpose of "territion", i.e. of terrifying. The more recent re-search work of F. T. Schulz, however, seems adequate proof that the spikes were a later addition and that the iron maiden was accordingly a pillory-like instrument for inflicting degrading punishment, a mantle of infamy for women. The iron maiden exhibited in the Crime Museum in

Rothenburg ob der Tauber presumably comes from Bohemia and to all appearances dates from the 16th century. In the past century it stood in the castle in Nuremberg, was sold to England in 1889, went from there to America, and came to Rothenburg in 1968. The iron maiden shown in Nuremberg up to its destruction in the war in 1944 was a copy of the one now in Rothenburg.

Couples who had not practiced abstinence, i.e. had indulged in premarital sexual relations, inevitably landed in prison. If they were willing to marry, the additional church penance was milder. Instead of a myrtle wreath, the bride had to wear a straw wreath or, if the child was already born, it had to be held in her arms during the wedding ceremony. If the wedding was held during imprisonment, the tipstaff conducted the couple to church. If the bride had been convicted of several sexual offences, the wedding took place in an inn or in prison. If the couple wanted to avoid the shame of "being coupled in an inn", the wedding could be held in church, but only as a "Whore's wedding". Then, after the prison sentence had been served, two tipstaff "wives" had to escort the harlot, adorned with a straw wreath with two straw plaits, to the marriage altar, not through the bridal gate, but through a side entrance (black gate). Under the Prussian criminal code of 1640, brides who unlawfully wore the bridal wreath, had their plaits cut off and nailed to the pillory.

The symbolic procession mostly followed the same invariable route decreed by the court. In Rothenburg it was the Herrngasse from the market place to the castle gate and back, or on the market place around the St. Georgsbrunnen (St Georges's fountain).

Defamation

If a debtor failed to pay by the agreed date and did not respond to repeated reminders, it was hardly possible for a creditor to recover his money in earlier times. True, there was already a judicial procedure for default and the possibility of distraint (Lex Salica *), but these means were not always effective, particularly in the case of noble debtors. The creditor could then publicly decry his debtor by having letters of detraction and disparagement put up (see colour plates). The latter presented the facts combined with a warning to all not to lend money to such a person, and bore illustrations of the debtor undergoing every conceivable, dishonourable punishment (hanging, breaking on the wheel). If the debtor was of noble rank, his coat of arms was often shown upside down, which was as much as saying that the family was extinct. The seal which the debtor had affixed to the document, thus promising to repay the money punctually, was besmirched by showing it in the picture on the hindquarters of a swine, an indication that the debtor was not worthy of a clean seal. Depicting a seal hung from the gallows had the same significance. In 1577, letters of detraction and disparagement were forbidden by the imperial police regulations.

In all ages there were manuscripts and, following Gutenberg's invention of printing in 1445, books whose contents were leveled at the official opinions of church and state. The secular and ecclesiastical authorities therefore practiced censorship. Literature that was not agreeable to them was forbidden (Index) and in many cases was burnt in public by the executioner. Such action was equivalent to public disgrace for the author and often had other unpleasant consequences for him personally. One very well-known case recorded by history was the public burning of the papal bull of excommunication by Martin Luther in Wittenberg in 1520. In this way Luther publicly expressed his contempt for papal power. It was a deed that had far-reaching consequences for the church.

If a lawbreaker deserving death by burning had evaded punishment by fleeing, a dummy was burnt publicly in his stead. Even today, this practice is still adopted by the people at demonstrations or uprisings. Persons who had made themselves unpopular with the authorities by voicing their opinion in public speeches were banned from public speaking. Thereafter, they were not allowed to voice their opinions in public on pain of punishment. It was an effective method of silencing political opponents. If the offence was particulary grave, regardless of whether the perpetrator had fled or had been convicted and punished, all mention of his name could be prohibited. This meant the complete extinction of his personality and irrevocable expulsion from the community.

Wearing or Carrying Objects
The crime or offence committed was formerly easily identified by the characteristic matching punishment. Especially the degrading punishments intended to lower a person in the eyes of his fellow-men and make him ridiculous were very imaginative and there was hardly any limit to human inventiveness. The instruments of punishment used were as numerous and varied as the offences. There were masks of shame in the most bizarre designs. The "dragon" was a mask of shame for gossiping, quarrelsome shrews: big ears = they heard everything, spectacles = they saw everything, big nose = they stuck their nose into other people's business, big mouth and long tongue = everything they got to know was maliciously told to others. Such masks also bore inscriptions, e.g. "The shrew who cannot hold her tongue has to put this muzzle on" or "Punishment of dishonourable and wicked tongues". All masks of shame had a common

feature, they characterized the wearer's offence and made it plainly visible to the observer. For instance, a man who had behaved like a swine was forced to wear a mask in the shape of a boar's head. There were also masks of shame for scamping, botching craftsmen. Many of them covered the face completely. This might give the present-day observer the impression that despite the public nature of the punishment the miscreant remained largely anonymous. It must be taken into account, however, that towns at that time were very small. In Germany there were only about 50 towns with more than 5,000 inhabitants, and every inhabitant knew all the others. The condemned person never remained unrecognized. The great rush of onlookers at such events is explained by the fact that in those days there were few opportunities for amusement and entertainment, and advantage was taken of every diversion from the wearisome monotony of everyday life. The musician who played badly had a "shame-flute" hung round his neck. Wicked women and girls were locked in the "neck-violin" and had to stand on the market place near the pillory for some time. Two women who continually quarrelled in public were locked in the double neck-violin until they promised to keep the peace in future. When married couples quarrelled, the neighbours put a beetle (a heavy piece of wood) in front of the house door and it could only be removed after they had buried the hatchet. Attendance at church services was obligatory. Absence without an excuse, which was easy to establish, because every one had his regular seat, was sentenced to a church punishment, e.g. the rosary, and the same applied to those who fell asleep during the service. The enormous rosary of large wooden beads was placed round his neck, and wearing it he had to stand before the church door on Sundays before the service started and below the pulpit during the sermon. Persons who had to stand in the pillory had "shame-boards" placed round their neck, which bore their name and the nature of their offence. Loafers and idlers had to wear a fool's cap. Those who cheated at cards or dice went to the pillory and were decorated with the cheater's chain. The slander-stone also belongs in this context. If, as an act of grace, banishment was not enforced, the condemned person had to carry a "slander-stick" in public. It was a sort of beggar's staff of barkless wood branded with the town's coat of arms. Though the modern observer may be amused at some of the seemingly comical humiliating devices, there was nothing amusing about them for those on whom they were inflicted. Although they very rarely caused physical pain, they pointed up clearly the negative traits of the affected person and his misdeed, and aroused in his fellowmen what is probably the lowest and most reprehensible form of pleasure, pleasure in the misery of others.

Ban on the Bearing of Arms and Knightly Accoutrements

The knights had a special standing within the empire. The legal status of a knight was incomparably higher than that of a simple commoner. For this reason, many of the punishments customary at that time could not be imposed on knights. Despite the decline of the knighthood in the 14th and 15th century, the knights succeeded in retaining their privileges. If a knight had committed an offence and was caught, he was brought to trial. If the crime did not merit corporal punishment, but only a degrading punishment, the latter differed from that of normal citizens. Such knightly punishments included: the ban on bearing arms, or it was decreed that instead of a dagger he was allowed to carry only a broken knife; riding without boots or spurs, without a saddle or with a bridle of bast; in serious cases, the shattering of the coat of arms or signet-ring.

Penal Servitude

Servile labour was a widespread punishment. Men were predominantly sentenced to entrenchment work on the fortifications, but also to temporary, and sometimes lifelong, galley slavery. But these were genuine punishments, often inflicted as an act of clemency instead of a death penalty. In addition, penal servitude developed into a degrading punishment for violation of public morals. The so-called public morals commissions in the times of Empress Maria Theresia often imposed such punishments. Men and women who led a dissolute life had their hair cut short and then had to sweep the streets and cart away the rubbish.

Punishment of Prostitutes by Penal Servitude, Switzerland, 18th century.

Loss of Rank and Relegation

A punishment that lay completely within the discretion of the judge was loss of rank, which was imposed especially in cases of offences by officials. A town councillor, for instance, who had taken improper advantage of his office, lost his seat on the council, and this often involved also loss of his honorary pew in church. The severest form of this punishment was banishment, often coupled with corporal punishment. Banishment could be inflicted for a limited period or for life. For non-local evildoers certainly a mild punishment, but for a local person it meant loss of his home and consequently destruction of his civil existence in most cases.

Burial

It is almost inconceivable nowadays that not even the dead were safe from punishment. In the case of people who had themselves to blame for their destitution, a so-called "silent burial" was decreed. Although the deceased was buried in the churchyard, there was no big funeral procession, no music and singing. Suicides were treated differently. In Germanic times, suicides were regarded as "harmless ghosts" who had to walk the earth until the time of their normal death. It was the Christian faith that first placed suicide on a par with murder and treated it as a mortal sin. The deed was considered reprehensible and the person was classified as a criminal who deserved punishment. Under the influence of such teachings, the notion that a suicide laid hands on himself out of his own initiative was also banished. Now the opinion was held that unearthly beings

Penal Servitude on Fortifications, Woman with a Neck-Violin, 17. century.

157

Public Morals Commission in Vienna, 18th cent., cutting of hair and street-sweeping.

or metaphysical forces had persuaded the suicide to commit the deed. In other words, under Christian influence he became in the superstitious minds of the people an evil spirit who was anxiously avoided and whom one attempted to banish for good. In the late Middle Ages, people believed in the power of the Devil, who had drawn the suicide down into his realm. For this reason, the deceased was also associated with bad weather, rain, hail or drought. It was believed at that time that ghosts haunted the scene of the crime and the place of burial. This superstition also explains the great aversion to the body of a suicide. If he had hanged himself, you had to box his ears before taking him down, otherwise your own neck would be wrung. It was not allowed to take the dead person out of the house across the threshold; he had to be pulled through a hole specially dug under the threshold or through a hole in the wall. The burial took place outside the cemetery in unhallowed ground, where possible at a crossroads, and was carried out by the knacker or executioner. The dead person was buried face down with a heap of thorns on top to make any return more difficult. And the objects used for the crime, such as a beam, knife and rope, were destroyed, as was the bier.

From the standpoint of the Catholic church, life and death were gifts of God for Christians. All suffering was regarded as a trial and the source of true salvation. Hence suicide was classified as a mortal sin, as breaking away from God. Formerly, and to some extent even today, that had consequences under (canon) law: refusal of Christian burial, no memorial services, ban on mentioning the name, exhumation from hallowed ground if suicide was established, all of which was equivalent to excommunication, although not formally decreed.

A suicide also had consequences under penal law. From the 13th century onwards, in a number of areas regulations appeared, which provided for confiscation of the property of suicides in favour of the sovereign. The Bambergensis also contained such provisions, but refrained from imposing punishment. The Carolina was the first code to abrogate these penal regulations. For a long time, however, the so-called ass's funeral was practiced. A criminal who had evaded punishment by commiting suicide was taken by the executioner to the gallows on an ass and was buried there. This was the most dishonourable form of burial.

Pillory

When and where a pillory was first used as an instrument of punishment cannot be established from historical records. The chronicles reveal, however, that its use spread gradually in the 12th and 13th century. In later times, pillories became a general custom and in numerous places they still exist even today, or their former location is on record. This instrument of punishment was known by a large variety of names. In north Germany it was often called "Katz", in south Germany and Austria „Prechel" or "Schreiat" , in England "stretch-neck" and in France "pilori" or "carcan". Pillory punishments were inflicted up to the end of the 18th century and in some towns even up to the middle of the 19th century, for instance in Flensburg, where the pillory was used regularly up to 1864, i.e. 7 years before the present penal code came into force. A large number of pillory sentences were passed after the promulgation of the Carolina. The Bavarian criminal law of 1751 prescribed the pillory considerably more often than that of 1616. Even Anselm von Feuerbach *, a proponent of liberal justice, still recognized the pillory as an auxiliary punishment in 1813.

How often a pillory sentence was passed can hardly be established. A record kept by the executioner at Ansbach shows that over a period of 25 years he put 309 persons in the pillory, that is, one per month. In this connection it should be noted that the executioner was called upon only in particularly sensational cases. How many punishments of this sort were carried out by the beadle can only be guessed, for records were hardly ever kept for minor offences.

In principle, the situation was the same as at present, only the big criminal cases remained in people's memory, everything else was soon forgotten.

The pillory had a great variety of forms. But for all the differences in construction, they had but one common purpose, i. e. conspicuous exposure of the person at the pillory to the eyes of passers-by. Of course, there were various degrees of punishment. In Rothenburg, the fool's cell was considered less disgracing than the pillory at the town hall. The main forms of pillory were:

1. a neck iron fastened by a chain to the town hall or some other public building.
2. a wooden post driven into the earth or standing on a platform with a neck iron fastened to it ("shame-post").
3. the pillory post of wood or stone, of somewhat more artistic design, frequently decorated with the town coat of arms or symbols of justice and often bearing warning inscriptions.
4. the stage-type pillory, a masonry platform with steps, mostly at the town hall (Rothenburg).
5. the stage of shame, an elaborate construction mostly free on all sides, very high to give a good view of those standing on it (stage-type pillory in Schwäbisch-Hall).
6. the sitting pillory, a "shame-stool" or "shame-ass", was a wooden structure standing on a public place, on which miscreants had to sit.
7. a cage in which offenders stood or sat, either standing free on all sides on a public place (Rothenburg fool's cell) or fitted into the front of a building (town hall) like the "Trülle" in Berne. These cages could often be rotated.
8. the stocks, a vertical block or board with holes for the legs and irons for the hands.

The offences for which people were sent to the pillory were as numerous and varied as the types of pillory. In this connection it should be noted that nowadays many of those offences no longer fall under criminal law and are not prosecuted. On examining the elements of the offences, we find that they can be classified essentially in five groups:

1. Criminal Offences
   For the first overt theft of property valued at less than 5 florins, Article 158 of the Carolina prescribed the pillory. For the second case of petit larceny, Article 161 of the Carolina called for corporal punishment (birching) and banishment, and in addition concurrent standing in the pillory. Flogging, branding or mutilation, e.g. cutting off the ears, was often carried out at the pillory.

At the pillory, from an altarpiece in Marburg, Lahn.

2. Imperilment Offences
   Violations of political regulations fell within this class. A person who polluted wells was sentenced to the pillory for endangering the supply of drinking and fire-fighting water. Those who violated the curfew or were found on the streets at night without a lighted lantern were similarly punished. Revellers who disturbed the peace at night while drunk were promptly put into the fool's cell. The inscription on the fool's cell in Ochsenfurt

A wrongdoer in the "Trülle" in Berne, 1780.

161

(a Bavarian town in the district of Lower Franconia) is typical: "Beware and don't go out / if you are caught / they'll put you in the fool's cell." Similarly, under the steps of the town hall in Nördlingen (a Bavarian town in the district of Swabia) is the picture of a fool with the inscription: "Now we are two." Work-dodgers and vagrants were sat on the wooden "shame-ass". Without having committed an offence in the true sense of the word, their misdeed consisted in not living as a normal person was expected to. A "shame-ass" of this sort stood in Rothenburg at the southern edge of the market place not far from St. George fountain. Sitting on a wooden ass was also a military punishment for disobedient soldiers. The stocks were also a punishment for work-dodgers and vagrants. The condemned had to sit on the

Prisoners in the stocks,
Tengler Laienspiegel

Prisoners in the stocks
Pen-and-ink drawing from the House-book of Prince Waldburg-Wolfegg, 15th century

ground with their legs through holes in the wood and their hands in the irons. With all their limbs thus immobilized, they had to sit out their time, while street urchins removed the defenceless men's shoes and stockings and tickled the soles of their feet with straws.

3. Sexual Offences

A very large number was sent to the pillory for violating ethical and moral rules. Unmarried persons convicted of sexual offen-

Whipping of unmarried mothers, 1782. Etching by D. Chodowiecki

Flogging, stocks and neck-violin, 18th century

ces had to go to the pillory the same as those who had aided and abetted, i.e. procured for immoral purposes, by tolerating an offence or providing a room. A man who had committed adultery for the first time with an unmarried woman went to the pillory. And the second time, too, unless the circumstances of his misdeed merited more severe punishment.

4. Defamatory Offences

Any person who injured the honour of another by slander, libel or false accusation was himself considered to be without honour and went to the pillory. If the offence had caused major harm to the affected person, the pillory was supplemented by imprisonment or corporal punishment. The corporal punishment was then inflicted at the pillory. Among these offences, the dissemination of insulting pamphlets ranked as particularly grave. Also disparagement or unjustified criticism of the authorities was punished with the pillory in less serious cases.

5. Religious Offences

Simple, non-malicious blasphemy was punished by the secular authorities with the pillory. Repeated and malicious offences entailed not only the pillory, but also corporal punishment and mutilation by cutting out of the tongue, which was likewise carried out at the pillory.

Often, as an act of clemency, a pillory sentence was passed instead of a deserved, more severe penalty. In most cases, the pillory could be avoided by paying a fine, with the result that mainly insolvent, poor people suffered this punishment. Nobles and persons of rank could not be sent to the pillory. The period of public exhibition averaged one to two hours, as far as possible on market days or Sundays when many people were on the streets. There were also judgments which decreed several periods in the pillory on various days. Above or beside the pillory, a board was hung, bearing the name of the wrongdoer, his offence and the sentence. In addition, humiliating objects were often placed or hung on the offender, e.g. masks of shame "slander-stone" or cheater's chain. The object of the pillory was primarily deterrence, but the idea of retribution and security played a by no means insignificant role. The concept of resocialization was completely alien to mediaeval law. The criminal was to be banished perpetually from the community of the honourable.

In connection with the pillory, it may be of interest that in schools, too, pillory punishments were customary, longer in fact than in penal law. There was sitting on the ass, standing in the corner, wearing a donkey's (or dunce's) cap, or hanging a wooden ass round the neck. One or the other of these punishments may be familiar to older readers.

Riding

The ass has been regarded from time immemorial as stupid, low and ignoble, a creature of ignominy. Riding the ass therefore numbered among the degrading punishments. Sitting on the wooden "shame-ass" has already been mentioned in the preceding section on the pillory. Another punishment was riding a living ass. A wife who had beaten her husband was set on an ass and led trough the streets of the town. If she had struck her husband in an overt quarrel and he had not defended himself, he had to lead the ass. But if the blows had been struck from behind so that the man could not defend himself, the ass was led by a court bailiff. Riding the ass was also imposed on adulterers sentenced to death on the gallows. They were set on the ass facing the animal's hindquarters and led through the streets to the gallows for execution.

Ducking

This punishment was used particularly on bakers, for which reason it was also called the "baker's baptism". The weight of rolls and loaves was prescribed by the authorities. If a baker sold too small rolls or underweight loaves, it was considered fraud. He was then put in the baker's cage or stool and ducked in a well or pond with a seesaw, the number of duckings depending on the amount of the weight shortage. The weight had to be exactly right; for example, the baker Gumprecht Steinmetz of Windsheim (now Bad Windsheim in Central Franconia, Bavaria) was fined 5 florins in 1540 for baking loaves that were too small, whereupon, according to the records, he made his loaves too large out of arrogance and was therefore fined double the amount, i.e. 10 florins.

Children who in autumn unlawfully shook fruit from trees or trespassed in vineyards, were punished in Rothenburg by being placed in a basket and ducked several times in the fountain at the market place.

Woman in the Ducking Stool, England,
18th century

Tarring and Feathering

The punishment of tarring and feathering should not be left unmentioned. The upper part of the body was smeared with tar or some other sticky substance, then the delinquent was rolled in feathers and subsequently placed in the pillory. For what offences this punishment was inflicted cannot be established from the available sources. Whatever the case, it was a degrading punishment.

Fines

In addition to the punishments enumerated so far, fines were imposed at a very early date. The old "folk" laws prescribed fines for violations of other's rights. The fine payable by the offender accrued to the injured person or his family who, on their part, waived vengeance on the offender. The amount of the fine was expressed in terms of money, but in keeping with the early economic system, was paid in kind, e.g. livestock and grain. The punitive character of the fine, however, is demonstrated by the fact that as a rule it was substantially higher than the damage caused and often resulted in impoverishment of the offender or his family. This is also evident from later regulations, which required part of the fine to be paid to the public authorities. In the case of the Franks, for example, one third of the fine had to be paid to the count, and in the case of the Lombards one half to the king.

Apart from these penalties for damage under the older bodies of "folk" law, in the times of the Franks sovereign interdictory power became a second point of departure for the development of fines. Interdictory power, i.e. the power to prohibit something on pain of punishment, was at that time the supreme expression of the king's powers, which even then could be described as governmental. Any person who disregarded and contravened a command of the king or of any official to whom he had delegated interdictory power had to pay a fine. The amount of the fine, however, was governed not by the protected legal interest, but by the rank of the person who had issued the command.

The social changes in the Middle Ages and the resulting impoverishment of the lower strata of the population caused a marked increase in crime. Since in most cases the offender was poor, and could therefore not pay a fine in cash or in kind, an attempt was made to combat crime with the punishments to life and limb laid down in the municipal and national public peace regulations, though still adhering to the principle that pecuniary penalties could replace other punishments. On account of the weaknesses in the public administration of penal law in the early Middle Ages, many breaches of the law were not punished at all, but were settled by a conciliatory agreement between the offender and the injured party. In consequence, conciliation was also occasionally included in the public peace regulations among the legal consequences of a breach of the law. However, replacement of the due penalty by payment of a fine was made dependent on the previous conciliation of the offender with the injured party or his family. It was not until the late Middle Ages that the hitherto applied conciliation system was gradually displaced by the sovereign power's right to punish. How slowly this process took place is illustrated by the fact that even in the 17th century the courts still had to declare expressly that, regardless of any conciliatory payment (damages) to the injured party, the offender was subject to punishment.

Although, as already mentioned above, most punishments could be replaced by fines in the early Middle Ages, from the height of the Middle Ages (13th century) onwards this was predominantly true only of punishments to the "hide and hair" (mutilating punishments). In step with this development, punishments to life and limb were also frequently laid down only for the event of insolvency. A distinction must be drawn between genuine avoidance of punishment by a convicted person who was able to pay and the decision of the court "in mercy" to allow a highly solvent condemned person to avoid punishment by the payment of money.

This development resulted in a decline in the payment of damages to the injured party in favour of the "peace money (comparable to the English term "amercement) payable to the public authorities. In various regions, this "peace money" was also called "pene", "Brüche", "Busse", "Wandel" or, in the Sachsenspiegel, "Gewette", but the most widely used term was "Brüche". The "Brüche" payable to avoid the due penalty accrued entirely, or at least for the most part, to the public authorities since they, the guarantors of the public peace, were considered the true injured parties, especially where the infringed right was vested in the king or territorial lords as the holders of public authority. Derived from the concepts of "Friedlosigkeit" (peacelessness) and "Huldverlust" (loss of favour), in the domain of sovereign judicial powers it became general practice for criminal court judges to impose predominantly pecuniary penalties at their own discretion and thus enable the offender to recover favour and peace.

From now on we can speak of fiscalization of the penal law. This led to court jurisdiction becoming a productive sovereign right which could be pledged, leased or vested in others. The financial interest was also the reason why, in the Middle Ages, the numerous prescribed punishments were predominantly inflicted only on poor persons. The police regulations issued by the cities and territories likewise provided for numerous fines, most of them expressed in pounds. The pound was a unit of account: 5 3/5 pounds equalled 1 florin. But since, as a rule, the fines amounted to 10, 20, 30 or more pounds, the receipts from the administration of penal justice were substantial. The authorities tried to increase this revenue still further by allotting part of the fine to the person who filed the charge in the case of offences that were prosecuted only when reported.

The Bambergensis and the Carolina tried to bring about a change. Article 272 of the Bambergensis forbade officials and judges the imposition of fines in penal cases. But this was probably done primarily to put an end to the abuse of fiscalization by the so-called "purse judges".* The Carolina prescribed only non-pecuniary penalties, providing for a fine of four times the value of stolen property only in the case of petit larceny (Article 157 f). Fines payable to the authorities for grave crimes were unknown to the Carolina. Thus fines were abolished at least in the field of serious crime. But neither the Bambergensis nor the Carolina changed very much. In the case of the nobility, for instance, corporal punishment could be regularly avoided by paying a fine. Moreover, by sovereign acts of clemency the sentence, though not quashed, was commuted to a fine. Especially in the domain of territorial and municipal law concerning the police and maintenance of law and order, fines were retained on account of the great financial importance.

Payment of Court Costs, woodcut from the Bamberg Halsgerichtsordnung, 1510.

Imprisonment

Even in the times of the Franks, deprivation of liberty ordered by the authorities customarily took the form of detention in prison. But essentially it was inflicted only as an act of clemency instead of a due death

168

sentence, especially for high treason, or as a coercive measure. In the 8th and 9th century, deprivation of liberty as a punishment was included in the laws only in isolated cases. Lombard King Liutprand, for example, laid down imprisonment for one to two years for theft in a law dating from 726; Anglo-Saxon law had similar provisions. In the German Middle Ages, deprivation of liberty remained a mercy punishment in all states with the exception of Bavaria, where it was a revocable statutory punishment in the form of imprisonment for persons of rank. It was only in the 14th century that it became more widespread in the cities. There deprivation of liberty was used with increasing frequency, first as an alternative statutory penalty in the event of insolvency, but later also as a punishment in its own right for other offences. Article 157 of the Carolina prescribed a period of imprisonment as an alternative penalty for petit larceny. By nature and in its effects, however, imprisonment was a corporal punishment, for conditions in the prisons at that time were appalling. This becomes evident on viewing the completely unlighted, damp and fusty dungeon pits in Nuremberg. In prisons like this, the prisoner, possibly in fetters or in the stocks, suffered untold ordeals from darkness, cold, hunger and vermin so that many of them longed for the deliverance of death. Famous jurists such as Schwarzenberg* and Carpzov* made efforts to remedy this deplorable state of affairs, but had little success, for the Theresiana* of 1768 still demonstrates by its regulations that the old conditions still prevailed in the prisons.

Commitment to prison
from Tengler Laienspiegel, 1511

Punishment at that time was primarily retribution; the idea of resocialization was still remote. All in all, deprivation of liberty played only a subordinate role in the penal system, the "pains" or painful punishments were clearly predominant. The prisons were used primarily for the detention of prisoners until they were tried and executed, i.e. as remand prisons.

A new form of imprisonment introduced in England towards the end of the 16th century had a great impact on the development of deprivation of liberty as a punishment. The social changes and the accompanying pauperization of the lower strata of the population resulted in hordes of beggars and mass criminality of unimaginable proportions. In the interests of social welfare, institutions were built in which beggars and the work-shy were to be forcibly trained to work. Following the English model, similar institutions were set up in Holland. The Calvinist work ethic called for combatting poverty by means of work procurement. Restless work was considered the sole means of escaping damnation and attaining eternal salvation. Those who did not

Friedrich Baron von der Trenck in the Magdeburg prison with his fetters weighing 68 pounds.

pursue that goal on their own initiative had to be compelled by suitable measures to seek salvation. The humbling of the obstinate by hard labour was intended to remedy their disturbed relationship to God. So in Amsterdam a house of correction for men was established in 1595 and one for women (Spinhuis) in 1597. As their name implies, these houses aimed at correction and teaching the inmates to work. They took in paupers and combatted begging and vagrancy. In view of the prevailing laws, this was already a step towards combatting criminality. The connection to penal justice was demonstrated particularly clearly by the fact that, from the establishment of these institutions onwards, also young, reformable thieves were sent to the house of correction rather than to the gallows. Viewed from this standpoint, the houses of correction of 1595 and 1597 were also penitentiaries. In these institutions, discipline was strict and the reformatory idea was predominant. Infringements of the institution's regulations were punished by confinement in a dark cell on bread and water or by whipping. Juvenile inmates were given school instruction and all were required to attend Sunday services, to join in the prayers before and after meals, and to take part in catechism lessons. The food was adequate for the work performed and medical care was also provided. The stay in the house of correction was intended to bring about a change of mind in the inmates so that they would pursue a normal, industrious life in the future. These institutions in Amsterdam were the first to put the modern idea of imprisonment into effect, that is, working towards resocialization of prisoners by work therapy.

Prisoner in the blockhouse prison in Berne, 1822

The Dutch model was then taken over in Germany in the 17th century. Soon after 1600, the Hanseatic cities of Hamburg, Bremen and Lübeck built similar institutions and their example was followed by numerous other cities and states. A new means of punishment had been introduced into the administration of justice. Initially, commitals to houses of correction and workhouses were undoubtedly decreed "in mercy", but gradually this form of penalty found its way into the statutes and the regulations of the sovereign powers. What a change of mind that was when we consider that for centuries it was held that punishment must be retribution alone. How profoundly this new punishment differed from the old ones. For in the last analysis, the latter amounted to destruction of the criminal. This was also true of sentences of imprisonment, fortification work and the galleys. The bodily torture or killing that was really of no benefit to the community in general, apart from the deterrent effect, was replaced by sentences to fortification work or the galleys. This afforded the opportunity to make use of the criminal's working capacity for the benefit of the state up to his death, which was mostly premature on account of the very hard labour and inhuman treatment. In consequence of this conception, the development of the house-of-correction system to that of the modern execution of punishment suffered a setback in the 18th century. The object of resocialization was thrust aside in favour of the idea of extracting the greatest possible benefit from the corrective institution. The houses of correction offered a large potential of extremely cheap labour, so what was more obvious than to utilize it in the interests of the state by setting up production shops. Things went so far that houses of correction were leased to private entrepreneurs who, however, had not the slightest interest in the crime-policy goals of those institutions, but only wanted to maximize their profits, even more so than the state. As a result of this misuse, these institutions declined into neglected confusion. Buildings and equipment fell into desrepair and low-grade super-

Prisoner with neckbrace, 18th century.

visory personnel let discipline decline. All this and the crowding together of great numbers of criminals and non-criminals made the houses of correction "hotbeds of crime". Despite this very negative development, which incidentally did not take place everywhere, the houses of correction remained the vehicles for the idea of modern prison punishment. The reforms of the 19th century, which had become urgently necessary, then brought the final breakthrough to the present-day system in the execution of punishment.

Animal Trials

Exodus Chap. 21, Verse 28 reads: " If an ox gore a man or a woman, that they die: then the ox shall be surely stoned, and his flesh shall not be eaten; but the owner of the ox shall be quit." These words from the Old Testament led to formal court trials of harmful animals being held in the Middle Ages, which were similar to trials of human beings. The accused animal was assigned a court representative. If he lost the case, brutal punishments were inflicted on the convicted animal, by both the ecclesiastical and the secular authorities. In cases of sexual crimes with animals (bestiality), the animal concerned was burnt with the offender.

The two illustrations show how in 1685 in the margraviate of Ansbach (formerly Onoldsbach) a wolf that had attacked people was taken, after it had been killed, to the gallows and hanged in human clothing and with a mask and wig. The population believed that it had recognized in this wolf an incorrect and hated burgomaster who had died shortly before the wolf made its appearance.

Torture

by
Prof. Dr. Dr. Friedrich Merzbacher

Torture, or torment, was action taken by a court to induce an imprisoned but impenitent criminal to confess by applying appropriate instruments to his body. If the court had failed to prove the guilt of an accused person and he refused to confess, denying the crime he was charged with despite circumstantial evidence and good grounds for suspecting him, and if the suspicion could not be disproved in any other way, the court proceeded to the "painful question". People were by no means unaware of the dangers of torture, especially since this procedure might result in condemnation of an innocent person and ultimately in his execution, if he was unable to stand the physical pain caused by the torture. For all that, as late as 1745 the big Universal Lexicon of all Sciences and Arts by Johann Heinrich Zedler asserted in all seriousness that, in the interests of the common weal, torture was a very useful and, indeed, necessary thing: "for if villains knew that, in the event of their guilt not being proved, which proof is often most difficult to obtain, they could not be tormented to obtain the truth in any other way, but would have to be released as innocent, the world would be filled with innumerable villains and evildoers to the greatest prejudice of the common weal." Contemporary theory in the 18th century placatingly averred that a completely innocent person could never be tormented with torture, since all preconditions for torture had to be weighed and thoroughly examined in accordance with the law. In the final analysis, torture, or the "painful question", was interpreted as a last, legal means of finding the otherwise undeterminable truth. Contemporary learned men considered it admissible to torture, or martyr, the body of a suspected criminal, as ultima ratio, in order of find the truth. In his famous "Notes on the Codex Juris Bavarici Criminalis", the great Bavarian legislator Kreittmayr remarked that although torture was a very dangerous and "deceptive" means and also not practiced by many nations, the fact remained that it had been introduced in the Electorate of Bavaria and, over and above that, there were clear indications that torture "was customary in Bavaria a thousand years ago". The Bavarian legislator refers here to the Lex Baiuvariorum*, Chap. VIII, 18, under which a bondsmaid who gave a woman a potion to procure an abortion was to be given 200 strokes of the lash (flagella).

Moreover, he supported the view that, in the light of experience, doubt could not be cast on the good use of this lawful means.

It must be pointed out that torture was not applied uniformly; essentially there were several degrees of torture. In the opinion of the experts, there were five degrees of torture. The first involved the mere threat of torment outside the torture chamber. For the second degree, the prisoner had to be taken to the torture chamber, the site of "painful" interrogation. In the third degree, the accused was stripped and bound. For the forth degree, the alleged wrongdoer was suspended and allowed to hang for some time. The fifth degree consisted in shaking the ropes or cords or striking the prisoner's body with them to inflict extreme pain.

In some areas, for the last, fifth degree the wrongdoer's feet were dragged down by a weight, thus stretching the body and aggravating the pain to an extent depending on the wight of the stone. According to another opinion, the degrees of torture were differentiated in that, for example, first the wrongdoer was subjected to "physical terror" by seizing, stripping and binding him. Then he was hoisted up and left hanging for a short time. The next step left him hanging for a longer period. The fourth degree involved shaking the rope and the fifth the fastening of a weight to his feet. Occasionally, however, torture was broken down into only three degrees: 1. "realterrition" (physical terror), i.e. removal of clothes and tying the hands; 2. hoising up and hanging; 3. shaking the rope or attaching weights. With respect to the use of the various instruments of torture, it is evident that the mildest form was the application of cords or thumbscrews. A more aggravated form was the Spanish boot or leg screw (pedicae ferrae), i.e. wooden rails in which a curved piece of wood with numerous notches and points on the inner side were pressed on the leg of the prisoner by means of screws.

The final degree of torture was racking on the ladder, that is, stretching, often including dislocation of joints, and, as a further qualification, burning with drops of sulfur or pitch torches. In Augsburg in 1381, for example, a land-shark and paederast was tortured for fraud and then burnt together with his accomplice, a hermit, and two Beghards. In aggravating the last degree of torture by burning with liquid sulfur, the executioner took six or more, or possibly less, goose feathers from a feather duster, dipped them in a pot of melted sulfur, then lighted them and finally threw them down at both sides of the prisoner's body. If the feathers adhered, the burning sulfur spread out at that point. Torture by burning was also carried out by inserting resinous wooden splinters under the nails of all ten fingers, lighting them and letting

them burn down. The most painful degree of torture was the application of pitch torches to the body or making the prisoner stand on glowing hot bricks.

The indications for torture had to be checked carefully. There were certain persons who enjoyed exemption from torture, the so-called "immunitas" or "liberatio a tortura". In principle, it was a general rule that everybody could be subjected to torture, unless expressly exempted by law. First and foremost, minors under 14 enjoyed immunity from torture; on the grounds of their weak powers of reasoning, it was not permitted to inflict torture on them. Similarly, sick and bedridden persons were

"Painful" interrogation. Left, torture by burning; right, by the pulley. Woodcut from Tengler Laienspiegel, 1508.

exempt from torture, because their illness did not permit the due execution of torture. It was not permitted to torture pregnant women, because the life of the foetus had to be preserved. Nursing mothers with breast-fed children were likewise immune from torture. The imperial common law provided that nobles and other worthy persons should have milder penalties inflicted on them and in many instances they could not be tortured. Benedikt Carpzov, the great Saxon legal practitioner, in particular, affirmed the admissibility of torture in the case of a noble killer where malice aforethought could be assumed.

The effect of torture itself varied greatly. The already mentioned Lexicon by Zedler remarks, undoubtedly not without good reason, that any one who survives torture without confessing anything can count himself fortunate. In many cases, persons who had survived torture and not been forced to make a confession were extolled as martyrs and thereafter con-

Illustrations opposite:
Top left: Torture by suspension; top right: Torture with leg screws; two woodcuts from Millaeus's "praxis criminalis", 1541.
Below: Preparation for torture, woodcut from the Bambergensis, 1580 edition.

sidered more innocent than ever before. For from the legal standpoint, it was now presumed that all previous accusations and circumstantial evidence had been invalidated and refuted by the torture suffered. The tortured person had to swear an oath of truce, vowing not to revenge himself for the imprisonment suffered, and then had to be released. In many cases, however, this did not make him safe for ever, since he had attained merely absolutio ab instantia, acquittal from that particular court, and if other grounds for suspicion were found he was liable to be accused and tortured again.

For the carrying out of the "painful" interrogation, the Carolina of 1532, i.e. the "peinliche Halsgerichtsordnung" of Emperor Charles V, proved a compass-bearing model. Art. 45 prescribed that in the event of a suspected and presumed misdeed the prisoner was to be subjected to ex officio "painful" interrogation. The torture, i.e. the „painful" interrogation, had to take place in the presence of a judge, two officers of the court and the clerk of the court. First of all, the threat of torture was prescribed in order to induce the accused to confess to the misdeed he was charged with. If the accused denied the crime, but the grounds for suspicion still remained and could not be refuted in any other way, i.e. when the court assumed that the accused prisoner was guilty despite his denial, it was provided that the proceedings should be continued with the "painful" interrogation. The scope of such "painful" interrogation is defined by Art. 58 CCC*, which states that the torture must be inflicted "according to the circumstances of the suspectfulness of the person, much, often or less, severely or mildly" at the discretion of a good, reasonable judge. It was not permitted to make a record of the statements of a prisoner under torture, but he had to repeat any confession he had made as soon as the torture was over. If he already had dangerous wounds or other injuries to his body, pursuant to Art. 59 CCC the torture had to be applied so that no new unjury was caused to his wounds or bodily injuries. In the event of violation of the Halsgerichtsordnung by undertaking inequitable "painful" interrogation, Art. 61 CCC provided that the initiator of unlawful proceedings should be punished with a penalty matching the violation.

From the 18th century onwards, a progressively more negative attitude to torture developed. These views, in concert with the spirit of Enlightenment, resulted step by step in the abolition of torture. In Prussia it was prohibited by Frederick the Great on August 4, 1754. Before that, in 1740, the monarch had already limited the use of torture to lesemajesty, high treason and qualified murder. In Würzburg, for example, torture was resorted to for the last time on July 7, 1778. In the Electorate of Bavaria, the formally customary trials by water, fire and lot and also judicial combat had long since been discontinued and abolished by the middle of the 18th century. But in Part II, Chap. 8 of the Codex Juris Bavarici Criminalis of 1751, there were detailed provisions on the "painful examination" or torture. The Bavarian legislation emphasized that torture was a legal instrument to induce an intractable evildoer, where adequate proof of guilt was lacking, to make a true confession or to clear him of the suspicion levelled against him. It stated that the customary torture of the land comprised partly the thumbscrew, partly suspension, and partly the pointed birch.

The first degree of torture was "territion" or the threat of torture. This was done by showing the instruments of torture in the torture chamber or by placing the hand in the thumbscrew without turning the screw. The subsequent second degree, the actual torture, consisted in tightening the thumbscrew or suspension or birching. The third, severer degree comprised either locking the thumbscrew in the fully closed position several times, renewed suspension, striking the rope and attachment of 25 - 50 pounds of weights, or twice repeated birching.

The law of the Electorate of Bavaria exempted nobles and "graduated" persons from torture. These included primarily high civil servants of the electorate, patricians and relatives of councillors in large towns. Moreover, mentally ill, deaf and dumb, old and sick persons, pregnant women and women in childbed could be subjected to "painful" interrogation only in the presence of a physician. To ensure that the torture was not more severe than the punishment itself, actual torture was called for only in the case of capital crimes for which the death penalty was prescribed, otherwise only "territion" was to be used. The torture had to be carried out by the executioner or his assistant. During the torture, the authorities were not permitted to withdraw and leave the prisoner alone with the executioner. If the accused came through the torture, he could be tortured again for the same crime only if new circumstantial evidence was produced. It was not until July 17, 1806, that the first Bavarian king, Maximilian I Joseph (1806 - 1825), abolished torture or "painful" interrogation in the former duchies of Bavaria, the Upper Palatinate and Neuburg and abrogated the provisions contained in Part II, Chap. 8 of the criminal code of 1751. At that time, the judges were instructed to endeavour to further the purpose of the inquiry by dispassionate and wise conduct appropriate to the circumstances and the character of the "inquisited" person. Undeniably, torture, i.e. the use of physical violence against defendants, is one of the darkest chapters of criminal history and, in the last analysis, grossly repugnant to humanity and humanitarian interests. Regrettably, the end of legalized, legitimate torture cannot obscure the fact that man in his abberations has resorted to such practices beyond the bounds of all legality.

Before the lion, in the role of judge, the animals bring a complaint against the fox.
From Reinicke Fuchs (Reynard the Fox). 1592.

The lion, as judge, breaks the staff over (= condemns) the fox, who is then dragged to the gallows. From Reinecke Fuchs, 1662.

Animal Fables

There is a causal connection between animal trials (see p. 173) and animal fables like that about Reynard the Fox and the so-called Belial (satanic) trials aimed at overcoming the devil.

Witches and Sorcery

by
Prof. Dr. Dr. Friedrich Merzbacher

According to early, pre-Christian conceptions, sorcery was any supernatural effect brought about with the aid of demons with the intent to gain an advantage or cause harm. The belief in the existence of demons was deeply rooted in the mythology of antiquity and of the early Germanic epoch. By no means the least important manifestation of such notions is the persistent belief in alps (= demons) and vampires. Controversy on whether witches existed persisted right up to the late 18th century. In this connection it should be emphasized that in the course of time the term witch was applied primarily to women who, with the help of demons or Satan, did harm to people, animals and things. The Mosaic law punished sorcery with stoning. The German word "Hexe" (Engl. hex) came into use in the 13th century, initially in the language area of the Alemanni. Following the establishment of the scientific concept of witchcraft, this term meant any alliance with the devil by virtue of which a person surrendered himself to the devil in exchange for benefits promised by Satan. The important Bavarian lawmaker Kreittmayr was compelled to concede in his commentary on the Codex Juris Bavarici Criminalis of 1751 that it had always been a highly controversial issue among savants whether any such alliance was possible.

In the days after the notion that the demonic world was reality had gained general acceptance and sorcery had been placed on a par with the crime of heresy, a fundamentally new assessment of sorcery took shape. Hence, in the central period of scholasticism, sorcery evidently evolved into a crime involving "conversation" and alliance with the devil. For the chief idea associated with witchcraft was undoubtedly the alliance which such people concluded and practiced with the devil. According to contemporary notions, Satan appeared to the witches in a variety of forms, sometimes resembling an animal and sometimes a human being. According to learned opinion, the compact with the devil could be concluded both publicly and privately.

The public compact was concluded in the presence of many other sorcerers and witches, while only the devil on the one hand and the

Conversation with the devil

witch on the other took part in the private compact. It was believed in all seriousness that the devil marked his confederates with a special witch-mark, growths and boils. These witchmarks were thought to be insensitive so that no blood flowed from them when pierced with a needle. Others believed that witches had to sign the pact with Satan with their blood and, in particular, that they had to commit themselves to have sexual intercourse with the devil. Elements of the belief in demons played a not inconsiderable role in this connection. However, such conceptions were far removed from the early ecclasiastical opinion of, say, Burchard von Worms in the 11th century, who energetically rejected such allegations as superstitious notions. Moreover, this bishop of Worms also castigated witches' brooms, flying demons and transformation into animals as unrealities. It was later believed that witches had to commit themselves to appear, with devilish assistance to carry them through the air, at witches' sabbaths and witches' dances at certain places, e.g., according to folktales, on the Brocken mountain in the Harz district of Germany. The big witches' assemblies were allegedly held on Walpurgis, May 1, in remote, lonely woods and on high mountains, or even under the earth.

Woodcuts from the late Middle Ages show witches riding on brooms and forks or on goats. Incidentally, from the late Middle Ages onwards, crimes of sorcery were also punishable under secular law. In addition, the papal inquisition proclaimed peremptory procedural principles which attained the character of guidelines for the ensuing ever more

frequent witches' trials. Since witchcraft had become punishable under secular law, witchcraft (crimen magiae) constituted a genuine delictum mixti fori, which could be prosecuted by both secular and ecclesiastical courts, the sole aim being prevention. Quite generally, the view was held that witches were capable of killing and inflicting dangerous illnesses. Reputable jurists like Benedikt Carpzov, the Saxon practical lawyer, believed in the reality of conversation with the devil and regarded intercourse between witches and Satan as a definite fact. The German law books of the 13th century, Sachsenspiegel and Schwabenspiegel, called for the death penalty for sorcerers, namely death by burning. In all segments of the European population, the witch mania spread rapidly, the seed falling on fertile soil everywhere. The French witch trials of the 13th and 14th century had their counterparts in the Italian trials of the 14th and 15th century. Sorcery and demons took on the dimensions of an epidemic. When the witch mania became rife everywhere, Pope Innocent VIII (1484 - 1492) issued his famous witchcraft bull "Summis desiderantes affectibus" of 1484, ordering the inquisition of sorcerers. The Dominicans Heinrich Institoris and Jacob Sprenger wrote a commentary for contemporary court practice, the so-called "Hexenhammer" (witches' hammer) or "Malleus maleficarum" of 1487, which laid down court procedure. Denunciation and torture were the dominant features of the proceedings. Divine judgment, with "proofs" and "sympathetic" agents were classified as evidence. The Constitutio Criminalis Carolina, the "Peinliche Halsgerichtsordnung" of Emperor Charles V dating from 1532, attained decisive importance for the prosecution of witchcraft in the Holy Roman Empire. It prescribed death by burning only for harmful sorcery. Witchcraft numbered among the crimina excepta and crimina laesae maiestatis divinae which had to be prosecuted in accordance with the divine law. According to prevailing jursitic opinions, which were largely followed in court practice, the crime of witchcraft comprised the four individual crimes of blasphemy, bestiality, sorcery and procuring for immoral purposes or, in the case of married witches, adultery. Quite generally, the crimen magiae was held to be a crime in which a human being made a pact with the devil under which the witch ceded him her soul while Satan provided her with benefits on earth. In Augsburg on September 25, 1625, when a witch was condemned as the seducer of her own child, an 11-year old girl, she was beheaded with a sword for proved conversation with Satan and the body was subsequently burnt. It was probably not without good reason that the chronicler remarked that it was a very fine day when she was led out and executed, but then a terrible storm came up, which caused terrible damage.

Suspicious things like oils, salves, powders, pots with vermin, human bones, magic wax candles, waxen images pierced by needles to bring harm to the witches' enemies, unconsumed and purloined sacramental wafers, crystal mirrors, letters of devilish alliances, mandrake and roots, sorcery books, incantations and the like were regarded as witches' "medicine".

Peculiarities considered typical characteristics of witches were listed point by point, e.g. aversion to men, non-observance of holy days, striking features such as bleary eyes, red hair, certain moles, aversion to cooking and washing, turning back at churches and crosses. Besides, in many cases witches were poison-mixers. The Germanic peoples in general believed that witches could raise storms and tempests. In contrast, Italian witches tended rather to practice the magic of love. The undeniably many-facetted, scintillating and highly varied picture of the witch included elements of oriental, Arabic and of Romanic

Witches making a violent storm.

and Germanic notions and rites. Superstition and soothsaying were also closely linked up with sorcery and witchcraft. The Carolingian laws (8 - 10 century) prescribed punishment of sorcerers for their alleged cannibalism.

The interrogation of witches for the purpose of obtaining evidence and, above all, their confession, was conducted in accordance with an interrogatory schedule. The "interrogatoria" were questions on which the examination of defendants or witnesses was based. They had their origin in canon law. They were laid down mainly in C. 2 "Praesentium" in VI⁰ de testibus II, 10, a regulation issued by Pope Gregory IX in 1239. Under this regulation, certain articles had to be presented to witnesses, which had to be formulated to match the facts of the case. A distinction was made between interrogatoria generalia and interrogatoria specialia. The term interrogatoria generalia was applied to interrogative formulae of a general nature. On the basis of these interrogative formulae, the court put questions to witnesses or co-witnesses concerning their names, age, domicil and abode, estate and craft or trade, and their property. These general questions also covered whether the person concerned was proscribed, related to the defendant by blood or marriage, whether he had offered to testify of his own accord, whether he had lent help or assistance, insulted the defendant or his family and was thus at enmity with the defendant or entertained jealousy or hate for him, and whether his co-witnesses were known to him as honest people. On the other hand, the interrogatoria specialia were formulae relating to the actual case, i.e. to the alleged crime of witchcraft, its causes, its commission and its lore. So in a witch trial, while a witness was questioned as to whether he knew the accused witch or had consorted with other suspected sorcerers, the interrogatories for the witch herself concentrated on typical special questions. Among other things, the judge inquired why the people in general were particularly fearful of the accused, or, for instance, whether the alleged witch was aware that she had a generally bad reputation and was hated, or why she had threatened her enemies, and especially their children with harm, and why, say, she had touched a certain child. Ever and again the questions were focused on the crucial issue of whether the accused admitted being a witch. The unfortunate woman was also asked whether and when she had surrendered herself to Satan, denied God and his saints and the sacraments, and whether she had practiced sorcery. She was likewise asked where she kept her salves and witch's paraphernalia, by whom and from what constituents they were produced. The witch was similarly examined with respect to whether she concerned herself with causing storms, rain, frost, thunder, lightning or hail, the name of her devilish paramour and the form in which she had conversation with

him. The court was by no means least interested in her answer as to whether she had appeared in the form of an animal to terrify or delude people and whether she knew how to use poison and induce obscene love by devilish deceit. Moreover, the court never failed to inquire when the accused flew off and where she met other sorcerers and witches.

Preparation of salves and mixtures from children's corpses.

In early modern times, criminalistic theory supported the view that witchcraft comprised several very serious crimes: apostasy, or renunciation of religious faith, idolatry, blasphemy and conversation with the devil, which could only be atoned for at the stake. The necessity of capital punishment for sorcerers was generally acknowledged. In view of the gravity of the charge, criminal jurisprudence advocated the most severe form of punishment, especially since the authority of divine law required it. Under the Peinliche Halsgerichts-ordnung of Emperor Charles V of 1532, however, only sorcery injurious to human beings and animals was punishable by death, for which reason punishment was left to the discretion of the judge in cases in which no harm had been caused. Frequently, for instance, galley punishments, life imprisonment, public flogging and banishment were imposed. Witchcraft deteriorated into a broadly interpreted comprehensive offence in the prosecution of which Catholic and Protestant territories vied with each other. It should be realized that witchcraft and sorcery were not restricted to any specific religious confession, or a given nationality or even to Europe. On the contrary, witches and sorcerers were characteristic phenomena typical of certain periods in the universal history of law, and their prosecution was concentrated temporally, for example, in the 15th century in France, in the 16th century in Spain, in the 16th and 17th century in Germany, and in the 15th and 16th century in Italy. A woman was executed as a witch in England in 1716, while in Scotland the last execution is recorded in 1722. In 1623, Pope Gregory XV (1621 - 1623) decreed that persons who had made a compact with the devil or had practiced malicious sorcery causing another's death should be handed over to the secular courts so that the latter could inflict the death penalty on them. Especially during the Thirty Years War, witch trials increased considerably in Germany. The last witch trials were held in Würzburg in 1749 and in Kempten in 1775. Especially Jesuits like Adam Tanner and Friedrich von Spee and Protestants like Balthasar Bekker and Christian Thomasius were resolute opponents of witch trials.

It should never be overlooked that, in the final analysis, the witch and sorcery trials had the typical character of demon and ghost trials in which torture was resorted to especially readily in order to overcome the demons in allegedly impenitent and recalcitrant defendants. Seen from this standpoint, a proper understanding and assessment of witches and sorcery is possible only against the background of their historical environment. Even the enlightened people of the 20th century have to admit, in the face of many phenomena and their interpretation, that despite the breath-taking advances in scientific research, even modern man has not lost his possibly innate leanings towards the mysterious and the occult. Superstition and sorcery are closely interwoven with historical legal life; both have effectively undermined official opinion and found historical espression in many legal phenomena and statutes. Legal chronicles and utensils, and also sagas and fairy tales have become living illustrations of this interesting, but often misinterpreted and distorted subject matter of universal history and law.

On Tuesday, the twenty-sixth day of the month of April in this sixteen-hundred-and-fifty-ninth year, the honourable and strict Johann Hieronymus Imhoff, city judge of the Holy Roman Empire in Nuremberg, once again convened the criminal court and appointed to it the gentlemen of the council hereinafter named:

Herr Christoph Derrer	Herr Georg Christoph Beheim
Paulus Harßdörffer	Georg Paulus Imhoff
Veit Georg Holzschuer	Jobst Wilhelm Ebner
Wolf Jacob Pömer	Johann Friedrich Löffelholz
Ulrich Grundherr	Johann Wilhelm Haller
Paul Albrecht Rieter	

When, following the usual preliminaries, the evildoer named in the following judgment was brought before the court, the judgment previously passed on her unanimously by the entire council was read aloud by the clerk of the court.

An honourable, strict and most wise council of the city, our lords by virtue of the authority vested in them and of their office, having had the here appearing Margaretha, now the wife of Hanssen Mauterer, yeoman of this city, arrested recently on March 23, legally and for good cause, in her abode and imprisoned in the jail, has found in the various interrogations of her, and she has testified — as is well known — that already eight years ago during the lifetime of her former husband, Georg Staudinger, former jailer of this city, she did proceed, out of frivolous contempt for God and doubt of his help and allpowerfulness and out of greed for worldly goods and vile profit, to call upon the most wicked enemy of God and mankind, the artful Satan, on whose appearance and enticement she did renounce the most sacred and extolled Holy Trinity with gruesome blasphemy, did give herself up to the devil and mix with him abominably, and did twice take the holy wafer from her mouth at Holy Communion and deliver it to the evil spirit; and at the devil's behest and with no special cause she did wantonly and consentingly dare to harm the body and life of one and another person by sorcery. In that she has once more confessed to all this and the circumstances, free and unbound, before the judge of the Holy Empire and two assessors and is thus subject to punishment by the criminal court, her body and life are forfeit.

In the light of all this, the assessors rightfully find that Margaretha Mauterin shall be taken to the usual place of execution and there, by special grace, strangled at the stake, and thereafter burnt with fire to powder and ashes that she may meet with well-deserved punishment and that others, then knowing better, may beware of committing such abominable crimes and atrocities.

Decretum in senatu et executio facta per carnificem ut supra.

Written judgment passed on Margaretha Mauterin for conversation with the devil and sorcery; she was sentenced to death by burning as a witch and was executed on April 26, 1659, in Nuremberg.
StAN, AStB No. 224 fol. 72b - 73a

Interrogatories at Eichstätt Witch Interrogations under the Rule of Prince Bishop Johann Christoph von Westerstetten, 1612 - 1636

Interrogatoria
On what persons suspected of and imprisoned for witchery are to be questioned.

Interrogatoria
On what persons suspected of witchery are to be questioned before they are informed of the inditia crimine.

1. What is her name?
2. Where was she born?
3. Who are her parents and what are their names? What is their estate, their occupation, whether they lived in concord or discord with each other, whether they are alive or dead? When they died and of what illness?
4. Where, by whom and how she was brought up in her youth?
5. In what form and to what end she was taught from her youth onwards, and what she has learnt?
6. What is her living and occupation? In what place does she live, how old she is?
7. Whether she is single and why she has not married?
8. Whether she married of her own will or with prior knowledge of her parents and friends?
9. Whether she is married and how long she is married?
10. Under what circumstances did she make the acquaintance of her spouse and become betrothed? Also who he is?
11. Whether they do not come together at night and converse with each other alone?
12. Whether she did not while still single indulge in improper love with him, mix with him carnally or have been willing so to do?
13. When, where and how often this was done and who procured their coupling?
14. Whether, on her wedding day, she did not make use of superstitious things before or afterward or have them used by others?
15. What brought them together and how did they make a living until now?
16. How they lived together during marriage, and, having lived in discord, what was the cause?
17. Whether during her marriage she did not indulge in improper love to others? How and by what chance was this occasioned? Whether she sought opportunities to satisfy her evil will? Through whom, where they met and what came to pass each time?
18. Whether in her marriage she has born children, how many, what are their names, how old are they, whether they are alive or dead?
19. What is the abode of the children, how are they being brought up, what have they learnt and how do they now find a living?
20. When did those who are dead die, what illness did they die of, whether during their illness remedies were sought and used and what they were?
21. Whether her spouse is still living or dead? When and of what illness did he die, how long did he lie ill, how did he become ill, what remedies were used, who attended to him?
22. With whom does she mainly keep company and by what means did she make their acquaintance?
23. Whether in particular any personae denunciantes are known to her and in what form?
24. Whether she is aware, as cannot be doubted, that such persons have been executed as witches?

Interrogatoria
for further examination of persons suspected of witchery after they have been presented with the Inditia - ex crimine.

25. How long is it since she succumbed to the vice of witchery?
26. Whether such has happened here or elsewhere and where?
27. By what occasion and chance did she succumb to the vice?
28. When did she commune with the evil enemy the first time?
29. In what form did he appear, what did he say to her? What did she think of his speech and shape and by what did she recognize him?
30. What did he ask of her? whether and how often she mixed with him carnally?
31. Whether she felt a lust therefor and how did it seem to her, where did it happen?
32. What he further asked of her and to what she agreed?
33. What she promised him, whether and how she sold herself to him? Whether such happened then or at other times and in what way was it done?
34. Whether she denies God and the saints? promised to do harm to people, animals and fruits, with what words and in what form was this done?
35. Whether she was baptized by the evil spirit, what happened in so doing, what material was used? How did he name her and she name him and who was present and what did such persons do?
36. Whether the evil enemy continued to come to her thereafter, what he did with her each time, whether he again mixed with her carnally, in what way, in what shape was it done?
37. Whether she had such communion with the evil spirit not alone, but in the presence of other persons and whether it happened in public or secret meetings, at what times did such things happen, at what places, for what occasion did they meet, what did they do at such meetings and how often was it done?
38. How did she come to such places, did she go there herself or was she led by the spirit?
39. Who told her of the arranged meetings? How she accoutered herself for the journey, on what was she seated, what did she need for it, where did she go forth and how could she travel in the dark of the night?
40. Whether her housemates had noticed nothing and what means she had used to that end?
41. When did she arrive at the meeting, what did she see there and what happened?

42. Whether she had prayed to the evil enemy, what veneration she had paid him, in what way this happened and who had instructed her to do so?
43. Whether she did this alone or with others and who, beside her, were such persons, when, where, in what way did it happen?
44. In what shape did the evil enemy appear and what did he do?
45. Whether she also attended meals, where and when did it happen, how was the table prepared, how did she sit down at the table, how did she eat, who sat beside her, to the left or right, at the head of the table or opposite and in what shape?
46. What food and drink was served, in what dishes, was there bread and salt, whether she partook of the meal, to whom did she bring it and who brought it to her?
47. What was the discourse at the table, what did she say to others or hear from others?
48. Who served at table, brought food and drink, whether and how she could see in the dark of night, what lights were there and whence did they and everything else come?
49. Whether minstrels were also present and in what way did they come there?
50. Whether she danced, with whom, in what manner, who else did she see at the dance, in what shape, how did she recognize who were evil spirits and who were human?
51. What strokes she witnessed at such meetings, what she on her part contributed thereto by word or deed, or heard or saw on the part of others?
52. Whether at such meetings she practiced fornication, with whom, in what shape, when, how often, whether it was seen by others or she saw others do it, where and at what time?
53. How long did such meetings last, in what manner did they disperse and how did she return home?
54. What she saw, heard or otherweise experienced on the way?
55. Whether she did not receive instructions from the evil spirit to blaspheme God, with what words, works or gestures was this done, on her own or with others, who were they, when and where did it happen?
56. What she thinks of the holy Mother of God, or blessed ladies and other blessed saints and what she said of them and in what way she dishonoured them, how often, at what places and times?
57. How she comports herself at divine service?
58. Whether she has attended holy mass, with what intention, opinion and devotion, whether and what she prayed?
59. Whether and how often in the year she has confessed, where and when, whether with gravity and penitence for her sins, whether she confessed also to this vice or why she concealed it?
60. Whether and how often in the year she attended communion, where and at what time, and with what opinion did she do so?
61. Whether she consumed the sacramental wafer or occasionally removed it from her mouth, when, where, how often she did so and what she did with it?
62. Whether she has dishonoured the sacramental wafer, when, where, in what way, how often, who else was present, gave help or advice?
63. Whether and by whom she was led into this vice, on what occasion, at whose instigation, advice or action, where and when this happened?
64. Whether of her own accord or at the instigation of the evil spirit she has caused harm to the body, life or goods of any person, when was it done, for what reasons, on what occasion, by what means, at what time, at what place, in whose presence or with whose assistance, how was it done and what followed thereafter, whether and how this can be remedied.
65. Whether she has not received salves, powders, poison and the like for the ends of the evil enemy, how often has she taken such things into safe custody?
66. Whether she has sought to take a life, from whom, for what reasons, whether and how she set about it, who advised or helped her, at what time, at what places was it done?
67. Whether she has killed her own or other children before or after baptism, for what reasons, with whose knowledge or assistance, at what time and at what place?
68. Whether she had bent any person, inflicted other physical harm, by what means, for what reasons, with whose aid, to whom, where and when was this done?
69. Whether she did not go forth into other people's houses and strike the sleeping with fear, when, where, with whom, how often was this done? What she saw, heard or otherwise experienced there?
70. Whether she has not caused enmity, barrenness and other misfortune between spouses and others, for what reasons, advice and assistance, with what means, where and to whom was this done? and how can this be remedied?
71. Whether she has helped to disinter children, where and when this was done, who was present, how she set about it or previously discussed it, where she put the children and what she did with them?
72. Whether she has buried anything to cause harm or misfortune, what it was, when and where it was done, who was present, gave advice or help?
73. When and how often, in what places she caused bad weather, with what intention it was done, with whose instigation, advice, assistance and presence, what she used to that end and what were the consequences?
74. Whether and how often she has descended into the cellar, when and in what places, who was present, what she drank, out of what vessel, how long, what she otherwise saw, heard or did there?
75. Whether she changed into a different shape, why, how, when, where and with what was it done?
76. What other sorcery and evil she has committed, what harm resulted?
77. Whether at times she ever regretted this vice, remembered the doom of her soul, what she thinks of eternal salvation or damnation? and what the evil enemy put into her mind in this respect?
78. Whether she has not taken to heart the daily example of the malefic person so that she has resolved to better herself; why has she not done so?
79. Whether she does not desire to return to the arms of God and by earnestly repenting her sins and suffering well-deserved earthly punishment to escape eternal damnation and attain eternal salvation?

for calling to account persons who have confessed to witchery and then revoked their confession.

80. Whether she remembers her previous confession?

81. For what reason does she revoke it?

82. When did the pretext she put forward occur to her? Who have her instructions and advice? Whether the evil spirit had not given her the idea, when was he with her, what did he say and do to her?

83. Whether other persons had instructed her? Who? She should give the right reason so that it is not necessary to extract the truth by torture and pain.

84. She should think of the salvation of her soul, since she cannot escape the authorities; it is better to suffer a slight earthly punishment than eternal damnation in the hereafter.

From Eichstatt Witch File No. 49, State Archives, Nuremberg.

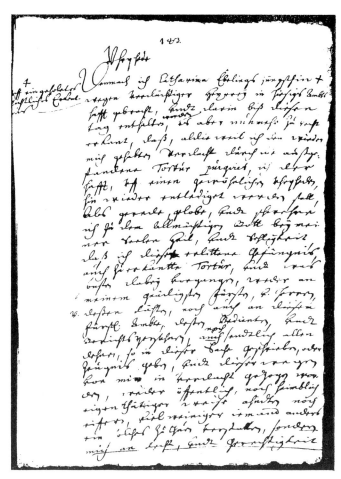

Translation

"Inasmuch as I, Catharina Ebeling, was recently consigned by order of the court and on suspicion of witchery to the local official prison and have been detained therein up to this day, and inasmuch as it has lately been legally established that I am to be released from prison against the swearing of a common oath of truce because I have been purged of the suspicion levelled against me by the torture I have suffered;

I therefore make oath and say and swear to God the Almighty by the salvation of my soul and my deliverance that I shall not, either openly or secretly, seek satisfaction or revenge, whether personally or by instigating others, on my gracious prince and his councillors or on this royal office, its servants and court officers and all those who have written or given evidence in this matter and whom I hence hold suspect, on account of the imprisonment I have suffered and the torture inflicted upon me and all other happenings, and I shall vent no threats against them or translate them into deeds, but shall be content with the justice meted out to me, so help me God, and it is my will to find salvation through Jesus Christ. Amen."

Oath of truce of Catharina Schlüter, nee Ebeling, of Bardeleben, sworn on March 26, 1659. Accused of witchcraft, she survived two hours of torture without confessing, was acquitted and set free after swearing the above oath.

Executioners

by
Prof. Dr. Wolfgang Schild

The executioner, also known as hangman, headsman, Jack Ketch (after a notorious executioner of the 17th century) or, depending on his activities, torturer, racker, etc., is probably one of the most fascinating and interesting figures in the history of criminal law. In fact, a bulky work on the history of criminal law could be written solely on the basis of the chronicles of the profession and on the still existing documents and instruments.

The activities of the executioner brought him into direct contact with the condemned and constituted officially sanctioned homicide. Both aspects therefore involved strong emotions and conceptions that reached right back to the old Germanic notions of the world.

For instance, the executioner was always a figure wreathed in superstition, a remnant of the magical-sacral conception of the world, although he himself did not make his appearance until the 13th century. Originally, the condemned person was handed over to the complainant for execution of the sentence, either personally or by his slaves. In many cases, undoubtedly the whole family took part unless – as in the death penalties of the Germanic peoples – the entire "Thing" was required to lend a hand. Stoning was always everybody's concern and sometimes hanging had to be carried out by every one pulling on the rope.

The court rendered assistance to the complainant at the execution: it provided the implements (e.g. the axe for the early form of beheading) or had a raped woman strike only the first few blows in striking off her raper's head with "axe and mallet". Sometimes the very youngest assessor had to place the rope around the neck or the youngest married man (in some Frankish towns); there were numerous variations. Whatever the case, for a long time the "Nachrichter" (lit. "after-judge"), i.e. the person who dealt out justice after the court, was a person who had not been trained to kill, unless possibly he was the count's slave and was often called upon to do such work.

Ducking cage in the yard of the Crime Museum. Punishment for bakers who sold too small loaves. For every lot (= 16.66 grammes) underweight the baker was ducked once.

Instruments for torture and punishment in the basement of the Crime Museum.

Letter of Detraction and Disparagement

a legal remedy of the 15th and 16th century for the collection of debts. If a debtor failed to fulfil his contractual obligation to repay borrowed money by the agreed date, the creditor (lender) was entitled to issue a reminder by way of such letters of detraction and disparagement, which were publicly displayed. In addition to a writ-

(continuation opposite page)

In the pillory in Rothenburg
left, a woman with mask of shame and slander-stone; beside her a woman with wooden ruff and "dragon" mask of shame. At the right, a man in the stock, above him on the wall the displayed judgment.

ten description of the facts, how the debts were incurred and when they should have been repaid, letters of detraction and disparagement contained illustrations decrying the debtor.
They showed:
The debtor's coat of arms upside down = the family is extinct; signet ring seal impressed on the hindquarters of an ass or swine, hanging on the gallows = the debtor is not worthy of a clean seal, because he had affixed it to the contract;
the debtor riding an ass = from time immemorial the ass was the symbol of infamy;
the debtor on the gallows or the wheel = boath particularly degrading punishments.

Two warning signs for gypsies; in front of the gate of Harburg castle near Donauwörth, 18th cent. They were a warning not to violate special laws for gypsies within a given sovereign territory.

Impalement of two adulterers, Statute Book of the city of Zwickau, 1348.

Shame-flute for bad musicians

Wooden ruff, punishment for women who violated clothing regulations

Iron neck-violin with bell

Chain for cheaters

Two single neck-violins, one double neck-violin. The neck-violin was a degrading punishment for women and girls. Such devices were put on women sentenced to the pillory as an additional punishment.

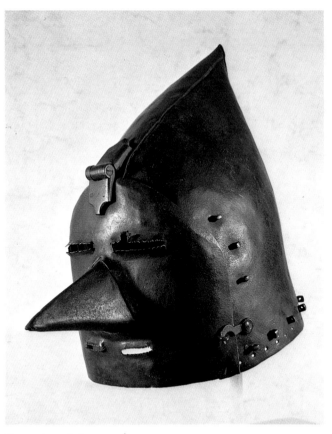

Executioner's iron mask

Irons for branding criminals

Mouth-pear, an instrument of tortu

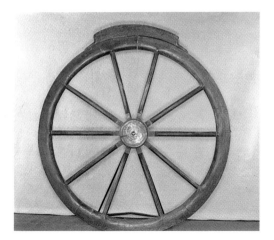

Wheel for breaking on the wheel.

Block with executioner's axe
for beheading

Executioner's swords for beheading

Executioner's swords, detail: inscriptions on the blades

Iron maiden, a mantle of infamy for women and girls, 16th cent.

Drinker's barrel for bibbers

Chair for the baker's baptism

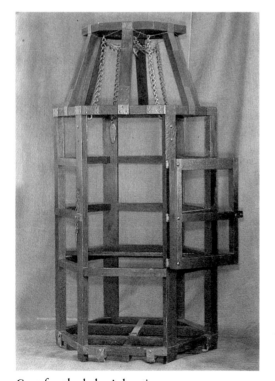

Cage for the baker's baptism

Stocks for two persons for feet-tickling

above: Mask of shame
left: Mask of shame, punishment for dishonest and wicked tongues

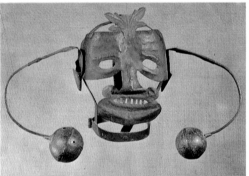

above: Rosary, an ecclesiastical pillory punishment

left — mask of shame with bells

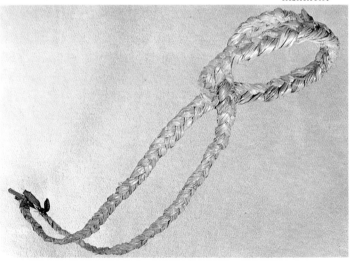

Straw wreath, a degrading punishment for "fallen" maidens.

Body hoop with handirons

Body hoop with neck-iron

Body hoop with shoulder hoops

Neck-iron with bell

Slander-stone

Slander-stone

Mask of shame for women with bell and long tongue

Mask of shame for men who had acted like swine

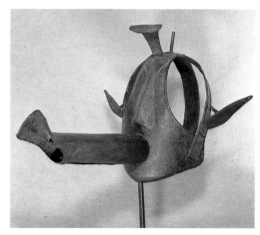

Mask of shame with long snout

Mask of shame for women, the "dragon"

Mask of shame for men

Spiked chair, an instrument of torture from the witchtrial era

Interrogation table with finger screw, 17th cent.

Fingerscrew

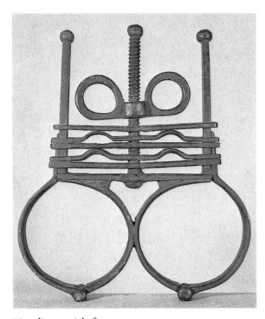

Handiron with fingerscrew

Legscrew

Execution following the sentence, Bambergensis, 1507.

Murder of Henry IV of France by Ravaillac, 1610.
In the foreground, the murder; top right, the offender riding to his execution on the tumbril; top centre, torture of the criminal; top left, execution by quartering. Contemporary pamphlet.

Breaking on the wheel and hanging of robbers, burying alive of a multiple murderess in St. Gallen.

Drowning of Peter Wunderlich in Zurich.
Pictures from the Lucerne Chronicles by D. Schilling, 1513, Bürgerbibliothek Lucerne.

Emperor Sigismund bestows fiefs in Constance. Spiez Chronicles by Diebold Schilling, 1485, Municipal library, Berne.

The count of Savoy does homage to Emperor Sigismund. Official Berne Chronicles by Diebold Schilling, 1484, Municipal library, Berne.

The emperor grants an amnesty to condemned criminals and takes them into the city.

King Louis of Bavaria declares a feud with the city of Berne. Spiez Chronicles by Diebold Schilling, 1485, Municipal library, Berne.

Burning of heretics in Schwarzenburg. Spiez Chronicles by Diebold Schilling, 1485, Municipal library, Berne.

Burning of Johannes Hus in Constance, 1415. Official Berne Chronicles by D. Schilling, 1483, Municipal library, Berne.

Execution by the wheel and boiling in oil. Spiez Chronicles by D. Schilling, 1485, Municipal library, Berne.

It was the towns, which knew no slaves within their walls ("Town air liberates"), and their inhabitants, worthy citizens more intent on commerce and crafts than on killing pernicious people, who brought a change. In 1276, the Augsburg Statute Book mentions the "hangman" for the first time in Germany; in addition to inflicting corporal punishments, he had other duties to perform, which will be dealt with later. There were some places, however, where a private person performed the executions until well into the 16th century. Only rich towns could afford their own executioner; the others had to hire one as occasion arose. At all events, the evolution of the penal system soon made it necessary to appoint a professional executioner.

Although the office of executioner was established at such a late date, his status was always a mystical one. People speak of the executioner's "taboo", meaning the superstitious belief that any physical contact with him released magical forces: evil and harmful, but also good and healing forces. This ambiguity – which is inherent in many taboos – resulted on the one hand in the executioner being avoided. He was not allowed to live inside the town (at most on the periphery), or drink with others at the inn (if at all, only at a specially designated table) or use the bathhouses or go to the fair (again, unless he had a specially marked place). He was not permitted to hunt (except for wolves), his livestock could not graze with the communal herd. Objects which he had touched were withdrawn from use; nobody wanted to place a hand on them. – And, of course, all these re-strictions applied also to his family. No one played with his children or wanted his daughter as a wife (apart from some other executioner). Even if he exercised the right of begging the life of a condemned woman by offering to marry her, it often happened that she preferred death, because the marriage would have been equivalent to death anyway as far as normal communal life was concerned. All this makes the punishment understandable which the town law of Ofen prescribed for fornication: a dance with the executioner.

The aversion to physical contact lasted throughout his life. If any one helped him – even unknowingly – in any activity, that person immediately lost his honour (for which reason the executioner often had to wear particularly conspicuous clothing to avoid mistakes). It persisted also with respect to his dead body, which is why it was so difficult to arrange his burial; just as diffi-cult, incidentally, as finding a midwife for his wife. This taboo undoubtedly had its origin in the notion that the condemned were creatures of demonic character and contact with them involved the danger of "infection" also for the executioner. For this reason the executioner wore gloves and in some cases a special mask to protect him against the evil eye, which was also why

above: Executioner, from "Kriegsbeschreibung" (Description of War), Count zu Solms, 16th cent.
below: Place of Execution, Urs Graf, 1513.

he delivered the mortal stroke of the sword form behind. The execution itself was therefore dangerous; there were rules intended to provide protection of magical nature. The rope had to be made in a specific way, the gallows constructed of debarked timber ("bright gallows") so that no demons could be concealed under the bark and initially the condemned person had to be naked to prevent objects with magical power being concealed in his clothes; sometimes his hair was removed prior to execution for the same reason; the wheel had to have a prescribed number of spokes, etc. The requirements for a successful execution also contained magical ideas: The body of a hanged person had to be exposed to the wind and animals, in the case of beheadings the head had to be struck off so that a wagon wheel could be passed between head and body (to prevent spirits from returning; the same purpose was clearly served by impalement), and similarly the head of persons broken on the wheel was often placed on a stake. In executions by burning, drowning and burying alive the danger was not so great, since it was counteracted by the purging power of fire, water and earth, which afforded protection. The custom of ringing a bell – the "poor sinner's bell" – throughout the execution is also indicative of a magical background, for the bell was invariably considered to drive off demons. Hans von Hentig also attributes the pre-execution meal to the fear of evil after-effects of the killing: the large and delicious meal was intended to put the candidate for execution in a friendly mood. For the same reason, at the site of execution the executioner asked forgiveness of the condemned person.

Furthermore – quite apart from the person of the condemned man – all objects connected with the execution of punishment possessed magical-sacral powers even before use. Consequently, it was a tremendous undertaking just to get the gallows set up. Accompanied by minstrels, all the craftsmen – without exception, and if any one was missing, a nail was saved, which he had to drive into the wood of the gallows on his return so that he, too, had taken part – proceeded to the chosen site, the councillors had to perform the first work in ceremonial form, and then the gallows was built by joint effort. The executioner's sword also had a special fascination: It is recounted that it took pleasure in executions and heralded its use by the ringing of its blade.

But all this was only one (negative) side of the executioner's taboo. On the other hand, the executioner was a medicineman who was often visited secretly, who could make healing potions and panaceas by magical practices and had control over the special power inherent in the paraphernalia of executions. The blood of an executed person was said to cure epilepsy and leprosy, a piece of his body or of the rope he was hanged with likewise had healing powers. Even in the 20th century, the Austrian executioner Lang was offered money for the gloves he wore at executions and for pieces of the rope used. We might mention in passing that even aristocratic ladies asked him for a rendezvous in order to be touched by him (and his gloves); and Casanova recounted that he had to be "of service" to his beloved during the execution of a regicide; at least in this form, sexuality was very closely related to magic.

In the era of the Christian-ecclesiastical conception of the world, in which the executioner's office first came into being, these notions were but part of the superstition which motivated large segments of the population; the "enlightened" Christians, especially in the towns, saw the executioner in a different light. For them his activities were suspect, a necessary evil, but in the final analysis immoral, because he killed for money and even made his living by it. True, following the peace movement the church adopted a more positive attitude to killing in behalf of the government – especially during war – and Luther* even explicitly voiced a positive opinion of the executioner's activities, but the moral discomfiture remained. In some places the executioner was refused the right to attend church and to have a church wedding and church burial. People did not shy away from physical contact, but wanted nothing to do with him and his family (except on a pure business basis, e.g. in connection with his other functions, which are mentioned below). Moreover, the holders of this office were often brutal alcoholics, in some cases even former, pardoned criminals, which did not make their company exactly attractive. The executioner was "honour-less"; hence he and his children could not practice any craft. So his sons were compelled to become executioners, too, which resulted in the well-known executioner's dynasties; in addition – since they could not live from executions alone – they were forced to accept work which nobody else wanted, which again impaired their social status. The executioner was also knacker, dogcatcher, "Cloacarius" (cesspool emptier), had to drive lepers from the town, was often also the brothel-keeper, and even supervised the public gaming events.

With the introduction of inquisitorial procedure, his duties as the enforcing agent for capital and other punishment were extended to include the work of the torturer. For this he needed from the very outset a certain degree of medical proficiency, as the killing of the victim was not permitted; such knowledge was especially important when no confession was extracted, for then he had to restore the tortured person to health.

In this way, many executioner's acquired a good name as doctors for humans and animals; they were even called upon by princes. It must be remembered that through their work at executions they also possessed anatomical knowledge better than that of learned physicians, for whom dissection was long forbidden. Some executioner's were even appointed town physician.

Thus, even in later times, this peculiar dual status of the executioner persisted: On the one hand dishonourable riffraff, on the other an organ of the town administration who was respected in a way. This contradictory image is attributable not only to the various bodies of law governing the executioner's status, but also to his position and functions.

As a rule, the executioner's themselves held a high opinion of their office (possibly a compensatory mechanism); they remained aloof from their "assistants", to whom they delegated simple tasks, e. g. execution of punishments to the "hide and hair". They considered themselves a guild of their own, held guild-days, and demanded strict training of candidates for their profession. It must be remembered how many jobs the executioner had to perform proficiently: torture, mutilation and killing techniques, and above all beheading, which was the "masterpiece" demanded of him and had to be explicitly proved when applying for an appointment. It called for physical strength and considerable dexterity to sever the head of a condemned person from the trunk freehand with a stroke between two neck vertrebrae, especially since it was necessary to turn the upper part of the body to get the proper swing, which made accurate aiming more difficult. Moreover, masterly proficiency was of vital importance: If the executioner "botched" and missed the mark, he was at least flogged and often killed by the enraged mob; if he escaped, he was discharged and also punished. If the stroke was eminently successful, however, it was quite possible for him to be cheered and celebrated. Under Art. 97 of the CCC, the judge was required to pronounce the so-called "executioner's peace decree", to the effect that no one should dare to hinder the executioner in the performance of his work and, in the event of a failure, do him violence. On the other hand, after executing a sentence, he had to ask the judge whether he had done so in a due and proper manner , and under Art. 98 of the CCC he had to be given the answer: "If thou hast executed as the judgment and the law demanded, I shall abide by it". Christian Helfer reports in his "Henker-Studien" (Hangman Studies) that for this reason some executioner's learned artistic abilities: For instance, a Nuremberg "master" succeeded with a single stroke in severing the neck of the condemned person and at the same time a bunch of flowers held in the latter's hand, or even beheaded two evildoers with a single stroke. Any one who has ever lifted an executioner's sword can appreciate what strength must have been necessary when in 1444 the executioner of Berne successively beheaded 72 men of the Zurich occupiers of Greifensee in a single day.

The executioner played an important role in the execution spectacle and many were perfectly aware of that. They endeavoured to play their role well and get favourable "reviews". It was probably the only way to survive in their business, for in the Christian-ecclesiastical conception of the world the self-confessed and penitent evildoer occupied a strange intermediate position. He had sinned and had to suffer for it, but he was no longer the enemy who had to be killed. It is reported that at times the reason for the failure of an execution was that the executioner had pity, was distracted by the condemned person's kiss of reconciliation or – especially in the case of women – could hardly find it in his heart to deal a calm and concentrated blow. In this respect, alcohol did not help much; probably a more effective means was to regard the activity as an art and hence an end in itself. Occasionally, of course, an executioner overdid things. For example, Master Augustin, the executioner in the Peasant's War, once tried to behead a condemned man who was standing erect; he failed completely and received no pay.

Even in the 20th century, the executioner went on stage in the professional garb of a virtuoso or magician, performing his act in white tie, tails and top hat, though he no longer had the public as an audience. While the Austrian executioner Lang was the "inventor" of a "humane" method of hanging – before the drop he stood behind the condemned person and broke the spine with his hands, causing immediate death – present-day executioners are technicians who use equipment to generate electric current or to fill the gas chamber. They no longer need gloves, because they have nothing to do with the person who is killed. In the mediaeval world the executioner admittedly performed a necessary function; in present-day practice, however, the inhumanity of the destruction of a human being is so blatant that no form of capital punishment should be permitted. Those who call for its reintroduction should think also of the man of whom they would make an executioner. Can they find any justification for that today?

By way of an appendix, here are a few figures that illustrate the work of the executioner: In Augsburg, in 1369 ten persons were executed, in 1371 thirteen persons, in 1373 five persons. In Nördlingen, from 1407 to 1500 there were one-hundred-and-thirty-seven executions, from 1501 to 1600 one-hundred-and-twenty; in Memmingen, from 1551 to 1573 thirty-eight death sentences were inflicted, from 1574 to 1661 forty-five, and from 1615 to 1683 thirty-nine. The records of Frankfurt on Main show one-hundred-and-thirty-five executions from 1366 to 1400 and three-hundred-and-seventeen from 1401 to 1560. The tally in Lübeck was four-hundred-and-

1. Judica Widmann, female executioner in Nuremberg, 1672.

2. Joh. Mich. Widmann, executioner in Nuremberg, son of 1., 1723.

[Handwritten document — Specification, an executioner's invoice signed by Caspar Friederich Kühn, Leitmeritz, 7 July 1757, and 8 July 1757.]

Executioner's invoice for the execution of a deserter, July 7, 1757.

215

eleven executions from 1371 to 1450. In Breslau, as many as four-hundred-and-fifty-four criminals were killed in 69 years (from 1456 to 1525), two-hundred-and-fifty being hanged, one-hundred-and-three beheaded, twenty-five broken on the wheel, thirty-nine burnt, thirty-one drowned, three buried alive and two quartered. For the period from 1402 to 1448 in Berlin, one-hundred-and-one executions are recorded (fifty-one by hanging, fourteen by burning, thirteen by beheading, eleven by breaking on the wheel, ten by burying alive), and it is doubtful whether these data are complete. In the margraviate of Ansbach (at that time approx. 100000 inhabitants), four-hundred-and-seventy-four people were executed from 1575 to 1603. Lastly, the sorry record of Hamburg should be mentioned: on four occasions more than seventy pirates were executed on a single day, and on seven occasions more than 25 pirates. How many people any given executioner killed is not revealed by these data. It is reported, however, that in the period of his office from 1501 to 1525 one Nuremberg executioner executed 1, 159 sentences; Peter Aichelin, the headsman of the Swabian League, beheaded three-hundred-and-fifty men with the sword in one month during the Peasant's War, but the "record" was probably held by the already mentioned executioner of Berne, who beheaded seventy-two men in a single day.

Breaking the Staff
Breaking the staff was a symbolic legal act; when pronouncing the judgment, the judge broke a staff and threw it before the feet of the accused. This act symbolized the breaking of the communal relationship between the criminal and his fellow men. The above picture shows the judge breaking the staff in the trial of Jew Süss-Oppenheimer in Stuttgart in 1738.

Actum Castra den 18 May 1707.

Nachdem früh nach 7. Uhren, der
krancks auch dem Pieß Seatze, in-
gleichen vor dem H. Auditeure
gestorben, würde und, erst
nach die folge zu abhörung der
armen Sünder abgestellt; auch
H. 9. Uhr erschienen die drey armen
vor dem gewöhnlich besetzten
Schmachpeinlichen Halsgericht
und nachdem selbel, wie ge-
bräuchlich, gehaget, der Urthel
denen armen Sündern noch.
mahlen und Gebrechen jeden ins
besondere des gelesen und
selbiger und das gebunden
fänklich und Gebrechen jeder ab
nachfen derselben befraget, derselbe
auch mit Lauter Stimme ihre
Gebrechen gestanden, würde Ihnen
hiernach die Urthel straffe nebst
denen ein geläuteren und fol.
lib. 45. des seg. erkandlich Hl. Religion frommenbil des gelesen,
die armen Sünder auch ihren

The foregoing page shows a sheet of the record on the execution of three criminals in Kahla in 1707 with the attached broken staff and the content of the record.
GDR State Archives, Weimar, Kahla local court
CI XIII. 1; 1707 No. 1 Sheets 82–83

Translation:

"Actum Cahla, May 13, 1707.

The court having assembled betimes after 7 o'clock on the Vicht Platze (square), that is, before the manorial council house, the court servants were sent at 8 o'clock to bring the Poor Sinners; at 9 o'clock the three Poor Sinners appeared before the high criminal court to which I, the official proctor, Actuarius (court recorder) H. Cagen, had duly appointed myself and nine (?) lay assessors, and the court, as is customary, having read the judgment to the Poor Sinners once again and to each in particular and having asked the said Sinners clearly and distinctly for their confession individually, the said Sinners confessed their failings in a loud voice and answered the question with Yes. Thereupon the death sentence together with the received descriptions (of the crimes) of which they were found guilty in accordance with Act. 45 et seq (uentes) were read out to them, whereafter the Poor Sinners were handed over to the executioner that he might execute the death sentence on them as decreed, the staff was broken and the high criminal court was adjourned in the name of the Holy Trinity.

Thereupon the three Poor Sinners, accompanied by their spiritual advisors of whom there were two for each Sinner, were led into the circle (area of the court) and, after each had prayed, then taken to the place of execution, each separately so that he could see nothing of the execution of the others, and the death sentence was carried out.
In the order of the execution of their death sentences, George Andreae was the first, Benjamin Kauffmann the second and Caspar Andreae the third. When the head had been struck from each of them, George Andreae was placed in the sack and, as decreed, most mercifully buried in a grave made in a special place, but the two others together with their heads were carried to the pyre and thereafter burnt.
After 12 o'clock the actu executionis was at an end and the three Poor Sinners had been sent to their blessed salvation, which is hereby duly recorded.

Actum Cahla ut supra.

E. H. Administrator
G. Abeyer manu propria"

218

Punishment of the Dead and Inanimate Objects and in Effigy

Punishment of the Dead

We do not punish the dead now. In the past, people thought differently. In some cases such punishment served to inflict a more severe sentence, in others the guilty person died before suffering the penalty, leaving only his mortal remains to satisfy the unquenched desire to punish. The dead had a right to a decent burial, for otherwise, according to ancient beliefs, they could find no peace. To deprive a dead man of a decent burial was torment, that is, punishment for him. From antiquity right up to modern times, a long series of punishments are recorded, which were inflicted on the dead. The preserved records, of course, relate to punishment, not of the "man in the street", but of some of the historical great. In 1660, the bodies of Oliver Cromwell, Bradshaw and Ireton were disinterred by order of Parliament. They were dragged on sleds to Tyburn, the gallows for common criminals. They hung there for all to see until sundown and were then buried beneath the gallows. Execution of the exhumed corpses had been delayed until January 30, the day of Charles I's death. After the bodies had been taken down from the gallows towards evening, they were beheaded and the heads placed on spikes above Westminster Hall.

At all times, the various forms of execution did not stop at extinguishing life. That alone did not satisfy the demand for punishment, and subsequent punitive treatment of the dead body was undertaken with great regularity. An old and hitherto unexplained custom was to place the head of an executed man between his legs. The head of Louis XVI of France was found in this position when he was disinterred after 1815. In some cases, too, the hangman boxed the ears of the severed head. But defensive magic was also practiced with heads on stakes and in such instances it is possibly not quite accurate to speak of punishment after death.

A very old custom was to leave a hanged person on the gallows. It was considered an act of mercy to allow friends and relatives to take down the dead person immediately. Illegal removal from the gallows was regarded as "aiding and abetting" the dead person.

The bodies of persons broken on the wheel were threaded through the spokes and the wheel then set up on a post. The ashes of those burnt at the stake were strewn to the four winds or thrown into flowing water. In later times, delinquents were strangled and only the corpses were consigned to the flames.

The urns of the Nazi war criminals were taken in 1947 to a lonely spot on the river Isar near Solln, broken open with axes and kicked apart. The contents were thrown into the water to float down to the Danube. The Bible contains evidence that even in antiquity a kick was a form of vilification.

Death "robbed" earthly justice of its victim, so what was more obvious than to visit retribution on the mortal remains. In Basle in 1552, a man who had killed his wife, children and himself was dragged to the execution site, threaded on the wheel, placed in a barrel and thrown into the Rhine.

The punishment of persons who died prior to execution and of suicides was reduced in the course of time from complete destruction to "dishonourable" burial". Among the Israelites, not to be buried at all was such a terrible disgrace that people would hardly wish it on their worst enemies. But mere burial in accordance with the rules was not enough to form such a firm bond between body and soul that the departed could find peace; the body also had to be intact and unmutilated. A practice that went far beyond placing an executed person's head between his legs was the custom of complete dismemberment. Even in old Nuremberg, executed criminals were handed over to the physicians and "anatomized". In Scottish court practice, the death sentence was aggravated by orders that the corpse was to be dissected in public and used for anatomical purposes. Unslaked lime was a no less thoroughgoing attack on the integrity of the dead body than fire or dismemberment. When rebuilding the choir in the chapel of St. Peter ad Vincula in the Tower of London in the early 19th century, it was discovered that most of the dead had no coffins and many were covered with unslaked lime. It was therefore difficult to identify the remains of Catherine Howard, fifth wife of King Henry VIII, who was executed in 1542.

Reversal of the normal posture was a further method of rendering the dead harmless. The power to do evil was "turned upside down". Ancient modes of thought re-emerged, and still do, when revolutionary groups temporarily gained the upper hand. In 1617, the rabble practiced mob justice on the French Marshal d'Ancre, hoisting him up on the gallows head down. The suspended corpse was pierced with a sword and beaten with clubs. In France, the hangman not infrequently hung criminal suicides head down on the gallows. The hanging of the dead by the feet is encountered again in a famous case of the present day. In the revolutionary turmoil that set in at the end of the war in Italy in 1945, the dictator Mussolini and his mistress were killed by revolutionaries and the bodies were hung by the feet publicly in Milan.

Punishment of the Dead (see text)

Caption: Trial of Marshal d'Ancre, held in Paris

Ancre, Marshal d', proper name Concino Concini, French statesman, died in Paris, April 24, 1617, son of a Florentine notary, came to the French court in 1600 for the marriage of Marie de Medici to Henry IV and under Marie's regency (1610 onwards) took over control of the government as Marquis d'Ancre and marshal of France. In the interests of the crown, he combatted the ambitions of the great; but finally he fell victim to a conspiracy led by Luynes with the knowledge of the young Louis XIII. His wife, Leonore Dori, called Galligai, the queen's lady-in-waiting, was executed on July 8, 1617, for alleged sorcery.

Punishment in Effigy

The term effigy means image or any form of human likeness. Under Roman law, for instance, only certain classes and individuals were accorded the honour of having public images set up. In contrast, Roman law knew neither the concept nor the practice of "executio in effigie", that is, punishment in effigy. This now familiar term gave rise to the notion of a well-established institution of the classical age. However, it is completely unknown to antiquity and the Middle Ages and was, in fact, introduced into the juristic terminology of Europe by the Humanists. Incidentally, punishment in effigy is not a peculiarity of German law; it can be comprehended only against the overall European background.

Effigies by no means aroused only feelings of fear and vengeance, but also love and respect. We look up to the statues on our public squares, we decorate them with flowers, and we even give them special penal protection. We pray to images of the deities and saints, speak to them as if they were alive or present. Images of deities were kissed and embraced, but also stoned and knocked down. Formerly, for example, people in Italy often threw stones at the image of their patron saint or hung it in the chimney when they suffered great misfortune. The patron saint was punished for his "failure". Even today, we place images of the dead on gravestones and honour them with flowers and candles. Identification of a beloved person with his image is something perfectly familiar to us.

In considering punishment in effigy we must draw a distinction between the well-regulated institution and outbreaks of public rage. To begin with, let us limit ourselves to the penal aspect of the phenomenon.

Execution in effigy: in place of the fugitive traitor, his image is hung on the gallows. The man punished in effigy later surrendered to the court, was sentenced to death by hanging, but was then pardoned and banished. 18th cent.

Scroll: Bigedini whose brother is a disloyal traitor

Verse: Although his brother escaped the death sentence.
         In his place his image shall be hung.
         But he remains a disloyal villain.
         Because he took part in the treason.
         Henceforth he dare not name his name.
         For the whole world will recognize him as disloyal.

222

"Strafe am Bildnis", "Leibesstrafe an seinem Bildnis", "im Bildnis voll-zogene Strafe" are the formulations found in German criminal regulations; they correspond to the French "en effigie" and the English "in effigy". All these terms mean pseudo-execution with the help of an image of the delinquent.

Punishment in effigy played a substantial role in Spanish inquisition proceedings. At the "auto da fé", the ceremonial public pronouncement of sentences and the subsequent execution, in addition to the condemned person, appropriately marked dummies of fugitive suspects and effigies of deceased accused and their bones were burnt as effigial reinforcement of the execution. We read that in Spain from 1481 to 1809, the Inquisition sentenced 31.912 persons to death, of whom 17.659 were executed in effigy.

In cases of bestiality, i.e. unnatural connections with animals, in some instances both offender and animal were executed by burning, the human being in effigy. In 1525 in Breslau, for example, a man guilty of bestiality was burnt on a wooden horse. The criminal animal, too, was punished in effigy, if it was impossible to lay hands on it.

The fully institutionalized execution in effigy of court judgments presupposed well-developed inquisitorial procedure for trials in absentia. The fact that the law provided for such execution only for crimes of lese-majesty (high treason) against the absolutist sovereign by the grace of God casts an interesting light on its origin and development over the course of time. While in Germany the Carolina made no provision for execution in effigy, the parliament of Paris, in its quality as supreme royal court, ordered pseudo-executions of fugitives convicted of lese-majesty as early as the second half of the 16th century, though they were not incorporated in the codified law until the 17th century, and from then onwards they were included in all central European criminal legislation.

In practice, executions (in effigy) differed from "Schandbilder" (vitupera-tive images), not in their plastic shape, but solely in the legal handling of the actual infliction of punishment at the public place of execution. It could be carried out either with painted images or with three-dimensional dummies. While the authorities of the Spanish Inquisition were content, when prosecuting blasphemy and heresy, to use symbolic, half-lifesize, papiermaché figures on poles and at mass executions even Janus-headed double figures, in 16th-century France they made life-size, clothable, straw-stuffed manikins with a realistic head (e.g. Admiral Coligny), which at the Danish court in the middle of the 17th century evolved into realistic wax effigies that were extremely lifelike. On November 13, 1648,

Chancellor Korfitts Ulfeldt was quartered in effigy. It is reported that the true-to-life figure representing him was filled with the entrails of animals to make the proceedings more graphically lifelike. They began with the cutting off of the right hand and head and the tearing out of the entrails, as was usual in punishing high treason. The head and hand were nailed to the wall of the city hall, where the remnants remained on view up to the great fire of 1729. At the time, these proceedings filled everyone with horror.

A second case exhibits a wealth of remarkable details. Kai Lykke had been indicted. He succeeded in escaping in 1661. The supreme court condemned him to death "in contumaciam" (in absentia). Execution in effigy was ordered. "It took place on September 5 at the castle courtyard in Copenhagen. A life-size figure had been made of wood or wax. It was an exact replica of the living man, with wig, white gloves, etc. The effigy was collected from the so-called blue tower of the fortress and drawn on a hurdle. The hurdle was drawn by a white horse . . . The executioner's assistant took the figure from the hurdle and placed it in a kneeling position on the sand. The neckerchief was then loosened, a blindfold tied over the eyes, and the hair placed under the jacket. Then the executioner first struck off the right hand. While the assistant held the hair, the head was struck off with two blows. The hand and head were placed between the figure's legs. The body was fastened on the hurdle, paraded past the castle and finally taken to the old market, where the head and hand were nailed to a post. First, the executioner put the body on show in his house against an entrance fee, then it was buried beneath the gallows."

It seems that the greater the similarity between the image and the living person, the greater the effect on the fugitive criminal. This association of ideas was certainly attained in the eyes and minds of the observers.

Execution in effigy remained a statutory punishment up to the great revolution. In 1777, Mirabeau was sentenced to be beheaded for rape and seduction. It was intended that the punishment should be carried out initially only in effigy. The sentence was to become effective only after five years, if by then Mirabeau had not surrendered to the court and been given a regular trial. It was a conditionally suspended death sentence, but was to be executed symbolically for the time being in order to serve as a deterrent.

In connection with the flight of Crown Prince Frederick of Prussia, the later King Frederick II (the Great), one of his confidants, Lieutenant Keith, was sentenced in absentia by a court martial in Wesel in 1730 to be "hung, quartered and nailed to the gallows in effigy".

In addition to the legal type of punishment in effigy, we find that practiced by incensed and revolutionary mobs. It is a remote echo of old court practice and lives on with enormous tenacity in the subconscious of the masses. It reaches out for the enemy who, though he has not fled, is protected by his powerful position and is thus beyond their reach. French history is full of such cases. In 1560, revolutionary feeling ran high in France. The cardinal of Lorraine was hanged in effigy a number of times by the incensed masses, once by the feet and once beheaded and quartered.

At the murder trial of Eugen Aram in London in 1745, a man was exempted from prosecution for appearing as king's evidence. A crowd gathered in front of this witness's house and it was only with great effort that it was prevented from demolishing the building. But they carried an effigy of the villain through the streets, which was dispatched with an axe and then burned.

In mob justice, the only forms of execution in effigy that have survived are hanging and burning. Possibly because it is easiest to imitate these forms of death. Hanging is the method resorted to by the American mobs when they want to punish an enemy. A case is known from the revolutionary period in which the traitor Benedict Arnold was shot, scalped and burnt in effigy (Philadelphia). Burning, which was used a numer of times in Arnold's case, indicates the profound bitterness of the crowds. In November 1918, the masses in New York burnt Emperor William II in effigy. But the present, too, is rich in examples of punishment in effigy by incensed crowds. In television reports on the revolution in Iran, scenes were shown repeatedly in which fanatic supporters of Ayatholla Khomeini carried out executions in effigy. They hanged or burnt dummies representing the deposed shah or the American president, Jimmy Carter. They even "punished" the entire American nation by publicly burning the star-spangled banner.

Ever since the 17th century, an explanation and the reason for this peculiar form of punishment have been sought. The idea of deterrence alone hardly seems sufficient. The pertinacity of this old type of punishment cannot, in the last analysis, be explained rationally, for indubitably its roots reach far back into the spiritual life of mankind. "What is done to the image is suffered by the imaged." This notion of magic practiced on images was familiar to all the peoples of the earth and still prevails among primitive groups. The belief in this form of magic is often so strong that people who learn what has been done to their images not infrequently actually die. In old Greece, a method of practicing this long-range magic was developed to an art: A wax figure was melted or pierced with many pins, with the result that the person represented by the figure suffered the same torment. Lead figures were placed fettered in the grave, to prevent any movement of the depicted enemy. At that time, the people believed that witches made wax effigies of persons they wanted to perish and then made them melt slowly over a low fire. When the figure dissolved into nothing, the victim, too, was intended to shrink and shrivel. Wasting away was a mysterious process, and withering a form of death familiar from the plant world. Witches, who were themselves emaciated, knew many a method of making others waste away.

Punishment in effigy is thus a left-over from the phase of human thought in which acts of magic were the most powerful means of self-preservation. The image and the original belong together. What happens to the one is suffered or experienced by the other.

The Roman emperor Nero called it "wiping out memory" when he overthrew the busts and statues of all former victors in the holy games and ordered them to be dragged on hooks to the latrines. In actual fact, it was the jealousy and hate of the living for dead rivals who were beyond the reach of his power. At times, the personality seems to be transferred completely to the image, which then shares all human emotions and quali-

Burning the Rumps at Temple Bar

Copper engraving by William Hogarth, 1697–1764, the great English painter and engraver, who was internationally famous for his moral and satirical works. Reproduced from "Les Satyres de Guillaume Hogarth", published in 1768 by Robert Sayer, Fleet Street, London.

The engraving depicts punishment in effigy by the "beastly rabble" at Temple Bar, the barrier to the old city of London.

ties. Sagas describing how mute images took vengeance on their calumnia-tors have been handed down by Aristotle, Theocritus and Plutarch. An old Greek legend tells of the double punishment of a hero's statue and the revenge it took for that vile treatment. "... there was a story about Theage-nes of Thasos and how, after his death, an enemy whipped his brazen image at night until at last the statue fell upon him and slayed him, whereupon the Thasians sank the murderous image in the sea, but thereafter, through the wrath of the hero, they were scourged by infertility until, after repeated instruction by the oracle of Delphi, they raised the sunken statue, set it up again and made scarifice to it 'as to a god'". The Middle Ages, too, knew such signs and wonders, which are found ever and again in the chronicles. In one case it is recounted that a villain wanted to take the sword from the statue of St. Paul. The statue swung the sword and split the scoundrel's skull.

It is really just juggling with words to speak of "fetishlike animation" or to depict the murderous Theagenes as being punished in effigy. But when statues killed, the situation is clear. Just as the represented persons murd-ered in effigy, they could also be called to account and punished in effigy.

Last meal before execution
Above their heads the penalties awaiting the condemned.
Bamberg Halsgerichtsordnung, 1507

Abschiedt

der Römischen Kayserlichen Ma=
iestat / auch Churfürsten/deputirter Fürsten vnd Sten=
de / für sich vnd in namen gemeiner des heiligen Reichs
Stende auff dem Deputation tag zu Franckfort Anno
Domini M. D. LXXI. auffgericht.

Mit Röm. Kay. Mayt. gnad vnd sonderm Priuilegio in zehen jarn nicht nach zutrucken.
Gedruckt in der Churfürstlichen Statt Meintz durch Franciscum Behm/
Anno M. D. LXXI.

Recess of the imperial diet of 1571, containing the imperial police regulations.

228

Police Regulations

Introduction

In the Holy Roman Empire, the term "police" connoted the good order to be maintained by the secular powers, i.e. provision for propriety and good morals, order and security in both private and public life, and all measures designed to promote the wellbeing of a country's inhabitants and economy. The word "police" did not come into use until about 1500. The statutory basis for this "good order" was the imperial edict of Worms of 1495, which has gone down in history as the "perpetual peace".* It set up the supreme judicial body for the entire imperial territory, the Reichskammergericht (Imperial Chamber)*, which was vested with the supreme executive powers of the imperial assembly. The territories of the empire were reorganized into districts, an imperial council was established, and the constitutional preconditions were created for sweeping, imperial police legislation. The imperial diet of Augsburg promulgated on Nov. 19, 1530, the first comprehensive imperial police regulations: "Römisch Kayserlicher Majestät Ordnung und Reformation guter Polizey im Heiligen Römischen Reich" (His Holy Roman Majesty's Order and Reformation of Good Police in the Holy Roman Emperor). A thorough revision of this imperial police code followed as early as 1548 at the imperial diet of Augsburg and at the later imperial diets of 1551 and 1577.

Authorities

In the imperial police statutes, the term "Obrigkeit" (authorities) played a special role, but without its meaning being clearly defined. All orders in the enactments of the empire were addressed to the "authorities", since the empire had no executive organs of its own; they were made responsible for implementation.

It is evident from a number of regulations, however, that "authorities" meant the responsible local bodies most closely related to the empire, that is, the princes and the lords, knights and towns directly responsible to the empire. They had to pass on the empire's rules and orders to the agencies who owed them direct obedience. The empire itself could not communicate direct with subordinate local authorities or member states of the empire, since that would have been considered intervention in the freedom of the imperial estates and would have been rejected by them. Hence, each imperial estate had to ensure implementation. It is thus evident from the imperial promulgations that the structure of the authorities was pyramidal. The supreme authority was the empire or the emperor. Below him, with no intermediate agency, were the imperial estates which, in their turn, constituted the "authorities" for an abundance of subordiate agencies.

Classification of imperial police regulations
The imperial police regulations can be generally subdivided into two groups according to their form:
1. those of precisely formulated content,
2. those containing only instructions of a general nature for the authorities. The latter called on the local authorities to remedy abuses or, for example, ordered the setting up of wage regulations for servants and bondsmen in keeping with local conditions. This type of police enactment justifies their classification as "general legislation" of the empire. The empire provided stimuli which the territories took over and enlarged upon or scaled down to suit their particular conditions.
The regulations of precisely formulated content, which were intended to apply throughout the empire, can be divided into two main groups: an economic and a social group. Both contain an abundance of individual provisions. The economic group contains regulations for the protection and promotion of comerce and crafts, it regulates money transactions, price-setting, trade in goods and conditions for crafts. The very extensive social group of imperial police regulations covers everything relating to welfare (in the broadest sense)[1]) within the empire.

At the end of the 16th century, there existed in the Holy Roman Empire a comprehensive, highly detailed imperial police law which was theoretically a useful legal basis for the preservation of good order in the empire. In practice, however, effective implementation facilities were lacking. But up to its very end (1806), the empire held on to its competence for police legislation, although it left the territorial lords a great deal of leeway for their own legislation. From the close of the 16th century onwards, police legislation gravitated to the territories. While the police regulations of 1530 and 1548 had conceded the territorial sovereigns the possibility only of moderating imperial law, the ban on making it more stringent was abrogated as early as 1577. From that time onwards, there was nothing to prevent the various imperial estates from creating their own police law.

Thereafter, in the space of three hundred years, every imperial estate issued thousands upon thousands of police regulations, and in the process a brisk interchange of law took place in order to attain a degree of uniformity. We find that in many instances the text of new ordinances was identical with that of older ones or that the more recent ones were merely more detailed and precise versions of the older ones.

Many ordinances contained long-range regulations, e.g. church regulations, marriage regulations, medical regulations, etc. Others were intended only as short-term remedies for current nuisances, were soon forgotten and lost their significance. The ordinances began with an indication of who had issued them, and had invariably a fixed preamble showing to whom they were addressed. Then followed a general description of the subject matter, and thereafter the mandatory or prohibitive provisions, which were usually coupled with the punishment regulations for contraventions.

In the following, a number of examples – with special reference to over 2000 ordinances from Rothenburg – will be used to illustrate the importance of police regulations for the administration and how they regulated life in the communities.

Public Health Police
Public health regulations prescribed all measures intended to prevent the community or individual persons from suffering harm to their health. The head of the medical system in those days was the "physicus" appointed by the town. On the one hand they were medical practitioners, and on the other they performed the functions of the present-day public health offices. They were responsible for supervising the surgeons, who had to bring proof of three years training and subsequent years of itinerant practice, the barbers and bathhouse keepers, the "stone and rupture cutters", and the midwives. The physici examined their knowledge and constantly supervised their activities. On taking office, the physici had to swear an oath committing themselves to call on the sick at all times. They were not permitted to make a distinction between poor and rich. Only in times of plague were they allowed to give medical advice in their houses. For this purpose, a messenger or relative brought a small glass of the sick person's urine, which the doctor used to make his diagnosis. The physici were not allowed to travel or stay outside the town overnight without the permission of the authorities. Moreover, they were admonished to remain in the town in times of plague and not to move outside the limits. Furthermore, they were required to report unusual diseases at once.

Once or twice every year they had to inspect the apothecaries to determine whether sufficient medicaments were in stock. The apothecaries were required to keep adequate stocks of herbs, roots and other basic materials for the preparation of medicaments and to store them in a due and proper manner. They also had to keep poison registers in which the had to enter the nature of the poison, the quantity, and when and to whom they were supplied. The sale of poison to juven iles was forbidden. The apothecaries were also required to sell medicaments only at the set prices.

The bathhouse keepers were com manded to consult a physicus in all cases of internal diseases. They also had to keep the bathhouses clean, which were mostly set up by the towns. The formerly customary bathing of men and women together was prohibited. The population was admonished to go to the bathhouses, not to in dulge their lust or to eat and drink, but only in the interests of cleanliness. If all these admonitions were in vain, all eating and drinking in bathhouses was summarily forbidden.

Plague doctor with protective clothing. Copper engraving, 1656.

Bloodletting, at that time practically a panacea, was carried to extremes and resulted in damage to health. The bathhouse keepers were therefore repeatedly admonished to exercise caution when bloodletting. A Rothen-burg ordinance of March 7, 1656 (Chapt. III, Art. 4) contains an interesting passage in this respect:

> "also up to now an abominable, irresponsible abuse has been practiced with impru-dent bloodletting / so that any person without distinction / whoever desired it / was let in 1, 2 or 3 places at once / also if the patient wanted (his veins) closed / but the bathhouse keeper imagined he knew better / not only refused but at times let out whole pannikins of blood from pregnant women . . ."

There were strict regulations on keeping the drinking water clean in wells and open fishing waters. The greatest dangers to the health and existence of the population in those days were the epidemics, above all the plague. At first, people were completely powerless in the face of them and sought help by prayer. Numerous plague monuments, chapels and altars still bear witness to the ravages of these devastating diseases. The number of dead was enormous. Towns lost up to half their inhabitants in a single epidemic. In 1634 alone, 2,314 persons died of the plague in Rothenburg, whose total po-pulation was then a little more than 5.000. As advances were made in medical science, it was realized that pestilences were spread by infection. This resulted in strict public health ordinances everywhere. The countermeasures consisted primarily in making it impossible for strangers to pass through or stay in towns. The object was to prevent epidemics from being

Physician with jar of urine and Capuchin monk with rosary at a sick man's bed. Woodcut from "liber pestilentialis" by Brunswig, 1500.

brought in by travellers. Every stranger had to prove on arrival by an official certificate that he had not come from a plague-ridden area, otherwise he was not allowed into the town. How unhygienic conditions were at that time is illustrated by the following admonition:

> Any person who carries dung, water or earth on to the streets or stepping stones must sweep it away from much-frequented streets withhin 3 days, from alleys within 8 days and ensure that the refuse carter can cart it away. Continually the orders prohibiting the throwing away of waste, rubbish and refuse are repeated, continually the pouring of urine from windows and shops is criticized. The decrees continually speak of "evil cloacae" which run out of the houses into the open alleys and of unpermitted dung heaps.

The Rothenburg council decree of 1663 reads:

> "But if, in addition, such filth is not only a great eye-sore and shame, but oftentimes gives rise to stench and other abominations and indeed to a dangerous pestilence . . . whereby considerable harm occurs and the way and streets are blocked so that it is nearly impossible to walk or drive past . . ."

The refuse piled up to such an extent at times that the council peremptorily ordered every peasant's wagon leaving the town to be loaded full with it and to have it unloaded at certain places outside the gates.

Domestic animals were not allowed to move around freely in times of plague. Detailed regulations were issued for the smoking out (disinfection) of houses. The citizens were alled upon to stay at home as far as

233

possible; markets, assemblies and dances were forbidden. If any one fell sick, the appointed bathhouse keeper had to examine the patient and decide what was to be done. If the disease was found to be infectious, the sick person was sent either to the pest-house or the hospital. The infected house had to remain closed for fourteen days and its occupants had to be supplied with food by the neighbours.

Doctors inspecting urine at the apothecary's shop, from "Hortus sanitatis", 1491.

If a person died of the plague, police regulations required him to be buried within twelve hours. In the funeral procession, the survivors had to stay a large distance from the coffin. The clothing, bed linen and all objects used by the deceased were not allowed to be sold or given away. A person who had recovered from an epidemic disease was not permitted to go to church or the bathhouse for fourteen days (quarantine).

The authorities also employed people who had to disinfect the houses in which the plague had claimed victims. The numerous public health regulations were based, of course, on existing medical knowledge, but on the whole they reveal praiseworthy circumspection on the part of the town authorities.

Apothecary's shop, woodcut from "Buch der Chirurgie" (Book of Surgery) by Brunschwig, 1497.

Fire Police

A basic distinction must be drawn between two types of regulations: on the one hand fire prevention measures, and on the other fire-fighting regulations. The mediaeval towns were constantly threatened by fire because, especially in the first two-hundred years of their existence, the houses were built mainly of wood and roofed with shingles and straw. Houses of stone were the exception; they were mostly monasteries and the houses of patricians, but for them, too, a great deal of wood was used. Disastrous fires are recorded in the history of nearly all old towns and some were ravaged by fires several times in a single century.

Fire Prevention: A large proportion of the fire-prevention regulations were building regulations. To reduce fire hazards, straw and shingle roofs were repeatedly forbidden; the roofing had to be of tiles. Chimneys had to be constructed of "baked" bricks, had to protrude three feet above the roof and have a crossection large enough to allow a chimney sweep to climp up inside it to the top. Ovens and wash boilers were not allowed to be built against hollow walls. To supervise observation of these regulations, the town administrations appointed fire inspectors who had to inspect all houses, in some towns twice and in others four times every year. Numerous "visitation" reports demonstrate how stringently contraventions were treated and how frequently fines were imposed. These preventive measures gradually bore fruit. Building craftsmen who contravened the fire regulations in performing their work were punished. The structure concerned was torn down and rebuilt in compliance with regulations at the delinquent's expense. In contrast to other towns, Rothenburg, for example, experienced only small fires and was spared disastrous conflagrations. This was due not least to its stringent fire regulations. A large amount of space in the fire regulations was devoted to the prohibition of certain actions. For instance, it was forbidden to place ashes on wooden floors, to walk around the house with open lights, to cut straw, thresh, break and comb flax, work with hemp or pitch, melt tallow, wax or other fatty substances, wash clothes and slaughter animals at night by lantern light, to wash oneself or prepare a bath behind the stove at night or before the horn heralded the day. The beer brewers were not permitted to dry malt at night, nor the ropemakers hemp, nor could the baker dry damp wood in the oven. The sale of powder was allowed only by lantern light, i.e., a closed-off light. It was forbidden to enter places endangered by fire, such as barns, granaries or storage rooms with a burning tobacco pipe. Even the hosts of inns had Fire Regulations, police rules for preventing and fighting fires, 1687 to continually warn their guests not to go around with open lights. If there were many guests in the house, a watchman had to be employed day and night. At parish fairs (kermis), weddings and dances, special safety precautions had to be taken.

Feuer-Ordnung/

Des

H. Reichs-Statt Rotenburg ob der Tauber.

Gedruckt daselbst

im Jahr Christi 1687.

durch Noah von Millenau.

The burning of hedges, grass and the like had to be reported to the burgomaster beforehand.

Firefighting: The fire regulations contained precise instructions on what was considered necessary for firefighting. The streets, in those days narrow alleys, had to be kept clear so that the water wagons could pass unhindered. For this reason all refuse had to be cleared away and the stacking of firewood or goods in front of houses was prohibited. Each house had to have one or two leather water buckets and a copper always filled with water. In summer, an additional trough filled with water had to be set in front of the door or in the yard. The citizens were commanded always to keep the wells in the alleys and yards in good order. The public wells were the responsibility of the town "well-master". In order to keep the wells ready for use at all times, not only for drinking water but also for firefighting, every type of pollution was punished, for "whosoever sullies and taints them wantonly with foul stinking things or with carrion shall themselves clean them and thereafter, if the cold permits, stand at the pillory in wet clothing until the harm is atoned for and one guilder fine has been paid". In the towns there was also a number of reservoirs (called "Wethen", Eng. wets) which were always full of water. The craftsmen, who needed a lot of water, were forbidden to take water from public wells. They had to haul their service water with wagons and buckets from rivers and streams so that water reserves for firefighting were not diminished. The town "water fountains" (fire-engines) and other extinguishing equipment had to be inspected every six months by the town's master builder and any defects had to be remedied immediately. The watchmen had to "remain in the alleys" all through the night, call out the hours and investigate any smell of fire. If a fire broke out, they had to rouse the occupants of the burning house and the neighbours and report the fire to the town watchhouse. The first watchman to report a fire received a reward. In the event of a great fire, the watchman on the town tower had to sound the alarm immediately and put up a flag by day and a lighted lantern at night, indicating the direction of the fire. If a fire broke out outside the town, the alarm was given by striking the town hall bell three times and continually repeating the signal. Every inhabitant knew what he had to do and where his place was. Some had to hurry to the fire with buckets of water, others had to appear at the market place with their weapons to rcinforce the watchmen on the walls and ensure security on the streets. The only exceptions were widows, the infirm and children, and neighbours who were themselves endangered by the fire. The keepers of the keys (the town councillors who had custody of the keys of the town gates and public buildungs), the gate-keepers and the watch had to surrender their keys at the town hall. The joiners, masons, roofers, painters, chimney sweeps and pavers had to proceed at once to the site of the fire, together with their journeymen, apprentices and labourers, taking with them axes, hammers and picks with which they could "chop, tear and break down". They were repeatedly reminded of this duty at craftsmen's assemblies, and masters, journeymen and apprentices were threatened with punishment and immediate banishment for failing in their duty. Carters or citizens who owned horses were required to stop anything they were doing and hasten with their horses to the armoury, fill the fire-engines and tanks with water and hurry to the fire, where the equipment was operated by other delegated citizens. To ensure this was done "with despatch", there were rewards; the first man received 1 guilder, the second 3/4 guilder and the third 1/2 guilder. Men who had no special assignment had to borrow "barrels and vats" from innkeepers and brewers, fill them with water and take them to the fire, and also to bring fire-ladders. To guarantee security on the streets at night, pans of pitch at corner houses had to be lighted, or if there was a wind lanterns, and every citizen had to fix a lighted lantern to his house.

The supervision and direction of extinguishing work were in the hands of the town's master-builder and the judge. They had to ensure that the water buckets were passed smoothly along the chains of men and that dams were built to take up the water in the streets. They also had to make sure that water was taken up to the attics of houses near the fire. A decision on the necessity of breaching a wall was likewise their responsibility.

Since many onlookers, especially children, stood around uselessly at such disasters, it was the job of the police to chase them away. To avoid theft, strangers spending the night in the town were forbidden to leave their quarters. For the same reason, armed men were placed in the streets, who had to keep an eye on everybody and the goods they carried. If a suspect "could give no proper answer", all he had with him was seized and he himself was taken to the watchhouse. Any person who concealed goods saved from a fire and entrusted to him paid for it with his life like a thief.

After the fire was extinguished, a fire-watch had to remain at the site. The master-builder had to collect all fire-fighting equipment, return what did not belong to the town, and have damaged articles repaired and lost articles replaced.

If a citizen had an accident while fire-fighting and was therefore unable to work, it was provided that he should be cared for from the alms-box or by the hospital. If a carter's horse was killed while fire-fighting without any fault on his part, the horse was replaced.

After the fire was extinguished, all concerned were called upon "both at home and in public churches to give heartfelt thanks and devotely pray for the gracious prevention of further misfortune", to quote the Rothenburg Fire Regulations of 1687 (see next page above).

CAPUT III.
Was nach Löschung des Feuers
zu beobachten.

WAnn nun vermittelst Göttlicher Güte die Brünst gelöschet / solle deroselben Männiglich so wohl zu Hauß/als in offentlicher Kirchen darfür hertzlich dancken/ und umb gnädige Verhütung fernern Unglücks andächtig bitten.

2.

Es soll auch / wer an dem Feuer schuldig / gebührlich inquirirt werden/und da befunden würde / daß es durch eines/ oder des andern Unachtsamkeit / Ungehorsam / Versaumnuß/und Verwahrlosung verursacht worden / soll derselbe ohne Ansehen der Person bestrafft werden.

From the Rothenburg Fire Regulations of 1687

The law of the rod: The width of all alleys was regularly checked by the authorities. If the rod touched the sides, immediate alterations were ordered.

Highway and Traffic Police

The regulations dealt with here were not the precursors of present-day road traffic regulations, for the traffic problems familiar to us did not exist in those days. The main streets of the towns were wide enough for the prevailing conditions and the many open squares provided sufficient room to park incoming vehicles. So hardly any ordinances can be found which can be compared with current road traffic regulations. Only in the "Rechtsspiegeln" (law mirrors) of the 13th century can anything similar to traffic rules be found. They prescribed that the king's highways must be broad enough for two wagons to pass each other without danger. The right of way was laid down to some extent by prescribing that an empty wagon should allow a loaded one to drive by, a lightly loaded one should give way to a heavily loaded one, a rider to a wagon and a pedestrian to a rider. At bridges, which often had just one lane, it was prescribed that the first wagon on the bridge must be allowed to pass over, whether empty or loaded.

In the towns there were special regulations governing the driving of livestock into or out of town. It was repeatedly ordered, undoubtedly for good reason, that this was to be done "without tumult and shouting". The animals were driven out at sunrise, first the horned livestock (cattle), then the community shepherd with the peasants' sheep and swine that were in his charge, and finally the butchers with their livestock. An hour before sundown, the bell was rung for the livestock to be brought in. First came the butchers, who were followed at intervals of a quarter of an hour by the community shepherd and then the horned livestock. Although it was otherwise forbidden for livestock to run around free in the town's alleys, there was a special dispensation for driving it out and in, because the animals found their own way to their stables. At sundown, the nightbell was rung and the town gates were closed.

In this connection it should be added that large-scale animal husbandry was necessary to supply sufficient meat for the population. In Rothenburg, a butcher was allowed to keep 40 to 60 sheep and drive them to the municipal pastures. Peasants could have 18 sheep or horned livestock, but only 12 if they had no more than 4 to 6 morgens of land (1 morgen = approx. 0.7 acre), and only 8 if they had no more than 2 to 3 morgens. Persons who owned no land could keep only 4 sheep. A citizen was allowed to keep 2 goats or swine, and so-called protectees (non-citizens) and day-labourers only 1 goat.

The term highway and traffic police therefore embraces mainly those regulations dealing with the building, maintenance and cleaning of roads and their financial aspects. In olden times, a mediaeval town differed from a village only in its larger number of houses and defence works. For a long

Proceedings before the Herford town court.
Behind the table with crucifix and sword, the judge and assessors; in front of the table,
the litigating parties and the clerk of the court.
Miniature from the Herford Law Book, ca. 1375; town archives, Herford.

Vome erue vozkynße vn vozpande.

Delivery to Jail. In the large doorway of the punishment tower the watchman awaits the new prisoner, who is driven into prison violently with kicks and punches by two catchpoles. (Soest "Nequambuch" (banishment register), 14th cent).

Opposite:
Members and clerk of the court at an "out-of-court" audience. Illustration of various forms: how a bond must be furnished to the court and opponent and how judgment must be enforced; legal transactions were concluded in the presence of the proctor and justices on account of the incontestability of the testimony of the court and as a form of security; pledging by physical transfer, here a costly goblet handed to the opponent; in the foreground, illustration of a "handfast" pledge, symbol for the keeping of a promise; adjacent: rejection of such a pledge, the man puts his hands in the sleeves of his mantle; on the latter's right, pledging gesture with outstretched forefinger; the enforcement of a judgment is depicted outside the building on the left, which is transferred by handing over the door ring or knocker (Hamburg City Law of 1497)

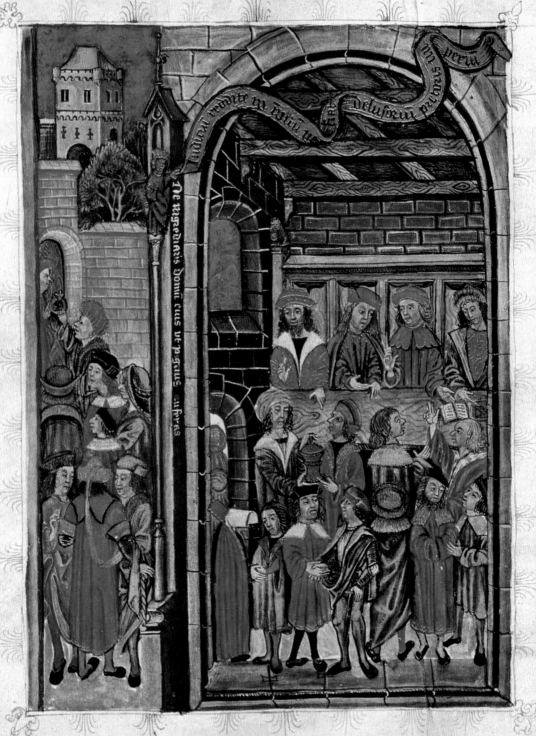

Wome hoelam vñ sekerheit to rechte bestedige

Banishment. On the right under the archway, two banished men, a hovering devil between their heads. The catchpoles with swords drive them out violently, the one with a kick and the other with hand raised ready to strike. (Soest "Nequambuch" (banishment register), 14th cent).

Opposite: Purchase of a rent (i.e. an annuity), right of inheritance, and neighbourly strife. The scroll text reads: "Thou shalt not lend thy money in usury, nor receive back more than thou hath given." Left, on the bench, the presiding burgomaster and two justices; an inspection date has been set. In the background on the right, a plumb bob is hung from the gutter, a master craftsman explains the case; it is a dispute among neighbours on gutter rights. Centre right: the elder, bearded man transfers the house to his heir; the legal symbol: the removed shoe. Foreground: a man in a green mantle counts coins on to the table, he is the purchaser of a rent, the recipient of the money is the seller (Hamburg City Law of 1497).

Van vomuderen,

Seesaw Punishment. With a seesaw the bald delingquent is catapulted out and falls from a great height into the water indicated by wavy lines. On the bank, the mocking spectators. (Soest "Nequambuch", 14th cent).

Opposite:
Guardianship. The council appoints and confirms a guardian, the open book indicating the importance of this official appointment. The guardians have to assume their duties towards their wards in public. In the foreground, a widow permitted to appear as representative of her child, but only with the help of a trustee. Left, a mentally deficient young man with torn clothing; right, a man with felt hat and green mantle who is choosing his attorney. (Hamburg City Law of 1497).

Breaking on the wheel. The wheel is fixed to a high post. The broken limbs of the naked, condemned man are threaded through the spokes and tied with ropes. Right: the mocking, grinning executioner with the ropes left over; left: three sympathetic spectators, one a woman wearing a kerchief on her head.
(Soest "Nequambuch", 14 th cent).

Beheading. In the centre, the executioner with his sword swung high, before him the delinquent in undergarment kneeling on the ground. In the tree on the left, two on-lookers; on the right others crowded together and in front of them another condemned man tearing his hear and lamenting. (Soest "Nequambuch", 14th cent).

The Count of Savoy is raised to the rank of duke by Emperor Sigismund

The courier of the Count of Valengin bringing a challenge to the city of Berne.

Judicial combat (divine judgment) between man and woman (Berne, 1288).

All three pictures from the Spiez Chronicles by Diebold Schilling, 1485. Municipal library, Berne

Nipping the condemnend man with red-hot pincers on the way to the place of execution; right: breaking on the wheel and impalement, Regensburg, 1534.

Burying alive and impalement of a woman; the man is being broken on the wheel, Freiburg, Switzerland, 1574.

Public stoning of a drunken executioner, 16th cent.

Witches: Conversation with the devil, trial and burning, Berne, 1568.

The pictures on this page are from the "Wickiana", Central Library, Zurich.

Execration of three monks by three bishops in Berne, 1509. Lucerne Chronicles by D. Schilling, 1513.

Two evildoers being led to the gallows in Baden "cut from the hand" of the executioner by the Coun of Montfort, 1509, Lucerne Chronicles, 1513.

Hans Spiess is convicted of the murder of his wife by the "bier proof", 1503. Lucerne Chronicles by Diebold Schilling, 1513. For the "bier proof", the suspected, naked murderer had to approach the bier and touch the mortal wound of the corpse. If the wound began to bleed again, the suspect was deemed guilty.

The torture of Hans Spiess, 1503.

The wheel with the body of the executed murderer Duckeli is raised on a post, 1492.
Pictures from the Lucerne Chronicles by D. Schilling, 1513, Municipal Library, Lucerne.

Drowning by throwing from the bridge, Constance, 1486. Lucerne Chronicles by Diebold Schilling, 1513.

Above and right:
Leading condemned criminals to the place of execution. Pen-and-ink drawings from the Volkach "Salbuch" (conveyance register), early 16th cent., town archives, Volkach.

Enclosed court site under a lime tree.

Beheading with the sword in Lucerne, 1509.
Pictures from the Lucerne Chronicles by D. Schilling, 1513, Municipal Library, Lucerne.

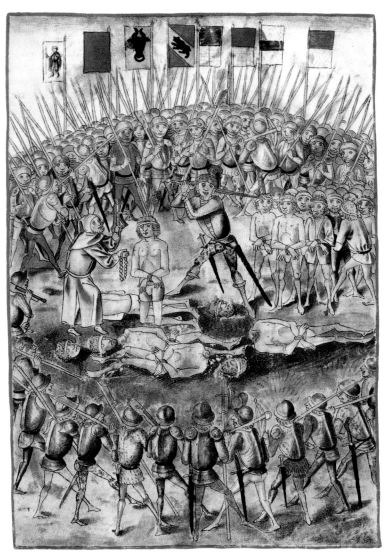

The Murder of Greifensee, 1444

An impressive picture of the mass execution of the Zurich occupiers of Greifensee by the Berne executioner, who executed 72 delinquents with the sword
on a single day (see also article "Executioners").

Berne Chronicles by Diebold Schilling, 1483, Municipal Library, Berne.

time, the streets had a rural appearance because the inhabitants still engaged in farm work in addition to their occupations as merchants or craftsmen. Right up to the modern era, the citizens still pursued a peasant's life in the vineyards and fields outside the towns. Prior to the beginning of the 15th century, street paving was the exception. In Germany, Nuremberg took the lead in 1377. As the building of paved roads cost a lot of money even in those days, very soon a whole series of ordinances appeared on conservation and cleaning of the roads. To finance and maintain them tolls were levied, road, bridge, paving, wagon, barrow and wheel tolls, and also the "wagon-shaft pfennigs". A good source of revenue for the town treasurers. Inside the towns, however, the authorities only had part of the paving laid at public expense, for instance the main streets and market place, at the public wells and town gates. For the rest, the house owners were obliged to pave the streets. The gutter laid in the middle was the boundary of the "stone ways" of the house owners. To supervise the streets, "way-masters" were appointed, who had to renew their oath of office every year. They had to swear to remain incorruptible and to observe the statutory road-building period, mostly from All Saints to St. Gertrude's day (November to March), with respect to all repair work ordered. To conserve the road paving, there were regulations called road acts, which prohibited the use of metal-tyred wheels. Only wagons "which go on day-long journeys on imperial highways" were excluded from the prohibition. The highway and traffic police also covers those ordinances dealing with the cleanliness and negotiability of the roads. Their provisions overlap those

Street-cleaning, carting off of refuse by peasants' wagons.

of the public health, fire and public order police. Dung, for example, was allowed to be deposited in front of houses only for a limited time. Some towns set up a "refuse cartage" system, i.e., a municipal "muck wagon" regularly carted off the refuse swept into heaps in front of the houses, against payment. During building work, timber was not allowed to lie on the street for more than three days. Free passage for fire-fighting vehicles through the streets had to be ensured at all times. To check this, a rod of specified length was held crosswise and carried through the alleys. Where it touched the sides the prescribed minimum width had not been adhered to and immediate alterations had to be made.

Street lighting regulations are of more recent date. Night-life was unknown in the Middle Ages. The day ended at sundown and the people went to bed. So there was no need for street lighting. If a citizen ever left his house after dark, he took his lantern. In Rothenburg, any person found on the street after dark without a lighted lantern was regarded as a "Fensterer" (a Don Juan who climbs through windows) and had to pay a fine of 4 imperial thalers (1617). And there were times in which parents were punished, if they allowed their children to roam around. The police regulations of 1745 read:

> ". . . young servants stay out late at night in the streets with no other intention than to seek wanton women . . . wherefore no young servant shall stay in the streets after 10 in summer and after 8 in winter, otherwise he shall be taken forthwith to the imperial court, and punished as a "Fensterer" with a fine of 4 thalers."
> "It has proved of late that among the young persons of the female sex there is no small number of brazen women who, forgetting God and all morals, run after soldiers, wherever they come from, not only in the streets but also in the inns, go dancing and offer their wanton bodies . . ."

Increasing numbers of thefts and attacks at night and the resulting diminution of security and order induced the authorities to urge a general duty to provide lighting. Soon, therefore, there were ordinances requiring permanent lighting of the streets. A lighted lantern had to be hung on every third house, all house owners having to take over this duty in rotation every three days. As observance of these ordinances was very desultory, repeated reminders had to be given. All this finally led to public street lighting provided by the towns.

Public Order Police

Numerous ordinances were issued to maintain peace and order. Many towns had promulgated town peace statutes to counter the settling of differences in public. Every freeman had the right to carry a weapon at all times, and in disputes the temptation to use it was naturally great. Since it was difficult to abrogate the right to bear arms, because in time of war the citizen was required to do so, the only possibility was to limit the carrying of weapons. For instance, strangers were forbidden to bear arms in the town. Innkeepers and their servants were instructed to draw strangers' attention to the ban and to report cases of non-observance. The size of the dagger permitted to be carried was laid down and to prevent arbitrary interpretation of the ordinance a "specimen dagger" was displayed at a place accessible to all (town hall or gate). The penalties were severe: "Should any man secretly bear a weapon by day or by night under his coat or in his trousers or in his shoes or in any way, he shall pay two pounds and if he does not have the money his hand shall be cut off."

Strife involving bloodshed was not to be kept secret and so the surgeons, bathhouse keepers and barbers were required to report every wound immediately to the authorities on pain of severe punishment. It likewise appeared necessary to protect meetings of the town council from armed demonstrations. How could a session be held in a due and proper manner, if a petitioner were accompanied by numerous armed men to lend emphasis to his wishes. For this reason it was ordained that no citizen might appear before the council bearing arms.

The authorities' constant fear of violent changes in the distribution of power found expression in numerous ordinances. Many of them made reference to the "Golden Bull" issued by Emperor Charles IV in 1356, which prohibited secret meetings and secret assembly on pain of punishment. Especially in periods of general unrest around 1525 (reformation, peasants' war), during and after the Thirty Years War and then again towards the end of the 18th century, such ordinances were the order of the day. In Rothenburg, for example, a town councillor had to be present at the regular meetings of craftsmen. Extraordinary meetings had to be agreed upon with the Burgomaster. The authorities fear of seditious influences from outside went so far that the sworn master craftsmen had to take an oath every year after the council elections that any letter to local craftsmen from another town would not be opened, but first submitted to the burgomaster for inspection. So as far as freedom of opinion was concerned, the citizens were really in a sorry state. To nip any unrest in the population in the bud, in 1778 the council of the imperial city of Rothenburg forbade discussion of public affairs in inns and on public squares. The ordinance reads:

> "It is generally and at all times improper and impermissible for private persons to venture to express open, hasty, untimely and biassed opinions on government business and affairs."

In this connection, however, it should be noted that on the whole the population obediently supported their authorities.

VOrweiser dieses

reiſe unter heutigem dato von hier / als einem von
aller Contagion und Seuche GOtt Lob! reinen und
geſunden Ort ab / welches / zu deſto beſſern fort=
kommen / unter hieſiger Statt angedrucktem Canzley=Secret hiermit
beurkundet wird.

Rotenburg auf der Tauber den　　Anno 172

DAß Vorweiſer dieſes

Alters ohngefähr　　　Jahr　　　Statur
Geſichts /　　Haaren
gekleidet / von hier / als einem GOtt Lob! geſund=
und uninficirten Ort mit einem beglaubten Paß komme
und zu raiſen willens / wird
hiermit atteſtiret ; daher Jedermänniglich erſucht wird /
frey / ſicher und ungehindert paſſiren zu laſſen.
Urkundlich des hierunter gedruckten Canzley = Secrets.
Geſchehen Rotenburg auf der Tauber den
Anno 171

Certificate of exit from a pestilence-free area
Two official forms of the town of Rothenburg, 18th cent. (see also p. 232)

260

It was the duty of the general public to suppress breaches of the peace. No one was permitted to evade that duty. In the event of a murder or serious wounding, the "hue and cry" was raised, the loud shouts in the streets. At the sound of the cry "To the rescue!", which passed from mouth to mouth, the watchmen closed the gates to prevent the criminal's escape, the citizens left their work and homes to answer the call, and the burgomaster sent the tipstaffs to seize the criminal. It is evident from some police regulations that, although it was the general duty of all citizens to pursue a disturber of the peace, money rewards were offered to those who brought in or reported such criminals.

In the daytime it was relatively simple to preserve public security in the town, but not at night. For then the lawbreaker could count on the protection of darkness in performing his deed.

As a means of general protection, therefore, regular internal watches were organized. The watch went on duty every evening. Half the men remained in the watch-house as reliefs, while the others, three or four men, depending on the size of the town, patrolled the streets singly, each in the part of town assigned to him. Patrols were relieved every two hours. The watch lasted from 9 p.m. to 5 a.m. in winter and from 10 p.m. to 4 a.m. in summer. Such night-watchmen carried the watchman's pike, a lantern and a bugle. A further security measure was the mandatory carrying of a lantern at night. The prevailing view at that time was that any one not carrying a lantern had evil intentions.

Since nighttime revellers impaired security, though mostly in a harmless manner, it was another logical step to restrict the opening hours of inns. Innkeepers were not allowed to serve anything after the second or third ringing of the evening bell. For this reason, the evening bell was also called the drink, beer or wine bell. But customers were allowed to stay for another hour. Thus official "closing hours" were born, 8 p.m. in winter and 10 p.m. in summer. People had to take the shortest route home. No one was allowed in the streets at night without good reason, streets and squares were deserted, only the night-watchman was on his rounds.

The functions of the public order police also embraced regulations covering strangers and local residence. If a stranger wanted to pass in at the gate, the watchman subjected him to a thorough check and questioning. If there were still doubts about the information given, he had to swear an oath confirming it. But despite the oath, he was not allowed into town unless he was completely unsuspicious and his stay was agreeable to the council. In times of political unrest, the innkeepers even had to submit to the burgomaster or the officer of the watch every evening a list of all persons staying overnight. A citizen was allowed to accommodate private guests only with the express permission of the Rothenburg council. Journeymen craftsmen wandering the country to satisfy guild requirements were not allowed to enter the town without further ado. They had to present at the gate credentials (the later "wander-book"), in which the last entry was not more than three months old. If they were allowed to enter, then only on condition that they leave the town again within a day, if they found no job. They had to leave their "wanderer's bundle", i.e. their personal property, at the gate as security.

The "residence police" of olden times had similarities with present-day passport and personal status registration systems. The old system, however, had nothing like the perfection of our present residents registration offices. It comprised rather ordinances permitting the authorities an overview of the population within their bailiwick and its composition. Even the capitularies of the Carolingian period contained provisions on the setting up of lists with which the make-up of the population could be determined, the first beginnings of the residents registration system. The towns also began to keep "Bürgerbücher" (citizens registers) at an early date. But only the newcomers were entered in the latter. Any person who wanted to claim the protection of a municipal community had to become a citizen. This personal right was not hereditary and could only be obtained by swearing the citizen's oath. Because admission as a citizen brought advantages, there were also conditions attached. The applicant had to prove that he was born in wedlock, not a bondsman or subject of some other sovereign territory, and not involved in a trial or dispute before an outside court. As the towns were committed to give support to relatives of a citizen in cases of hardship, though to a much less extent than now, the council demanded that applicants provide proof of their capital. Craftsmen, who on settling down mostly had but little capital, had to submit their apprentice's indenture, provide proof of three to four years itinerant journeyman's practice, and to make a "master-piece". All this to demonstrate that they could earn their own living. For all that, initially they were granted citizen's rights only for a limited period. On the expiry of that period, the citizen's rights were made permanent or denied. On his acceptance as a citizen, the applicant had to swear the "citizen's oath", with which he vowed:

1. to stay loyal to the town
2. to obey the town council
3. to seek his rights only before the town court
4. to report immediately all that might harm the town or council
5. to pay taxes punctually
6. not to move away without the council's permission (mostly coupled with the obligation not to move away before the expiry of a certain number of years)

7. on relinquishing his citizen's rights to pay the so-called "Nachsteuer" (retroactive tax).

After taking the oath, the "Bürgergeld" (citizenship fee) had to be paid, the amount of which varied.

Since, with a few exceptions, every citizen was obliged to defend the town in the case of war, every new citizen had to possess his own weapons and prove that he was well-versed in their use. Exceptions from these conditions of acceptance were made only in isolated cases, for example where the admission of individuals or groups was of special interest to the town on account of their abilities or vocations. Such exceptional agreements were concluded individually between the town and the applicant. For instance, for the so-called "Pfahlbürger" (pale citizens), most of whom were day-labourers, who lived outside the walls but within the protective pale of the town and were indispensable to the citizens for garden and field work, particularly low tax rates were laid down. To stimulate the town's economy and increase the tax yield, special tax concessions were granted from time to time to attract wealthy persons to the town.

If a person wanted to give up his citizen's rights and leave the town, he had to prove that he had paid all his debts in the town, pay the retroactive tax and swear the valedictory oath.

Based on the view that the property of the individual citizen had to serve the community, the towns tried to extract further benefits from those who moved away. It had always been forbidden to sell land or rights to land to non-citizens, and on relinquishing citizen's rights such land or rights had to be sold to a resident citizen within a year, after which they were forfeit to the town.

Citizen's rights could also be withdrawn as a punishment. They were abrogated permanently for betrayal of the town, burgomaster and council, for disobedience and participation in riots, for answering a summons to an outside court, and for capital crimes such as murder and manslaughter. Temporary loss of citizen's rights was imposed for severe bodily harm, contravention of the bans on money-lending, serving wine, and playing dice and games of chance.

Public Morals Police

Theoretically it is perfectly conceivable that a community could prosper, if the laws were restricted exclusively to vital essentials and the individual member of the community were allowed absolute freedom in his personal way of life. But from what has been said up to now, it is apparent that there were many ordinances which influenced and governed the human way of life. This is even more true, however, of the police regulations dealing with customs and morals. In order to assess the "public morals police" it is necessary to know its historical development.

People in olden times lived in tribes, entrammeled in the customs and usages of their "folk". There was no uniform religion nor even a more or less official class of priests, and the concept of "sin" was largely unknown. Germanic law, for example, knew practically no punishments for breaches of customs and morals with the exception of adultery. A change in thinking on "good" and "evil" was first initiated by contact and partial mixing with other tribal peoples during the period of the great migrations (4th to 6th century). Christianity, prized as a new philosophy and new morality from the 2nd century onwards, then exerted the strongest and most decisive influence. How could a new world of thought and moral doctrine be inculcated into a person in those days in any other way than by commandments. The secular lords who had been converted to Christianity placed their power in the service of the church and thus helped to convert those tribes who still clung to their old beliefs and to wipe out heathen customs (Charles the Great, king of the Franks from 768, Holy Roman Emperor from 800 onwards, died 814). Because they were imposed from above by the authorities, many of the new, and now ecclesiastical rules of life were similar to the later police regulations. The advancing civilization in the towns and the congealing of the spirit of the church into superficial forms then resulted in the authorities actually issuing regulations which governed not only the behaviour of people within the community, but also their "private lives" in so far as they ran counter to church conceptions. The mediaeval notion that no "sin" should go unpunished and that a sinner had to be called to account here on earth in order to establish a good relationship of the community to God gave the final impetus for the promulgation of those "public morals" police regulations which, on pain of punishment, regulated private life, in some respects right down to the smallest detail, which really should have been a function of church education work.

Marriage Regulations
It is not the purpose of this essay to give a thorough insight into Germanic marriage law. But for a better understanding of the later marriage regulations it is necessary to explain the basic forms of concluding marriage and marriage structures under Germanic law. Germanic law knew several forms of concluding marriage and hence various types of marriage; but up to the present, scientists have been unable to reach any final agreement on their significance. However, on the basis of the procedures leading up to marriage we can distinguish among four forms of marriage.

1. The "mund" marriage; this was the most usual mode of marriage. The leading role in concluding the contract fell to the bridegroom, while the bride was merely an object of the contract by reason of the existing ties under tribal law and her consent carried no legal weight, although not infrequently her wishes were taken into consideration. The contract between the bridegroom and the bride's family, for which the term "Verlobung" (betrothal) is used in later folk laws, committed the bride's family to hand the woman over to the bridegroom and give him marital authority (mund) over her. The bridegroom was committed to take the bride home and set up a marital community with her.

At the betrothal, the bridegroom had to pay a "bride-price" or at least a down payment to the bride's family. The changes in the significance of this bride-price, or bride-gift, over the course of time must be neglected in this essay; it would seem important, however, that the bride-price paid to the family became the so-called dowry, later given to the bride herself, and served as the foundation for her widow's subsistence, which was not provided for by the law of succession. Breaking of the betrothal had legal consequences. Infidelity of the bride during the betrothal period was regarded as adultery. If the bridegroom or bride married another person, a fine was payable.

The marital community was established by formal legal acts. The wedding ceremony gave the bridegroom authority over the bride. It took place in ceremonial form, the bride being handed over to the husband by symbolic actions such as setting her on his knee and other rites customary at an adoption. The marriage was consummated, however, by the ceremonial leading of the bride to the man's home, which was followed by the wedding repast and by the couple repairing to the marriage bed in the presence of the relatives (cohabitation). The leading home and cohabitation made the bride a wife with all that involved with respect to the family, house and personal status. On the morning following the first night, the husband handed the wife the morning gift in recognition of her status as mistress of the house; the morning gift mostly comprised cattle, a harnessed horse and weapons. In later times, it often consisted of other objects, which again became part of her widow's fund.

2. Marriage by capture. The match-making effect of the capture of women can be explained as follows: the folk laws made no distinction between capture and abduction. According to the Lex Salica, capture was any removal of a girl from the power of her guardian (holder of authority)

against his will, without any importance being attached to the will of the captured girl. Capture resulted in initiation of a feud by the woman's family. Whether or not the object was to recover the woman is a matter of conjecture. The folk laws imposed a fine on the abductor, but initially did not require the return of the woman to her family; this could only be compelled by the feud. If avenging action was not taken or was unsuccessful, the marital community undoubtedly persisted because it was not the capture, but the manifestly established conjugal community which created the marriage. In the case of a marriage by capture or abduction, the wife lost her right to inherit from relatives. The husband had no "mund" (Latin: manus) over her unless he acquired it subsequently from the holder of authority. The marriage resulting from abduction was more or less a marriage by consent.

3. The marriage by consent (Friedelehe) was based on the free will and mutual consent of the man and woman. In this case, in contrast to concubinage, the marital community was established by publicly leading the bride home and by cohabitation. There was no wedding ceremony, because the woman was not under the man's control, nor was a bride-price paid. But on the morning following the first night, the wife received the morning gift. The social function of this sort of marriage was characterized by the fact that there was no manus involved in the marital relationship and the wife's legal position relative to her husband was much stronger than in a "mund" marriage. For instance, she had the right to take unilateral action for divorce. Marriage by consent appears to have been chosen primarily by women of rank who did not want to place themselves under the control of a man who was possibly of lower rank, and when a man "married into" the house of the bride's father. This marriage by consent permitted the practice of polygyny by the nobles, since in addition to a mund marriage the man could have any number of "free consorts" (Friedel). A marriage by consent could be transformed into a mund marriage, if the husband subsequently paid the mund-dowry. This form of marriage by consent resembles the "morganatic marriage" ("left-handed marriage") which made it possible up to well into the 18th century to conclude marriages with a woman of different rank without her being raised to the husband's rank or acquiring the right to inherit from the husband.

4. Marriage by unilateral disposition was made possible by the fact that the freeman was given control over the unfree woman by the law of property. This gave the lord control over the conjugal relationships among his bondmen and bondwomen, which at least in the Frankish era was regarded as marriage. Moreover, the freeman could also take his own bondwoman,

who was subject to his authority also in sexual respects, as his consort. This gave rise to concubinage. Originally it was certainly not a marriage, but where there was a suitable possibility of termination it could take on marriage-like features. Such marriages were based on the command of the man.

The assertion that the mund marriage was the only legitimate type of marriage in the age of the Germanic law and that in comparison all other forms must be considered inferior can no longer be upheld. However, the special importance of the mund marriage, especially in the light of its so-called "marital effects", justifies our disregarding the other forms of marriage in this essay. Under Germanic law, the relationship between spouses was characterized by the inferior legal status of the wife. In a mund marriage, the wife was under the control of the husband. The mund marriage gave the husband rights over the wife such as punishment (death penalty), repudiation or sale in the case of genuine need. Only the wife was committed to monogamy and marital fidelity and generally she also had no dispositive authority over the children, had no legal capacity, and the husband took her property under his control, administered it and enjoyed the benefits. He was also liable for any offence committed by the wife.

These rights which were vested in the husband, above all the right of polygamy, were a challenge to the church to intervene. In point of fact, the church ought to have recognized the marriage by consent, which required the consent of the woman to marriage, as the only legitimate type of marriage. But the church's degradation of marriage by consent to concubinage and fornication had its origin in the structure of this type of marriage, which was in contradiction to the Christian notion of marriage. Christ had raised monogamous marriage to the dignity of a sacrament, i.e., an unbreakable bond between one man and one woman in a physical and spiritual community. Marriage by consent, on the other hand, favoured polygamy because in addition to his mund marriage the husband could have any number of "free consorts" (Charles the Great and Himiltrud). Also the ease with which it could be dissolved, the frequent abstention in Frankish times from public conclusion of a marriage, and also the equal status of man and wife brought about by marriage by consent were contrary to the holy scriptures according to the then prevailing view. All this explains the influence exerted by the church on the recognition of the mund marriage as the only "right marriage".

Furthermore, the differences in the assessment of impediments to marriage should not be forgotten. Germanic law knew only a limited number of impediments, e.g. sexual immaturity; peacelessness which made it impossible to take the bride home in public; marriage among very close relatives (with a person's own issue); and polygamy on the part of a woman. Over and above this, there was a number of countermeasures to hinder marriages regarded as contraventions of the law or a disturbance of community order. The latter included marriage to the wife or bride of another during his lifetime, marriage of a free woman and unfree man (only the freeman could take his bondwoman as a consort), and occasionally marriage of members of different tribes. Church influence was responsible for extending the impediment to marriage between relatives and also for including relatives by marriage. In addition, new impediments were introduced such as ecclesiastical kinship or the vow of celibacy. The recognition of the mund marriage as the only lawful marriage by the church likewise explains why the church clung to the observance of the procedures customary in the mund marriage such as betrothal, dowry and wedding ceremony. The idea of making marriage dependent also on the consent of the woman resulted in the introduction into secular law in Frankish times of a ban on marrying a woman against her will. With the growing importance of canon law for marriage law, the woman received the right of self-betrothal. The marriage was concluded by both parties expressing their consent within the circle and with the approval of the relatives. All other requirements (wedding ceremony, taking home and cohabitation) were now only of subsidiary importance for the conclusion of the marriage. Gradually the position of the holder of authority was taken over by a chosen guardian who gave the couple to each other. The position of the "Trauvormund" (marriage guardian), however, was transformed; he became the one who asked whether the parties consented. The "Trauvormund" could be either a member of the clergy or a layman. Then, in the 12th century, church regulations forbade marriage by a layman and made participation of a priest and the posting of banns obligatory. The object was to supervise observance of the impediments to marriage. The introduction of the consent of the woman to marriage and the lack of any public form of concluding marriage, however, then resulted in declarations of consent to marriage made informally and without witnesses being regarded as valid, which led to considerable abuses despite the threat of spiritual and temporal punishment.

The transition from the Middle Ages to modern times brought a loosening of family ties and the old, geographically restricted social groupings. The political, social, economic and religious upheavals of those days caused disorder in married life as a result of the degeneration of morals. The personal marriage law that had been under church influence since the Middle Ages and had been developed along ecclesiastical lines lost much of its authority as a result of the Reformation. In large segments of the population it had been forgotten or had at least become unclear. It was the function of the police regulations to remedy this deplorable situation. Their object was to enlighten and, by threatening punishment, counteract disregard of church norms. It was intended to strengthen the importance of marriage for the existence of the community. The marriage law of the pre-Tridentine period was very reticent on this point. The Tridentine Council held at the instigation of Emperor Charles V took a decisive step in its third group of sessions (1562/63) by making the validity of a marriage dependent on its publication by the church. The marriage regulations subsequently issued by the authorities, however, went much further and attempted to hinder marriages which seemed objectionable to the community, to ensure public conclusion of marriages, and to ensure the disclosure of impediments to marriage by appropriate measures. The betrothal was deemed to have marriage-establishing force. A promise to marry or the marriage bond created by betrothal was so strong that it could be cancelled only by a resolution of the council. Persons who failed to keep their promise to marry were punished. A promise to marry entailed the obligation to marry in church. A mutual declaration of willingness to marry by the parties was sufficient for concluding a marriage, but the marriage regulations also required that the future spouses must have it proclaimed from the church pulpit at once and after the third reading of the banns have themselves married in church within three months. The wedding had to precede consummation. This was also the reason for the order: "but beforehand and before this has happened, they shall abstain entirely and in all circumstances from all and any witting and other dishonourable deed, fornication or cohabitation." In old records, entries can often be found, which show that married couples were punished because the wife gave birth to a child too early (before the end of 7 months).

The marriage ceremony was not an act establishing rights, but merely a declaratory one, although it presupposed that the church had established the willingness to marry by questioning the couple. Performance of the ceremony was therefore the public declaration of the marriage and its confirmation. The attempt made by police law to compel marriage in church by means of the marriage regulations was mainly in order to prevent secret marriages. Secret marriages were perfectly possible under pre-Tridentine law. But they were a great danger to the "order of marriage" and hence also to the community. Because they were difficult to prove, they could, under certain circumstances, entail disadvantages (inheritance rights) for the secret spouses and also for any issue. They facilitated bigamy and avoidance of impediments (marriage between relatives) and entailed in general a great deal of harm and moral confusion. Secret marriages concluded by the partners promising marriage on their own and without witnesses were punishable. The clergy, parents and heads of houses were instructed to warn young people, their children and their servants against such secret marriages. The clergy were forbidden to read the banns for people who had joined themselves secretly in matrimony, to say nothing of marrying them in church. Persons who left the territory to avoid the ban and conclude a secret marriage in some other sovereign territory were not allowed to return to their home.

It was laid down that a marriage could be entered into only with the approval of the parents. In this respect, however, there were differences in the marriage regulations; some prescribed approval for every age group, others called for approval only until the children had reached a certain age. Even in the case of widowed children who wanted to remarry, the approval of the parents was still demanded, though more out of a sense of decorum than for legal reasons. If children were still minors, approval could be refused without giving any reason. In the case of older children, reasons had to be stated for a refusal. Inequality of personal status, rank or origin, a disorderly life, bad reputation or a hereditary disease of the other party were grounds for refusal. A further ground for refusal was justifiable doubts as to whether provision for the future family was ensured. But approval could not be denied without cogent reasons. If this happened, the approval could be optained from the authorities.

In that case, the parents could not evade their duty to provide a dowry. If parental approval had not been given and the children had wilfully and deceitfully promised each other marriage, the parents could refuse the marriage portion. In addition, the couple was punished and it often happened that such a promise of marriage was officially "abrogated and declared null and void".

The marriage regulations devoted a lot of space to marriage impediments. In the majority of cases they were identical with those of marriage law, but some were first introduced by police law.

Under canon and secular marriage law, capacity to marry was dependent on sexual maturity and a mental capacity which was mostly related to the legal majority attained at a later age. But the marriage regulations often went further. Some marriage regulations prohibited marriages between too young persons, even when the parents' approval had been given. The reasons were that young persons had no property, had not yet learnt a vocation and were not in a position to run an orderly household; they married in a downright beggarly condition, became a burden on the alms box and thus deprived other needy persons.

The marriage law of the church was applied with respect to the impediment of close relationship. Every one was obliged to make sure whether such impediments to marriage existed. Before reading the banns, the clergy had to ascertain "whether such people can marry without impediment in accordance with divine and natural law so that they need not subsequently part from each other as a result of ignorance or of shame and scandal". In doubtful cases, the priest had to take the couple to the burgomaster and await his decision.

If widowed persons wanted to remarry, they could do so only after the end of the period of mourning and previous settling of children's property. But often a long period of mourning could not be observed. In the case of widowers owing to lack of care for the children, in the case of widows owing to financial difficulties. So the needs of everyday life made early remarriage urgent. The marriage regulations therefore prescribed that a new marriage could be concluded only after the expiry of a period of mourning of at least three months. Widows who were with child from their deceased husband were not allowed to remarry until after the birth of the child. Remarriage prior to the end of the mourning period entailed loss of the estate of the deceased spouse.

Serfs could be married only with the permission of their master. If serfs belonging to two different masters wanted to marry, the approval of both masters was necessary. Since the wife, despite her marriage and possible moving away was not released from the bondage into which she was born, the children resulting from the marriage had to be divided between the two masters. In this respect, the police marriage regulations made allowance for the continued existence of mediaeval land law.

Marriage between nobles and ordinary citizens required the approval of the territorial sovereign. If it was not procured, the marriage still remained valid, but the marriage contract regulating property rights and the right of succession of the woman and children was null and void.

Similar provisions to those banning marriage between too young people were applied to the sick and invalids. It was realized that harm could result from the marriage of epileptics, so the authorities were instructed to prevent the marriage of such persons. The inmates of hospitals for incurables could hardly be legally forbidden to marry, but obstacles were placed in their way by ordering that they must leave the hospital after their marriage. This was done to prevent families from moving into the hospitals and imposing an additional burden on the poor relief system.

To summarize, the marriage law of early modern times (from 1500 onwards) was characterized by the introduction of mandatory formal provisions on the declaration of consent to marriage, observance of which was a precondition for the validity of a marriage. The consistent further development of modern marriage law then led to the civil marriage (obligatory or mandatory civil marriage). This type of marriage makes validity of a marriage dependent on declarations of consent before a government agency. The breakthrough to civil marriage, i.e., obligatory civil marriage, was brought by the French Revolution (1793), since the revolutionary state no longer considered itself a Christian state and rejected the Christian wedding and any church claim to competence. This was reflected in the Code Civil of 1803. Following similar demands made by the Frankfurt national assembly in 1849, civil marriage was introduced at first in isolated places (e.g. Frankfurt on Main, 1850) and then in the entire German empire by the imperial act of February 6, 1875; it was later taken over by the Civil Code (1900) and the Marriage Act of 1938.

With regard to divorce, the notion that marriage was an indissoluble legal bond between spouses was alien to Germanic legal thought. The marriage could be dissolved, not only by the death or outlawing of a spouse, but also by unilateral or bilateral termination of the marital community. A marriage by consent could be dissolved at will by either the man or the woman. In the case of the mund marriage, divorce was effected by an agreement between the families (though only as long as the latter retained their legal significance) or, later on, between husband and wife. It was also possible by unilateral action, though as a rule this was an exclusively male prerogative (repudiation). If the repudiation was not based on grave unlawful conduct of the woman (as laid down in Roman law: adultery, witchcraft and desecration of graves) or on a "failing", e.g. barrenness, the man evoked the vengeance of the woman's family. Under the folk laws, he was liable to atonement. The woman's right to leave her husband gained acceptance only in isolated cases, above all in consequence of the influence of Roman law. A separation brought about by a woman was not merely unjustified dissolution of the marital community, but also a violation of the husband's mund.

As Christianity spread, the influence of the church on divorce law gradually made itself felt, leading to the obstruction or abolition of divorce in keeping with the principle of indissolubility. The tenet of canon law that a duly concluded and consummated marriage between Christians could be dissolved only by death did not become fully effective, however, until the church attained exclusive legislative and jurisdictional authority with respect to marriage.

It was not until the Reformation that divorce was reintroduced. The significance of marriage as a sacrament was denied by the reformers, thus destroying the theological foundation of the conception of the indissolubility of Christian marriage. True, the Protestant church still clung to the basic idea of the indissolubility of marriage, but where there were serious reasons it granted divorce and the right to remarry, inferring this from the Bible, Matth. 5,31 and 32; 19,3–9 and Corinth. I, 7,15. This development was furthered by the fact that in Protestant states, which also included the imperial cities, the secular authorities were simultaneously the authorities for the church. They appointed and discharged the clergy and also made church "visitations" (inspections). The situation was different in the Catholic states. The facilitation of divorce and its general introduction in the 18th century under the influence of the Enlightenment could not be emulated by the Catholic states. Out of tolerance, however, they permitted divorces of Protestants, but not of Catholics. If a marriage was ruined, Catholics' attention was drawn to the possibility of separation a mensa et thoro (from bed and board). The decisive breakthrough for Germany came with the imperial enactment of February 6, 1875; under Art. 77 dissolution of a marriage was then possible. But it was not until the introduction of the Civil Code in 1900 that a divorce law became valid and effective for all citizens regardless of their religion.

Other public morals regulations

The degeneration of morals and growing licentiousness, especially during and after the Thirty Years War, resulted in numerous ordinances. The clergy were instructed to read the marriage regulations from the pulpit several times a year and appeal to the conscience of their congregations not to lead a reprehensible, licentious and un-Christian life. In rural areas, the spinning-rooms were forbidden from time to time because, in the words of the ordinances, "useless gossip and voluptuousness was practiced there". Punishments were also inflicted on "nightly gallivanting with wanton women and loose window-wooing at night". The night-watchmen were instructed to keep a special eye on haunts in which suspicious or licentious activities could be practiced. A frequent subject of prohibitions was the mixed accommodation of servants in rural areas because "most pregnancies in the country are due to their lying together". They provided for fines to be paid by the masters, if the servants were not separated by sexes. Procuring for immoral purposes or tacit toleration of fornication were also made punishable. In the public account books, whole series of fines are recorded, which had to be paid by parents for tolerating such things. The basic object of all these ordinances was to permit sexual intercourse only within the legal marriage system and otherwise to prevent it. Only in this way could public nuisances be avoided, the Christian moral law be observed, a sound population policy be pursued and the wrath and punishment of God be averted from the country. Hence, it appears understandable that on moral issues, in contrast to other spheres, the authorities were very strict and did not shrink from inflicting punishment. In addition to tower (prison) and pecuniary penalties, therefore, church punishments were imposed, of which there were numerous variations. By way of illustration of this type of punishment, here are a few examples from Rothenburg's history: For starting malicious gossip about a woman, a certain Thomas Merklin of Tottenheim was condemned and swore in an oath of truce:

> "that in Tottenheim in the church, on a Sunday on which mass is sung, I shall stand in public below the pulpit and say what I have said and spread around about the woman thereby causing her harm and out of envy and hate doing her wrong though she is perfectly innocent ... Friday after Simon and Judas, 1406." St.A.R.U.No. 695).

Peter Karbacher, former forester of Schweinsdorf, was convicted of extramarital intercourse on May 28, 1671, sentenced to a fine of 818 pounds and the further punishment:

> "that during the morning sermon he must stand beside the town tipstaff before the local church door with bared head, arms and legs and carrying a rod in his hand until divine service is over." (St.A.R.Rech.Bd. 1671).

In 1543, a woman charged with slander and blasphemy had to

> "run around the baptismal font a number of times with a wax candle to the derision of all . . ." (St.A.R.Bd. 332, Fol. 8 b.)

Under canon law, derived from Exodus XXII, 16 and Leviticus XXII, 28 and 29, extramarital intercourse obligated the seducer to provide the dowry for the seduced woman and, if the father or guardian agreed, to marry her. The parents of an illegitimate child invariably had to pay a fine. Illegitimacy was a lifelong blemish. As a rule, for instance, a person born out of wedlock could never attain citizen's rights or admission to a craft (guilds). The majority of cases that came before the courts were morals cases and the revenue from fines collected in this field was correspondingly high.

Despite this ordained moral stringency, it was impossible to avoid concessions to moral corruption, i.e. with regard to the attitude of the authorities to prostitution. Of course, one disapproved of what the doctrines of Christian religion termed a sinful thing, but placated one's conscience with the thought that it was an unavoidable necessity. It was the policy of choosing the lesser evil which persuaded the towns to tolerate, or even grant privileges to, houses of ill fame, which were also known as bagnios, bawdy houses, whorehouses, "courts of the frail sisterhood", or "nunneries". Presumably the town fathers were sufficiently realistic to believe that they could supervise a phenomenon which had proved impossible to stamp out anywhere in the world more efficiently by collecting the harlots in closed houses. These houses were mostly the property of the town and were leased out to the "procurers" or whore-masters for a certain, by no means low weekly rent. All procurers had to give their oath that the regulations would be observed. The "inmates" had to be recruited exclusively from non-residents and only unmarried female persons could be taken in. The procurer was responsible to the authorities for everything that went on in the house. He had to feed and pay the prostitutes properly, was not allowed to take away presents given them by customers and had to care for them when they were ill, but had to report infectious diseases immediately. He also had to allow the prostitutes to move out of the house at any time, if they wished. The official supervision of the brothels was often taken over by the town council itself or by its lowliest official, the executioner. The courtesans, wenches or ladies of easy virtue were compelled to wear conspicuous clothing characteristic of their calling. In Rothenburg a red-and-white kerchief, in Augsburg merely a strip of green material two fingers wide on their veil, and in Leipzig short yellow mantles on which blue cords were sewn. The social status of the "filles de joie" varied greatly. In some towns they were treated very strictly and on their death they were buried at the knacker's yard. In other towns they enjoyed certain privileges, as in Nuremberg where they were entitled to attend dances at the city hall, or in Frankfurt where they were allowed to take part in patricians' weddings.

Bathing in mediaeval towns was also governed by police regulations. The bathhouses or bagnios were very popular and a visit to them was not only a hygienic necessity, but also one of the biggest amusements of those times. The only objectionable aspect was that the sexes bathed together and that drinking bouts and extensive feasting were carried on. Eventually, such lustful debauchery developed in the bathhouses that they became haunts of lechery. The police regulations took action against this. Mixed bathing of men and women was prohibited, and it was ordered that men might be attended only by men and women by women. The growing incidence of venereal diseases, especially syphilis, made strict regulations essential. The bathhouse keepers had to refuse to admit persons obviously suffering from any such disease, and knives and instruments with which such patients had been treated were not allowed to be used in the bathhouse.

The so-called "shameful dances" were also a great annoyance to the authorities. This term was applied, not to the sedate, ceremonial round dances of the patricians, but to the earthy, leaping dances with which the common people amused themselves. The most popular were the "Hoppeldei", the "Heierleis", the "Firelfei" and the "Firlefanz", wild, rollicking and very unrestrained dances. The church declaimed such unruly frolics and condemned them as devilish. And so the authorities could do no less, especially since, under the influence of alcohol, leaps and whirls became ever wilder and skirts flew too high. Under such circumstances, the necessity of such bans is understandable, particularly considering that in those days the women wore no drawers under their skirts. Here are just two examples: Saxon-Meissen police regulations of 1555:

> ". . . wherefore we order, desire and lay down that where henceforth dances are held, whether in towns, hamlets or villages, they shall be chaste and modest; men and women shall be chastely and properly dressed and covered, and unseemly twirling, shouting and other improper conduct shall be completely abstained from and shall be permitted by no man in his courts regardless of his estate . . ."

The Rothenburg police regulations of 1761 prohibited the so-called "schlaiffers-Tantz" . . .

> "through such hefty leaping and dancing which at times nearly exhaust all human strength and through throwing their women dancing partners into the air many a person has already suffered an accident and the days of their lives have been shortened . . . prohibited . . . otherwise every contravener of this well-meaning prohibition shall pay an unabatable fine of 5 imperial Thalers, one third of which is hereby assured to the denunciator or person delivering up the offender."

Observance of such regulations was supervised by the town tipstaffs. The growing prevalence of gambling was also curbed by police regulations. Games of chance were highly popular among men and women of all classes, and even among the clergy. All warnings not to overdo things at gambling were fruitless. As many gamblers lost their homes and land, plunging their families into bitter poverty, the authorities saw themselves constrained to intervene, if only to protect the general public from the resulting burden on the poor relief system. Games played on boards and ball-shooting for low stakes were tolerated, and also card games and dice-throwing for nuts or apples. Persons who played for high stakes were punished by a fine plus the amount won or loss. In some areas, a prison sentence was imposed, its duration depending on the amount won or lost. Innkeepers who had tolerated gambling were likewise punished unless they swore an oath that the gambling took place against their express will. Pursuant to the Rothenburg Statue Book I, for example, it was permitted to lose only what one had on one's person at the time, including the outer garments.

Any promise to pay what had been lost on the following day or within a period set by the winner was null and void;" he can only be stripped of his clothing". Even the present Civil Code, Art. 762, reads: "No liability shall be created by gaming or betting." The community's revenue from fines was quite substantial. To preserve this source of revenue for the public treasury, they finally hit upon the idea of authorizing a concessionaire to organize games of chance, i.e., in effect to contravene the prohibition, against payment of a respectable fee. The passion for gambling was thus diverted into orderly channels and the work of the administration and courts was reduced, for the concessionaire was responsible for due and proper conduct of the gaming. The precursor of the present-day government-run gambling casino was born. In the prohibition of lotto and lottery gambling issued in 1780 in Rothenburg, we find:

"The enormous attraction of respectable winnings and stakes that cannot be compared with the winnings; the resultant greed and persuasive idea of the possibility of receiving such winnings; the deceptive hope of making good losses with the eventual winnings, of progressing from small winnings to larger ones and of thus finally attaining a considerable increase in property without any effort, work or exertion of one's own strength, etc. Such and other like visionary notions have stimulated the passion for gaming in well-to-do and impecunious persons . . ." Secret informers were promised that their names would be kept secret and that they would receive half the fine.

Drunkenness was also recognized at an early date as the cause of harm to health and social downfall, and was combatted with police regulations. The granting of credit by innkeepers was either completely forbidden, so that drink could be served only for cash, or the amount of credit was made dependant on rank, i.e., the rich could be granted higher credits than the poor. If the innkeeper went beyond the credit limit, in the event of a legal dispute with the debtor he was denied the right to the amount in excess of the limit and had to pay that amount as an additional fine. In contrast to the provisions of current criminal law, drunkenness was not recognized as mitigating circumstances. Offenders who advanced the excuse that the crime was committed while drunk were locked in the tower on bread and water for up to a month in addition to the normal punishment. So drunkenness was considered grounds for more severe punishment. Quite generally, the inns were subjected to strict supervision by the authorities. For according to Christian doctrine they were hotbeds of vice and sin. It seems remarkable that, especially in the Middle Ages, despite strict church discipline, no improvement in morals was achieved; on the contrary, rowdyism spread, which found expression in immoderate drinking bouts and uninhibited bad conduct. The sociableness coupled with moderate alcohol consumption, which originally improved interpersonal relations and gave pleasure, deteriorated into profligacy. Blasphemy was the order of the day. Countless regulations in the

In the "drinker's barrel"

17th century contained provisions on cursing, impious swearing and blasphemy. The clergy and the authorities held the view that such action brought the wrath of God on mankind and would entail such punishments as scarcity, war and pestilence. While the regulations on cursing and impious swearing were still formulated in general terms before the 16th century and the citizens amicably admonished to give up their vices, in the 17th century they were much stricter. A person who failed to report a blasphemer was threatend with the same penalty as the offender. And around this time a preciser definition was given of what the council deemed blasphemy, for example in 1612:

". . . that not only God's martyrdom, his cross, sufferings, wounds, baptism, and sacrament, but also God's throne, seat and house as named in the Holy Scriptures, namely heaven, the stars and the firmament are profaned."

According to the statute book of the town of Rothenburg, Title 66, the punishment for a curse was one schilling and the neckiron. In Statute Book I, Title 66, it was laid down that every citizen was entitled to demand one Regensburger (former small coin) from any other citizen he heard "swearing by God". If he failed to pay, on the case being reported the town bailiff had to distrain three Regensburgers. Pursuant to the ordinance of 1654, every offender had to reckon with a fine of 40 pounds after the first curse, the fine and an additional church penance (mostly standing in front of the church door) after the second curse, and with the punishment to life and limb laid down in the "peinliche Halsgerichtsordnung" after the third curse. Even mocking and impertinent talk about religion was still punished in 1764 with deprivation of civic rights, discharge from employment and punishments prescribed by the Halsgerichtsordnung. Persons with well-grounded conscientious doubts, opined the councillors of Rothenburg, should turn to their spiritual adviser and request advice.

It was forbidden to go to fortune-tellers and exorcists for advice and help. The ordinance of 1685 reveals much about the superstitions which were then widespread and persisted stubbornly among the people.

"And as it is not our will to tolerate sorcerers, fortune-tellers, exorcists, blessers, planet-readers, crystal-gazers or hand-readers, sieve-diviners and the like, and in particular gypsies, either in the town or in our rual areas, on discovery not only they shall be unfailingly punished with the tower, pillory, birch, sword and fire in accordance with the divine, ecclesiastical and secular laws and primarily pursuant to the Peinliche Halsgerichtsordnung, but also those who call on their devilish services and no less the blasphemers . . .''

". . . those who run to any fortune-tellers or exorcists in the neighbourhood and seek advice and help there and even from deceitful vagrants in order to enrich themselves all the quicker, and those who buy the so-called devilish mandrake and other magical and superstitious things . . .''

In 1672, for example, Georg von Berg was expelled from the town and the rural area belonging to it

". . . because he bought from an executioner's assistant the thumb of a thief and a piece of a coat and smeared the cocks of beer and wine barrels with them that he might get better receipts."

Similarly, Margareth Nehen was fined 30 pounds for visiting an exorcist.

Ever and again, admonishments to attend divine service and observe holy days were repeated or the ban on going to an inn, a winehouse and the beer brewers during divine service in order to eat, drink, gamble, dance or indulge in other frivolities. Contraventions entailed a fine for the host, too. All trading was forbidden during divine service. The general stores had to stay closed. No work was permitted either in the house or in the fields, nor could livestock be driven anywhere. Untiringly the council admonished the people to observe the Sabbath by zealously listening to the word of God and after church to avoid opulent living by extravagant eating and noise-making in the inns. Meetings of craftsmen and guilds were prohibited on Sundays and holy days, as were dances and other amusements. In 1696, the council ordered citizens outside the town to attend church there. In view of the generally profligate and sinful way of life, on occasions the council even ordained special days of repentance and prayer, on which everything that gave pleasure was forbidden.

It should be noted, however, that formerly there were considerably more public holidays than at present.

"It is the will of the honourable council that the days hereinafter named be proclaimed holy days and observed in a manner befitting Christians. The New Year's day, Epiphany, Candlemas, St. Matthew the Apostle, Annunciation (Lady Day), in Passion Week Wednesday, Thursday, Friday, Holy Easter Day together with the following Easter Monday, St. Phillip, St. Jacob the Apostles, our Lord's Ascension, Holy Whitsunday together with the following Whit-Monday, Holy Trinity, Post-Trinity, St. John the Baptist, St. Peter and St. Paul the Apostles, Visitation of Our Lady, St. Jacob the Apostle, St. Bartholomew the Apostle, St. Thomas the Apostle, St. Somonis and Judae the Apostles, St. Andrew the Apostle, St. Thomas the Apostle, holy Christmas day together with the following St. Stephan and St. John's day."

Since Rothenburg was Protestant from 1544 onwards and according to Luther's teachings the clergy were subordinate to the temporal powers, the council was the superior authority of the church. Every year, therefore, a so-called church "visitation" took place at which the consistory, comprising 3 members of the council and 3 clergymen, examined not only the minister, but also the whole community. Every one had to appear. "Woman and man, child and servant, young and old, and no one excepted". Knowledge of the catechism was tested and woe betide anybody who could not answer correctly. However, devastating conditions must have prevailed at divine service. This is demonstrated by the ever new ordinances which were issued; they were full of admonishments and prohibitions. A few examples: "Dogs may not be taken into church; no one shall dare to wear slippers to church for Holy Communion; it is forbidden to step on the organ; on Ash Wednesday one should go to confessions not only in outwardly honourable clothing, but also with inward repentance; boys will kindly sit on the long benches, the little girls on the women's chairs; do not enter the church with a tobacco pipe in your mouth;" . . . and so forth.

The complaint by Superintendent Ludwig Hartmann concerning deplorable conditions at divine service in 1668 provides an interesting insight:

I. ". . . . The minstrels go to church as if to an inn, without prayer or book; before service there is a lot of gossip . . . during prayers the one stands here the other there and no one thinks of joining in . . . During the sermon, a number are on the organ, others in other corners, gossiping in pairs. In winter they gather together with others who run out around the coal fire, and one after the other they have their say without considering the sermon . . . After evening service, the minstrels run out to all the inns where they know they will find the drunken violaters of the Sabbath; and there, those who are loth to stay awake for an hour in church spend half or the whole night!
II. As far as the schoolchildren are concerned, during common prayer they run in large numbers to the organ with great din and thereafter hardly 2 or 3 of them sing.
III. Over and above this it is most deplorable that all sorts of people without distinction seek a place on the organ and neither the organist nor others fend them off . . ."

It should not remain unmentioned that in those days the church services lasted considerably longer than nowadays and the daily hour of prayer began in summer three hours, in spring and autumn two hours and in winter one hour before sunrise, and the weekly sermon an hour later, but in all circumstances while it was still night, because as soon as full daylight arrived the working day started.

While the measures taken by the authorities in the sphere of the "public morals police" seem perfectly understandable even today, because they set out remedy abuses and nuisances, the following morals police regulations go far beyond what the responsible citizen would accept at present in the way of government intervention in his private life.

There was a certain connection between the measures against licentiousness dealt with in the foregoing section and the regulations on marriage and child baptism. The perfectly understandable need to celebrate occasionally had become corrupted in the course of time, i.e. extravagance knew no bounds. At marriages and baptisms, people ate and drank excessively and every host attempted to outdo the others. The actual occasion for the festivities, the ceremonial act of marriage or baptism, became a purely subordinate matter. Citizens who had attained prosperity vied with the great to such an extent that they often went far beyond their financial capabilities. It was this that the authorities' countermeasures set out to remedy. Limits were set to extravagance by marriage and baptismal regulations which prescribed precisely with what outlay such family festivities were to be celebrated. One of the reasons for these regulations were the then emerging social tensions between poor and rich. Such luxurious feasts could not be felt to be anything but challenging and a source of hate and envy in times of general want when especially those without property were particularly badly situated. Hence these regulations, which made allowances for the social position of the individual, served the purpose of all police regulations, i.e. as mentioned at the beginning, the preservation of "good order" as had always been customary.

However, when we read what was still allowed by those regulations, those festivities were downright orgies compared to ours in the present day.

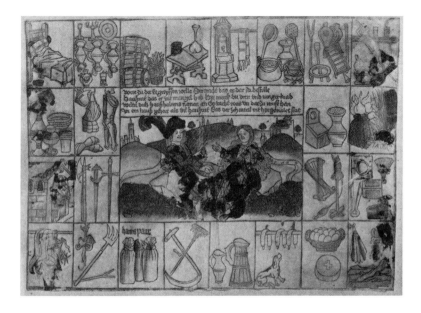

How intemperate people were with food and drink in those days is evident from the following. At the inauguration of a newly elected council, the town gave a "council banquet" in which all the councillors, that is, forty to fifty persons as a rule, took part. The bill for such a council banquet (Town archives, Vol. 361, fol. 193 et seq):

For the forthcoming council banquet the following goods are needed.

	Guilders	Kreutzers
2 calves at 2 Reichstaler each	4	48
3 calves at 1 guilder each	3	
8 geese at 4 Batzen each	2	8
8 young capons at 14 Kreutzers each	1	52
6 old fowls at 10 Kreutzers each	1	
27 young fowls at 4 Kreutzers each	1	48
4 sucking pigs	2	
4 larks and fieldfare	1	12
8 measures of fat	1	36
4 pounds of butter at 5 Kreuzers		20
150 eggs		36
for lemons, limes, capers		36
2 pounds of bacon		36
for spices, gherkins, etc.	1	30
for salt, vinegar and light	1	48
for greenstuff		40
amount	25	30
The cook and servers	2	30

15 guilders for 2 1/2 pails of wine to be paid for in cash, and the taxers will have to be asked that in addition they provide

1 pail of good and 1 pail of poor wine, and also 4 measures of spelt for bread and fine flour.

Further, for the master-builders the fish and for the burgomaster the game and hares.

Note:
1 Rothenburg pail = 71.68 litres
The consumption of 4.5 pails of wine was therefore equivalent to 322.56 litres!
1 guilder = 15 Batzen = 60 Kreutzers
1 Reichstaler = 72 Kreutzers

Let us now turn our attention to the Rothenburg marriage regulations; those of other territories differed in one point or another, but on the whole were very similar.

To enable better understanding of the following, let us briefly explain the frequently used term "estate". In former centuries, the people were divided up into estates, that is, social classes. The "Order and Reformation of Good Policy" promulgated at the imperial diet of Augsburg in 1530 laid down in XI, Art. 1 the classification of town populations in three estates. In big cities like Frankfurt and Nuremberg, but also in Schwäbisch Hall, there were five estates. In accordance with the imperial police code of 1530, Rothenburg had three estates which were here named "Grade" (grades). It proved unnecessary to extend the system to five estates because, due to the influence of the largely aristocratic upper class, there was no middle class. The people lived on the farm produce from the landed property, which had the respectable area of 400 square kilometres and included 167 villages, most of which was owned by the upper class. Wholesale and external trading was suppressed, and even forbidden, by the upper class in the interests of preserving the property relationships. So there were no merchants, and at most general stores in the town. In the villages belonging to Rothenburg there were initially three degrees: 1. Mayors and well-to-do peasants, 2. middling peasants and so-called "Kobler" (cottagers), 3. day-labourers and servants. In 1688, they were reduced to two grades by combining grades two and three.

One was either born into one's estate or grade, or one could climb to a higher one by vocational training and education, e.g. university studies and graduation, or in the case of women by marriage. In this connection it should be noted that there was not only the classification in three degrees, but within each degree there was a further rank system. The latter had to be taken extremely seriously, for there were even court actions on who had to give whom precedence or the chair on what occasions, e.g. funeral and other processions or public ceremonies. All this is best illustrated by the following Rothenburg Ordinance on Precedence dating from 1694.

> In as much as there have for some time been differences between various persons of the first and other grades concerning rank and precedence, a noble and most wise council sees itself constrained to forestall other inconveniences arising in such matters and to issue the following ordinance, which is binding upon all, but in such manner that each person shall be given precedence and chairmanship in accordance with his present rank, but any changes occurring in future shall be observed.

The persons belonging to the first grade shall rank in the following order:

1. The burgomaster in office
2. the four past burgomasters in the order of their election
3. the Superintendent
4. the jurisconsults in rising order with the gentlemen of the inner council up to the superintendent
5. the three inner offices, i.e. tax, building and imperial judge's offices.
6. senators, vesper and hospital preachers in rising order with each other up to the inner offices
7. the doctors of medicine
8. young doctores cuiuscunque facultatis rank after the inner council.

1. The four external offices and 4 deacons of St. Jacob and Rector Gymnasii in rising order according to their date of election.
2. The external burgomasters in the order of their election
3. Monastery and hospital administrators on an equal footing
4. Actuary and archivist
5. Deacons of the hospital and St. Leonhard's
6. The gentlemen of the external council who are from families of rank in this town and demand no office or other similar conditions.
7. Registrar
8. Con-Rector
9. The clergy of rural areas and other office employees, guardianship and hospital clerks, monastery administrators, town lieutenant and master forester in order of their appointment, then
10. following the gentlemen of the external council for literature
11. the two praeceptores tertiae et quartae classis in the order of their status in the ministerium scholasticum and their functions
12. praeceptores quintae, sextae et septimae classis
13. the other gentlemen of the external council except those for literature.

For the third grade – tradesmen, craftmen and council employees – there are regrettably no exact classifications.

The now usual, fairly long period of betrothal was not customary in those times; moreover, a betrothal could only be celebrated for one day and only the closest friends, whose number depended on the social estate of the betrothed couple, could be invited. It was permitted to serve the guests only simple dishes of fish, roast and baked foods. In the 1st estate, 12 persons with 8 courses; in the 2nd estate, 10 persons with 6 courses; and in the 3rd estate, 8 persons with 4 courses, the numbers including the couple and their parents.

The wedding, on the other hand, was a festivity that was celebrated lavishly, in contrast to present custom. The duration of the festivities depended on the approval of the council, the respective estate and whether the times were good or bad.

They lasted two to three days. Once the date of the wedding was set, the invitation went out to the guests. The wedding-summoner had to hand the bridegroom a copy of the valid marriage regulations so that he could familiarize himself with the various provisions. These regulations went so far as to require the bridegroom and the wedding-summoner to appear before the judge after the wedding ". . . to swear an oath" that the regulations had been observed. The number of guests to be invited varied according to the "grade" from 27 to 60 persons, e.g. 1st estate 48, 2nd 40 and 3rd 32 persons. So that the wedding did not cost the newly married couple too much, the guests had to defray part of the expenses. The amount of this contribution to the wedding breakfast was different for men and women. In 1685, the rule was:

> "... considering the present low prices, 10 Batzen per man and 9 Batzen per woman / then in the case of those of low rank, 9 Batzen per man and 7 1/2 Batzen per woman to be laid out to pay the bill."

and in 1705:

> "a man 1 guilder 10 Kreutzers in Rhenish money, a woman at most 1 guilder of Rhenish money".

Any person who had been invited by the wedding-summoner and accepted was obliged to attend, failing which he had to pay half the contribution to avoid inconvenience to the bridal couple and innkeepers. The wedding presents (called "Verehrens") were left to the discretion of the guests, although in this respect, too, it was laid down for a while that gifts should not exceed 2 imperial talers from a married couple, 1 guilder from a single man and 3/4 guilder from a single woman, but this did not apply to very close relatives.

The wedding guests had to appear after the first tolling of the bell to take part in the public church service, for the couple was accompanied on their way from home to the church. Anybody who arrived late had to pay a fine. As a rule, drinks beforehand were forbidden. The time of the wedding was precisely laid down, because immediately afterwards, in summer at 12 a.m. and in winter at 11 a.m., the wedding breakfast was held. Depending on whether times were good or bad, the marriage regulations were modified. For example, the duration of the festivities ranged from one to three days, with many or few dishes. Generally speaking, wedding celebrations were not allowed to last more than two days. When guests had come long distances, a third day was added, probably in consideration of the fact that long journeys were very wearisome in those days and relatives saw each other only very rarely.

For each estate, there were precise rules on what foods could be served to the guests, for example, in the Rothenburg marriage regulations of February 10, 1635, i.e. during the Thirty Years War:

> "... but in these expensive times the costly meals should be reduced and (served to) no more than the closest friends / and only one full table of them / and should be content with the little that God gives us."

As a rule, two meals per day were allowed, which could consist of several courses. Cheese, bread and pancakes could be served additionally and without restriction.

Ordinance of 1721:

1st grade: 1st meal with 8 courses;
            2nd meal beginning at 4 p.m. with 6 courses and choice confectionery.
2nd grade: 1st meal with 6 courses;
            2nd meal beginning at 4 p.m. with 5 courses and a little confectionery.
3rd grade: 1st meal with 4-5 courses;
            2nd meal beginning at 4 p.m. with 3-4 courses and a cake (no confec-
            tionery).

How abundant these meals were can be seen from the following example.
In 1654, in the first and "other" (2nd) grade the following was allowed.

". . . all manner of delicious, choice food (may be) served comprising fowl, game,
tarts, pastries and the like . . . in the lower grade they shall fare perfectly well here-
with / and no more than tame poultry / veal and lamb roast / common fish / baked
foods and the like shall be served."

The first meal was not to last more than three hours, the evening meal was
to begin at 4 p.m. and terminate in summer after four and in winter after
three hours. The wedding-summoner had to indicate and call out the
"expired time". When the time limit was reached, everybody had to rise
immediately. Guests who remained seated after that had to pay a fine of
20 pounds. In nearly all marriage regulations, wedding guests were forbidden to take home any part of what was served for children and the
servants. Even the small presents to be given to bondwomen and children
at weddings were prescribed. In 1685, the rules read:

"that at times shameless men and women / who lay claim to some standing / put
whole roasts in their trousers / or other bags secreted on their persons / at times have
bondwomen and children whom they have called especially for that purpose and
often wait half the day / carry off things in full handkerchiefs / so that they often
have double as much taken home / as they have given or paid in value / which,
especially before strange guests, is very disgraceful and grievous / and causes considerable harm to the innkeepers and wedding hosts; wherefore we solemnly forbid
all such things on pain of a fine of 36 pounds. And to prevent such abuses the
innkeepers shall not allow the bondwomen or children into the rooms / much less
to sit at the tables / but shall give them their presents outside the rooms / and give
them only one glass of wine / a bread roll and 1 kreutzer / on pain of a fine of
10 pounds . . ."

The musicians or minstrels were instructed to "refrain from all unnecessary,
and especially all gross and annoying talking and singing." The number of
minstrels was prescribed, two to four depending on the grade of the
wedding. Observance of the rules on the wedding dance was watched over
distrustfully. There were times when dancing at weddings was completely
forbidden. If dancing was permitted, only the wedding guests could take
part; the object was to avoid the infiltration of uninvited guests. In the case
of the third grade, the wedding dance was permitted only in the dance hall
and a tipstaff had to supervise it so that he could report uninvited guests to
the judge on the following day. An exception was allowed only when a

wedding guest invited an onlooker to dance. But here again, the onlooker had to "withdraw discreetly" immediately after the dance. In accordance with the already described ordinances of the council, dancing had to proceed decorously and was not allowed to go on longer than until 10 p.m. Subsequently, everybody had to return home quietly.

A whole series of marriage regulations imposed restrictions on or entirely prohibited traditional wedding customs such as loosening of hair ribbons, toasting, and shouting, singing and knocking at the house of the newly married couple, which was primarily done by young persons in order to beg wine and bread. The wages for the wedding-summoner, cook, servers and musicians were also laid down precisely. Marriage regulations usually consisted of 15 to 20 sections, each prescribing a fine for contraventions, which was mostly expressed in pounds, the pound being a unit of account, e.g. 5 3/4 pounds = 1 guilder. Under certain circumstances it could be very expensive for the bridal couple and the guests, if one or more regulations were violated out of negligence. The basic object of all marriage regulations was to counteract excesses. Naturally, the bridal couple were at liberty to abstain from all festivities and meals for the sake of economy. The marriage regulations for rural areas were similar to those for the towns, only the permitted outlay was considerably reduced.

Child baptism regulations issued by the autorities were patterned on church regulations to a great extent. For instance, they required baptism as soon as possible after birth. The godfathers of the child had to be "honourable, God-fearing and brave men" who had attended holy communion at least once. Depending on the parents' estate, up to three godfathers were permitted. The reason for this rule was that out of avarice some parents chose more godparents. The father was also required to take part in the christening "in consideration of this sublime act . . . and not to concern himself with other things". The aim of all such regulations was to restrict child baptism to the actual, ceremonial christening and to prevent all incidentals which might detract from or adulterate the significance of the act. In the course of time, of course, concessions had to be made. But as soon as incidental matters were overemphasized, the reins were tightened again. At times, therefore, it was forbidden to serve wine or give meals to guests after the baptism. The custom of sending cake to the homes of near relatives also fell under this ban. The church, in its turn, complained that in consequence "there was no one to help the child by prayer during the christening, apart from the godfathers".

In prosperous times, therefore, a banquet was permitted for which, as in the case of marriages, the number of courses (1st estate 8, 2nd 6 and 3rd 4), the duration of the banquet (at most 5 hours) and the number of guests

(1654: 1st estate 14 persons, 2nd 12 and 3rd 8-10; 1721: 1st estate 30 couples, 2nd 20-25 and 3rd 10-15) were prescribed. The contribution to the cost of the banquet was likewise laid down (1654: 1st estate 5-6 Batzen, 2nd 4-5 and 3rd 4). The so-called "god-parent's money" was limited by the baptismal regulations to a certain, not too high amount (1685: 1st estate 2-3, 2nd 1-2 imperial talers and 3rd 9-13 Batzen; 1721: 1st 4-5, 2nd 3-4 and 3rd 1-2 guilders; see p. 285 for comparative values), as was the value of other christening presents such as shift, dress, bonnet, spoon or shoes. At times they were even completely forbidden. Gifts to the child's mother were also forbidden; at most the nursing mother could be sent an "old fowl" and a quarter of a litre of wine to repair her strength. The midwives were ordered to report contraventions of these regulations and, in particular, illegitimate births to the judge without delay. After the baptism, the child's father had to appear in the judge's office and testify that he had fulfilled his "civic duty", i.e. that he had not violated the baptismal regulations; cf. marriage regulations.

New Year's Gift Regulations

The custom of making gifts to friends and acquaintances at New Year was already widespread in pre-Christian Rome. And Christianity brought this usage to Germany. As at weddings and christenings, everybody tried to outdo their neighbours in the sumptuousness of their gifts to demonstrate their own wealth. Even in ancient Rome, offence had been taken at the fact that Christians participated in the bad habit of making New Year gifts and they were called upon to give alms instead, so how much more annoyance must have been caused by the excessive practice of this custom in times of general economic want. None of the many church admonishments to practice moderation had any effect, so the authorities issued New Year's Gift regulations. Above all during and after the Thirty Years War, it was completely forbidden to give presents at New Year. The regulations called the attention of those who felt they were living in plenty to the possibility of giving alms for the poor relief system. But as it was evidently impossible to do away with the custom of making New Year gifts, later regulations permitted presents, but at least specified their maximum value. In particular, they laid down what godparents were permitted to give their godchildren, e.g. a coin, fruit and pastries. Heavy fines were imposed for contraventions.

Mourning and Funeral Regulations

The last opportunity to satisfy human vanity is the funeral. Funeral ceremonies afforded opportunities to demonstrate one's wealth and often ended with an extremely lively reception for the mourners, the so-called funeral repast or wake. The widespread habit of holding such extravagant funeral celebrations was practically a challenge to the authorities to intervene. These regulations required burial to take place within three days after death. An excessively luxurious coffin was forbidden, for which reason it was laid down what a coffin was allowed to cost (1721: 1st estate 3, 2nd 2 guilders 30 Kreutzers, 3rd 1 guilder 30 Kreutzers to 2 guilders). In some towns even oak coffins were forbidden. It was also prohibited to place exaggerated decorations on the coffin, e.g. crosses, wreaths or costly palls. Maximum amounts for coffin decorations were laid down according to the dead person's estate (1685: 1st estate 3 guilders, 2nd 2.5 and 3rd 2.). People who offered wreaths for sale were permitted to make and offer only 9 variations, 3 for each estate; in 1685:

"for the finest sort 12 Kreutzers, for the medium 9 Kreutzers and for the lowest quality 6 Kreutzers", all other, or especially made wreaths were forbidden on pain of a fine of 40 pounds.

Particularly at funerals, strict distinctions were observed among the estates. Only for the 1st and 2nd estate was a whole procession and singing in front of the house allowed; in the 3rd estate, singing at the house was permitted only for old citizens, but with the restriction – to distinguish them from the finer people – that only one or two verses could be sung. When a baby died, a funeral procession and singing at the grave were not permitted. Persons who had lived on public relief or were themselves responsible for their needy circumstances had to be buried quietly and without singing. In the case of suicides it was decreed that the "desperatus" should be "carried at night by several day-labourers without procession and singing to God's acre and there be buried".

At public burials the bells were tolled. Singing schoolchildren walked in front of the coffin, behind it the close relatives followed by the others. Expressions of sympathy at the grave had to be kept as brief as possible and abstained from entirely in times of pestilence. It was permitted to accompany the mourning family members to their home, but not to enter the house of mourning or attend the funeral repast. Thanks for the accompaniment had to be given outside the house door and could be accepted only by the funeral-summoner. The length of mourning cloaks was exactly specified and varied for the different estates. The wearing of "Leydbinden" (elaborate mourning bands), which cost a great deal of money in those days, was occasionally forbidden. To keep such unnecessary expenditures under control, the town of Rothenburg procured eight sets of mourning clothes, including hats and bands, which were hired out to all for a small fee. The duration of mourning was also specified exactly by the mourning regulations. The object of all these regulations, in the words used in 1685, was to prevent

"this being taken sometimes merely as an opportunity to display external splendour rather than Christian sympathy."

Excerpt from the ordinance of November 3, 1783:

Mourning period	deep mourning:	total mourning:
Spouses	6 months	12 months
Parents for children	6 months	12 months
Parents for children under 1 year		2 months
Grandparents and great grandparents for grandchildren	2 months	2 months
Brothers and sisters		4 months
Parents-in-law for son- or daughter-in-law		3 months
Stepchildren among each other		3 months
Sole heirs		2 months
Legatees		1 month

Spouses mourn the blood relations of their spouse like their own.

Mourning dress:
Deep mourning:
For gentleman of high estate:
"Black cloth or woollen clothes, cloth head-covering, no cuffs, black gloves, black shoe buckles, tarnished or cloth-covered sword or stick, crape-covered hat, woollen stockings and rough shoes."

For women according to their estate:
"Single-piece crape veil hanging down over the face, black crape neckerchief, black crape cuffs, black gloves and rough shoes."

Total mourning:
For men:
"black coat, vest and trousers with spun buttons, cuffs, uncovered hat, stick and sword, and ordinary shoe buckles."

For women:
"Cloth, black-material or woollen dresses, black kerchief, and in the last 3 weeks or 14 days a white kerchief with patterned or other black cotton or striped clothing."

The wearing of mourning crape on hats or as neckerchiefs is permitted only at burials of persons belonging to the council.

Clothing Regulations

In connection with the rules on mourning clothing, the clothing regulations must be mentioned. Clothing was originally only protection against the exigencies of the weather. But its symbolic significance from the standpoint of legal history is as old as clothing itself. Clothing became an integral part of various ceremonies. At coronations, the granting of fiefs or inaugural ceremonies they became the outward sign of the powers conferred. In the event of dethronement or removal from office, they were removed from the person concerned. The memory of such customs is preserved in some of our figures of speech; for instance we speak of vesting a person with authority or divesting him of his rank, especially in official, military and spiritual spheres. The criminal law of the olden days also provided for the wearing of certain clothing as a punishment. Evidence of how closely clothing is still associated with (government) power can be found in Art. 132a of the German Criminal Code. It forbids the unauthorized wearing of uniforms, official robes or specific professional clothing. So the indication of the rank, position and wealth of a person by the type of clothing worn, so that it was visible to one and all, has been customary from time immemorial among all peoples. Over the course of time, clothing has undergone many changes (fashion) in its form, materials and design. This led to exaggerated expenditure and extravagance. The attempts to deceive others as to one's true rank by wearing false clothing are as old as man's desire to wear splendid and beautiful clothes. The old adage that "clothes make the man" was of much greater significance to people of earlier times than it is today. To counteract the deplorable extravagance and deceit, the authorities promulgated the clothing regulations.

While the clothing regulations of the 14th century were still simple and contained predominantly bans on certain items of clothing, later on they became ever more detailed and extensive. Even the imperial diets of 1497, 1498, 1500 and 1530 dealt with clothing regulations. The imperial diet of 1530, in particular, was of great significance for this field, because it resolved the division of urban populations in the empire into the three estates, simultaneously with the clothing regulations. The chief purpose of those regulations was to preserve the distinctions among the estates, that is, "good order".

Nowadays people can wear what they like, their choice of clothing is merely a matter of personal taste, propriety and what they can afford. The clothing regulations of earlier times may therefore seem amusing in many respects. It seems absolutely ridiculous to us that burgomasters and town councils concerned themselves seriously with even the fine details of the cut of clothes, types of material, finery and fur trimmings, and undoubtedly had hot debates on the subject. What rage must those gentlemen have stirred up in women's hearts each time they issued another new clothing regulation. Let us cast a glance back at the clothing regulations of those days: In 1390, Constance prohibited the wearing of bonnets adorned with pearls, precious stones, golden rings and bows costing more than 50 guilders. Incidentally, this regulation clearly demonstrates the goal of combatting extravagance, for 50 guilders was a tremendous sum of money; at that time, one guilder would buy 100 pounds of beef or veal.

The same regulation forbade women to wear any jewelry other than their wedding ring and banned in particular belts and necklaces studded with silver. Neither dresses nor men's and women's coats were allowed to trail on the ground, and more than two colours were forbidden. The sleeves had to be no longer than the arms. In Breslau in 1505, the use of gold brocade, velvet, damask and atlas (silk satin) was forbidden. Berlin allowed costly sable only as trim for the hats of men of quality, damask and atlas silk was permitted only to the doctors. Hildesheim made the wearing of fur-lined garments subject to official permission and the applicant had to prove that he owned no more than two such garments and had no other clothing adorned with pearls.

To ensure observance of such regulations, the craftsmen were forbidden to make clothing which did not comply with the clothing regulations and contraventions were punished. In addition, they were required to report contraventions by members of their guild which came to their knowledge to the council without delay.

Footwear was likewise the subject of regulations. In 1453, Frankfurt on Main decreed: "Coloured shoes and shoes with points are forbidden for journeyman artisans and craftsmen, but they may wear doeskin shoes." Nowadays it is beyond our understanding that in 1468 there was a hot dispute between the journeyman tailors on the one hand and the journey-man bakers and shoemakers on the other as to whether the former were entitled to wear so-called "divided shoes", i.e. one white and one black. What grave deliberation must have been necessary on the part of the authorities to settle this dispute.

The punishments inflicted for contraventions were mostly fines, which were quite high. In Rothenburg, the tipstaffs had to supervise observation of the clothing regulations and to report contraventions to the judge immediately. Some regulations even allowed them to remove forbidden garments from miscreants on the open street. The simplest procedure was adopted by a council which punished men who wore clothing that was too costly and beyond their station by setting them "in consideration of the excess committed, two or three hundred guilders higher in the tax and assessment" (1685). The "masters and mistresses of houses" were ordered not only to conduct themselves in accordance with their estate with respect to clothing, but to admonish their children and, above all, the servants not to wear such "unseemly" clothing. The reason given was that no difference in estate and origin would be apparent and that experience had shown that as a result of the puchase of costly clothing debts were incurred all too quickly, wages were spent and the nest-egg was used up. What did the council in Rothenburg find fault with in particular? The question is best answered by the regulations themselves:

> 1624: "sundry, in part common and in part craftsmen's wives and their servant women not only have round their neck and wear, contrary to their estate, corals and the like, but also appear with unusual collars and with coloured and even silk knitted stockings, costly garters, tripping and peg-heeled shoes and also with shoe cuffs; in particular they wear sumptuous trappings on their heads."
>
> 1659: "Prohibition of all new, strange attire of gold and silver embroidered coifs adorned with tinsel and spangles, whether they be good or false, twining the hair with taffeta ribbons, silver hair pins, hair bows or chignons, tuckers with wide sleeves, much lace and braids, veils with large corners, long, hanging silk flowers and taffeta ties, stockings and skirts of bright colours, and shoes with large, almost one-hand high leather heels; all this to be abstained from completely on pain of a fine of 20 pounds in each case."

Nowadays, the necessity for the authorities to intervene in clothing matters may be controversial, and in those days, too, many people were certainly annoyed at the regimentation. However, the provisions of the clothing regulations which countered fashion trends that were in contradiction to notions of public decency and morals were definitely justified from the standpoint of those times. If the rules on the length of dresses were

Insonderheit hat solch stinkende Hoffart am meisten bei unverheiratheten Leuthen, Bürgerstöchter und Mägden statt, mit Haarkräuseln, Halshembdern, übermäßigen Spitzen, und andern allamodischen Trachten, dadurch ihr Liedlohn verschleudert wird: Als befehlen wir allen Hauß- Vätern und Müttern solch unziemliche Kleider nicht zu gestatten, im widrigen wir sonst durch Unsere Stadt- Knechte ein wachsames Aug auf sie werden haben lassen müssen.

Decretum in Senatu.
Rotenburg A. 1654.

Translation

In particular such stinking arrogance is found mostly among unmarried persons, citizen's daughters and maids, with crimped hair, tuckers, excessive lace and other accommodable finery whereby their wage is dissipated. We therefore order all fathers and mothers not to permit such unseemly clothing and in the event of contraventions we shall have to have our town tipstaffs keep a watchful eye on them.

Decretum in Senatu
Rotenburg, 1654

Von Hoffart in Kleidungen. Weilen der Mißbrauch in Gold, Silber, Perlen, Bändern, Näfteln, Röcken von höchster Farb und dergleichen Sachen, sonderlich bei denen Weibsperſonen, ſoweit überhand nimmt, daß auch die gemeine Handwerksleute, desgleichen die Dienſtboten und Ehehalten, der Hoffart ſich dermaßen ergeben, daß faſt kein Unterſchied des Standes, Würden und Perſonen mehr zu verſpüren iſt; durch ſolch ſchändliches Laſter aber der Allerhöchſte Gott billich zu Zorn, dann zeitlicher und ewiger Straffe gereitzet, auch mancher Menſch in das Verderben ſeiner zeitlichen Nahrung darüber geſetzet wird. Wir wollen Unſeres obrigkeitlichen Ampts halber männiglichen hiervon abgemahnet und ſeinem Stand, Herkommen und Vermögens gemäß ſich zu halten hiermit erinnert haben, mit dem Anhang, daß hinfür auf alle ſolche Übermaß ſcharpfes auff- und einſehen genommen, auch die Stattknechte, da ſie an ein und andrer Perſon, dero es nicht geziemet, dergleichen Hoffart und Pracht ſehen, ſolches anzeigen oder mancher Dirne von dem Kopfe zu reiſſen Macht haben ſollen.

DECRETUM BEI GANTZEM RATH,
FREITAG DEN 18. OCTOBRIS A° 1667

Translation
On Arrogance in Clothing. Whereas the misuse of gold, silver, pearls, ribbons, lace, coats of many colours and other like things, especially by female persons, is becoming so prevalent that even the common artisans and the servants and their spouses are given to arrogance to such a degree that scarcely any difference is perceptible in estate, dignity and person, but by such shameful depravity our Almighty God will be provoked to wrath and punishmend on earth and in eternity and many a person thereby brought to his destruction and the loss of eternal salvation; we, in the exercise of our authority and office, warn all against such practices and remind all to conduct themselves in accordance with their estate, origin and fortune and hereby decree that henceforth strict supervision will be exercised of all such excesses and that the tipstaffs shall be empowered, on seeing such arrogance and splendour on one or another person for whom it is not seemly, to report the same or to tear it from the head of any woman.

Decree of the Senate in Plenary Session
Friday, October 18, 1667

Right: Excerpt from a list of punischments dating from 1750; taken from the book
"Kleiderordnungen in Bayern"
(Clothing Regulations in Bavaria), by V. Bauer.

	Reichstaler
die Weissgerberin allhier ist in einer halbreichen belzhauben einmahl erschinen, 1 fall dan	5
blantzschin Lisel hat einmahl eine Reiche hauben getragen, 1 fall	5
die Marckhtschreiberin allhier welche nur 100 f: besoldung hat ist einmahl in einer sehr reichen mit goldt gestückhten hauben, nebst einer ebenmässig gestickhten schlafrockhfürtel /: so alles über 40 f. geschäzet würdt:/ erschinen, hiemit 1 fall	5
dessen Ehemann der Marckhtschreiber einmahl in einem mit goldenen Knöpfen /: so von faden goldt :/ beseztem Klaid, und goldt bordiertem huett erschinen: 1 fall	5
die Riedelböckhin tochter Rossina einmahl in einer sehr Reichen hauben ersehen worden, hiemit 1 fall	5
die schafler Windtin in einer Reichen hauben einmahl erschinen, 1 fall	5
die Unttertarberin in einer Reichen hauben einmahl erschinen, so dan hiemit 1 fall	5
burgermaisters Lumbergers tochter eine reiche hauben mit Silbernen Spitzen getragen so dan 1 fall	5
allhiesigen Rod: Abdeckhers tochter in einer sehr reichen hauben einmahl erschinen, hiermit 1 fall	5
Theresia Sondermeyerin Weingastgebin allhier in einer reichen hauben einmahl ersehen worden, 1 fall	5
dessen EheMann Johan Achati Sondermayr WeinGastgeb allhier, in einem Klaid mit von faden Silbern Knöpfen 2 mahl erschinen, 2 fall	10

Translation

	Reichstaler
The tawer's wife of this town appeared once in a "semi-rich" fur bonnet, 1 case	5
Liesl Blantzschin wore a rich bonnet once, 1 case	5
The market scribe's wife of this town, whose wage is only 100 f., appeared once in a very rich, gold-embroidered bonnet and a similarly embroidered morning gown girdle, altogether estimated at 40 f., 1 case	5
her husband, the market scribe, appeared once in a dress with golden buttons / of gold threads / and in a hat edged with gold, 1 case	5
the Riedelböckh daughter, Rossina was seen once in a very rich bonnet, 1 case	5
The wife of Windtin, the cooper, appeared once in a rich bonnet, 1 case	5
Untterfarber's wife appeared once in a rich bonnet, 1 case	5
Burgomaster Lumberger's daughter wore a rich bonnet with silver lace, 1 case	5
The local knacker's daughter appeared once in a very rich bonnet, 1 case	5
Theresia Sondermeyer, winehouse keeper of this town, appeared once in a rich bonnet, 1 case	5
her husband, Johan Achati Sondermeyer, winehouse keeper of this town, appeared twice in a dress with buttons of silver threads, 2 cases	10

observed, the ladies began to be more "open-hearted" with their necklines. Many of the chroniclers deprecated this folly of fashion in the powerful, pithy language of their times. Naturally, such clothes aroused the displeasure of the clergy, and the secular authorities hastened to counteract this immoral trend with ordinances. Towards the end of the 15th century, the city of Nuremberg decreed that women should have their dresses "cut no deeper than the breadth of a finger below the little bone at the neck at the front of the collar and at the back a quarter of an ell deeper."

As far as fashion was concerned, the men were on a par with the women. Their hose became more and more close-fitting and "plastic". In those days, the trouser-legs were not sewn together and there was no gusset; hose covered only the legs like long stockings. It is no wonder, therefore, that in Constance in 1390 it was decreed for men that "whosoever goes dancing or on the street clothed only in a doublet shall do so honourably and cover his shame at the rear and in front so that it cannot be seen". When the hose took on its present form and became trousers, a new indecorous habit appeared, the coloured fly-flap adorned with bows and fringes, which emphasized precisely what it was supposed to conceal. After this indecent fashion had disappeared, another came into being. It was morally less offensive, but nevertheless caused annoyance. I refer to the wide, slit breeches so popular in the second half of the 16th century. Especially the lansquenets, who invented them, were extremely immoderate and wore breeches that hung down to their ankles and needed up to forty ells of silk material as backing for the slits. The citizens took up this fashion enthusiastically and the authorities had to intervene with regulations. Threats of punishment had little effect, so more severe action had to be taken. In Berlin, the servants of Elector Joachim II of Brandenburg cut the waistband of the opulent breeches of a noble dandy on the open street. The voluminous garment fell to the ground, leaving the vain fop just in his shirt, the laughing stock of the onlookers. Other towns dressed their executioners in red, wide breeches, so that they lost their attraction for the citizens.

Apparently, all these clothing regulations rarely brought the desired results, as evidenced by the continual repetitions. Perhaps this was also due to the fact that there was no effective way to enforce them and the only penalties imposed for contraventions were fines. To some extent they probably achieved exactly the opposite of what was intended. They standardized for each estate the maximum expenditure for clothing and finery. As a result, everybody felt they were impairing the honour of their estate, if they were dressed more poorly and simply than the regulations allowed. In fact, the extravagant luxury in clothing diminished when the clothing regulations finally disappeared at the close of the 18th century. The clothing regulations that have been preserved can now only be regarded as cultural curiosities. From the standpoint of folklore, however, they are an important source of information for the history of costumes and costume research, for their abundant and precise particulars disclose much about clothing and jewelry of the various social strata of earlier times.

Market and Food Regulations

A large proportion of police regulations dealt with market matters, supplies for the population, trading, and weights and measures. The privileges to hold markets, which were granted by the territorial sovereigns, made a substantial contribution to the emergence of towns. Trade and commerce were the sources of urban prosperity. The authorities' commitment to safeguard and promote that prosperity led to the promulgation of the market regulations.

The most urgent task was to strengthen and protect domestic trade. For all that, the participation of external competitors in economic life was definitely desirable. But for non-residents such participation was rendered difficult by the many regulations and was limited to the few market days. For the duration of their stay in the town, outside merchants had to find bed and board at an inn and were not permitted to live on supplies they had brought with them. Their wagons with merchandise could not be guarded at night by their own servants, but only by persons engaged in the town. Some towns required the goods to be unloaded and placed in the town storehouse. Loading and unloading then had to be carried out by men from the town, and in addition storage fees were levied. To avoid such handicaps and in order to get into business in the town more effectively and, above all, on a permanent basis, outside merchants sought business connections with a citizen, who then sold their merchandise. In consequence, in some towns, e.g. Rothenburg, the practice of "mercantile associations" with non-residents was prohibited.

To ensure an adequate supply of goods and especially food supplies for the population, there was a whole series of ordinances. The export of certain goods, particularly grain and livestock, was forbidden from time to time or made subject to authorization by the authorities. The peasants from the rural areas belonging to the town were compelled to sell their surplus produce exclusively in the town. Sales ex farmyard were prohibited as were sales agreements on the way to market and subsequent delivery direct to the houses (mandatory market). To set up reserves for times of need, from time to time it was required that whenever grain was sold a certain quantity had to be sold at a lower price to the town storehouse or, in the case of exports, that one third of the exported quantity had to be sold cheaper to the storehouse. Another important factor was the forestalling of "cornering" or "advance purchase", i. e. the buying up of the entire supply of a certain sort of merchandise in order to be the sole source (monopoly). To this end, Nuremberg decreed in the 15th century:

"Our gentlemen of the council hereby solemnly order and decree that henceforth no one shall purchase anything of whatever nature in advance either here in the town or within one mile of the town; for whosoever makes advance purchases for one Haller-pound or less shall pay to the town a fine in the amount for which he made such purchases. But whosoever makes purchases in advance for more than one Haller-pound shall forfeit half of such advance purchases whatever the amount may be. And whosoever makes advance purchases more than once within a week and is caught doing so shall pay the aforementioned fine and in addition shall remain five miles from this town for one year . . ."

In the case of "eating things" (food) more severe punishments were inflicted. It was punishable to cause artificial scarcity of goods by holding them back in order to obtain higher prices later on. To safeguard food supplies there were also regulations which required butchers to hold sufficient stocks of meat for sale. The city of Munich's baking regulations of 1536 allowed baking only on four days of the week, but in order to provide the population with adequate supplies of fresh goods at all times the bakers had to work in rotation. The market regulations paid special attention to Jews and pedlars, for owing to the limited possibility of supervision the danger of contraventions was greatest in this group. For this reason, hawking and peddling was greatly restricted and at times completely forbidden.

To guarantee precise control, the entire market had to be held on open areas prescribed by the council, e. g. green, milk, meat, fish, flour, grain, swine, cattle, horse, wood market, etc. The controllers of free trading were on the one hand the town "under-buyers" or agents, who had to keep account of all wholesale transactions concluded and were themselves supervised strictly by the council. And then there was the town "market-master" with his assistants, the inspectors, the surveyors and gaugers. He assigned the dealers their places, set the stand rents, and also had to ensure observance of the maximum-price regulations. To prevent sellers from claiming that they received higher prices in other towns, a notice was put up at the town hall, indicating comparative prices at outside markets. The market-master also had to check the quality of the goods offered, both foods and crafted products, and finally, when everything was in order, to open the market for sales., In Rothenburg, a flag was hung out as the visible sign of the opening of the market. First, the citizens were allowed to cover their private requirements, but only in quantities needed for the household. In the case of fish, for example, the quantity sold to one person was not permitted to exceed four small whitings. Any one who needed more for a family celebration had to get special permission from the judge. Only after the flag had been taken down could the tradesmen buy for their businesses.

The authorities devoted special attention to the quality and condition of foods. The butchers were forbidden to use additives to make their meat look fresher. The fishermen were not allowed to offer living fish and crabs for longer than eight days, and salt fish could be sold only after the inspector had taken samples and branded the barrels with the town coat of arms. The bakers were forbidden to mix "poll" (presumably "pollard", a fine bran) into the dough for rolls and pretzels. Beer brewing was likewise subjected to supervision. Brewers had always needed the authorization of the authorities, probably for fiscal reasons. The brewing regulations – the oldest in Germany are of those Augsburg, dating from 1155 – also prescribed the constituents and the quantities of them. Probably the best-known, and still valid, regulation is the Bavarian purity requirement of 1516, the vital clause of which reads:

"... that nothing more may be taken for brewing than water, barley and hops."

Violations of the purity requirement were often punished with the abrogation of brewing rights. Quality control of wine in Nuremberg was carried out by three sworn inspectors appointed by the council. They themselves collected a jug of wine from every innkeeper. The price asked was written in chalk on the jug and the innkeeper's name on the bottom, so that judgment could be reached objectively. The jugs were placed on a table with chessboard-like markings in a room of the town hall and arranged in the order of the prices. Then the wine was tasted and the best one selected by a majority decision. The price of that wine and the name of the innkeeper who served it were then made known to everybody by means of a public notice. It should be added here that even in those days the adulteration of wine was severly punished.

Orderly trade is possible only if weights and measures are laid down. In the Holy Roman Empire there was a great number of states: principalities, counties, free imperial cities, etc. As an expression of their sovereignty, so to speak, each of those states had its own weights and measures. To ensure uniformity of the measures to be used by dealers at town markets and to enable supervision of them, the customary standard measures of length were often posted on the wall of the town hall and the standard weights were deposited at the council scales. Every seller had to orient himself to these standards and compliance was supervised by the "gauger". When large quantities of goods (e.g. grain) were sold, the council scales had to be used. The use of false measures resulted in relentless punishment.

298

The false weights and measures were smashed or burnt, the goods were confiscated and, in addition, a fine was inflicted. In the case of particularly serious offences, it was possible for expropriation of assets, deprivation of civic rights and expulsion from the town to be decreed. Bakers who sold too small rolls or underweight loaves of bread were sentenced to a fine and the so-called baker's baptism (see Degrading Punishments).

The regulations in the economic sphere which have been dealt with so far had the sole object of ensuring the orderly course of trade and commerce and providing a sound foundation for the livelihood of the citizens. In view of the great variety of problems that communities had to solve even in those days, it was only natural for the authorities to attempt to extract benefit from prospering business life. Levies were introduced, some in kind and some in cash. Apart from the road, highway, bridge or paving tolls dealt with in the section on highway and traffic police, merchants who wanted to bring merchandise into the town had to pay the so-called "principal duty" (import duty) at the district custom houses. These custom houses were situated at the boundary of the town's rural district. In Rothenburg, for example, the principal duty ranged from 1 pfennig for a sheepskin or a measure of flour or 1 head of livestock, increasing with the value of the goods up to 30 kreutzers for a wagonload of armour and arms. The rates for exports were similar: 1 pfennig for a goose or a pound of wax or wool, up to 12 kreutzers for a fattened bacon sow. As a receipt for the duty, a customs token was handed over, which had to be shown at all check points. In periods when food exports were prohibited, goods for which no token from the tax office or corn-master could be shown at the customs check point were confiscated. Merchants who were only passing through the town district had to pay no duty other than the road toll.

There were special provisions for Jews. They had to pay double duty for all goods they had with them and an additional "body toll". The rates were:

1 Jew on foot, not trading	=	2 kreutzers
1 Jew riding, not trading	=	4 kreutzers
1 Jew on foot, trading	=	8 kreutzers
1 Jew riding, trading	=	16 kreutzers

Body duty had to be paid even for the passage of a dead Jew. The rate was extraordinarily high, namely 60 kreutzers = 1 guilder. On reading this section on customs duties it should be remembered that there were numerous states in Germany and each of them levied similar duties. Under certain circumstances it could be an expensive matter for a traveller or merchant. When the authorities considered it necessary, the rates were amended. For example, to increase livestock movements, the tax rate was lowered for precisely specified livestock markets and the pre-emptive rights of local residents were cancelled. On the other hand, on account of the large number of visitors to the privileged annual fairs the tax rates were doubled, taking advantage of the opportunity for higher revenues.

The towns received other revenue from the weighing fees. It was ordered that every sack of grain that went to the mill and every sack of flour that came from the mill had to pass over the town grain and flour scales, and each time, of course, a weighing fee was due. Since in those times the mills were mostly owned by the towns and only leased to the millers, the scales was also a control instrument. The miller's remuneration was the so-called "Mitz" (OE, meed), a portion of the grain to be milled. The compulsory weighing enabled an eye to be kept on the millers, for the amount of the meed was a constant bone of contention between the millers and the authorities. The millers considered it too low and the authorities too high. The millers sought their own advantage in a great variety of ways and often resorted to unfair means. For this reason, on taking over a mill they had to swear a very strictly formulated oath and vow that they would observed the "mill regulations". They were required not to keep ducks, geese and chickens, not to fatten more pigs than needed for their own household, not to mix the "milled goods" of various "mill guests" (customers), not to misappropriate the grist of others, and to give priority to local customers over those from other sovereign territories. But contraventions must have been committed continually because, whether rightly or wrongly, the trade of the miller was considered "dishonest" for a long time. Incidentally, this opinion is also reflected in German fairy tales.

The foregoing description of supervision by the authorities brings us to the "trade police". The town administrations delegated a large proportion of these functions to the guilds. The guilds had attained ever greater importance in the economic constitution of the towns and were vested with certain powers with respect to trade law and the trade police. They exercised supervision over their members through the medium of their own guild court jurisdiction so that the authorities no longer needed to control individual tradesmen and craftsmen, but only the guilds. If they failed to satisfy the authorities' requirements, they were liable to have their guild rights cancelled.

The guilds attached special importance to good craftsmanship of their products. Supervision of craftsmanship was the responsibility of "master inspectors". Every master craftsman had to place his identifying mark on the goods he produced. No one else was allowed to use the same or a similar mark. The marks of all masters were therefore engraved in a lead plate deposited in the town hall of the guild hall. Towns with a particularly good reputation for certain articles demanded that each product made must be submitted to the "Geschworene" (jurors). If it was found to be flawless, it was given the "townmark" as an outward sign of guaranteed quality (e.g. as in silver hallmarks). Contraventions of the rules were punished severely. No one could carry on a craft or trade without the guild's approval. If he did so without approval, he was "put out of business", i.e. the workshop, tools and materials of the "botchers" or "mischief-makers" were destroyed. Ever and again, bans on the use of low-quality materials were issued. But for all the powers of the guilds, where the regulation of wages and working conditions was concerned they had at most an advisory function, for such matters were dealt with by the authorities. Just as maximum prices were laid down for goods, to curb rises in the cost of living, maximum wages were fixed, especially for crafts and trades which supplied only services, e.g. masons, joiners and roofers. If a journeyman left his master without observing the set period of notice, no other master in the town was allowed to employ him. In the event of contraventions, the crafts firm was compulsorily closed for a certain period. If a master enticed away the personnel of another, similar provisions applied. Enticement of servants (male and female) entailed a fine of 6 imperial talers in Rothenburg, and during the harvest season 12 imperial talers. Servants who accepted such offers were even liable to corporal punishment. The earlier regulations provided that in such cases bondmaids had to wear the neck-violin. Bondmaids and bondsmen who left their master's service before termination of the service contract lost their back wages, were put in prison for several days and had to leave the town. Servants had to give notice three months before the end of a service-year, otherwise their service was prolonged for a further year. The authorities called upon the masters to give servants their wages "duly and properly", to feed them adequately and not to overwork them. If they fell ill, the master had to be indulgent, but in the case of prolonged illness he was not expected to retain the sick person, to say nothing of paying full wages.

Credit Regulations

The transition from the barter of the early epoch to buying and selling with the help of money lent the credit system ever increasing importance in the Middle Ages. But as in all spheres of everyday life, there were abuses and excesses in this field, too. Following the teachings of Aristotle, the church forbade the charging of interest in the Middle Ages. The Jews, the chief moneylenders in those times, regarded themselves as non-Christians and therefore not bound by the ecclesiastical ban on interest; hence they were suspected of usury from the outset. For this reason, the imperial police codes of 1530 and 1548 forbade them to grant credit against interest and forbade Christians to enter into credit transactions with Jews. The territorial authorities, who were entitled to increase the severity of imperial enactments, sought to supplement the regulations of the imperial police codes by issuing police regulations to combat abuses in their areas. The main purpose of all of them was to protect potential borrowers from usurious exploitation and the careless assumption of guarantees.

Usury in those days was any interest rate in excess of 5 %. But the interest regulations were often avoided by contracts in which no excessive interest rate was agreed upon, but a lower amount than that named in the contract was paid out to the borrower. In the case of loans secured by standing crops or grapes on the vine, the value was set lower than the harvested crops actually brought in later on. Such contracts were therefore declared null and void. Following the Thirty Years War, such contracts were permitted, but only with the proviso that the agreed value of the product serving as security must be equivalent to the market price or the price that would prevail fourteen days after the harvest. It happened sometimes that a peasant became destitute as the result of a bad harvest and had to borrow the seed for sewing his land. The lender not only provided the seed, but helped with the field work. Instead of interest for the seed and wages for his work, he demanded a substantial portion of the anticipated harvest, so that in the end the peasant (borrower) had less than beforehand. On these grounds, the town of Rothenburg decreed on December 3, 1628:

> ". . . often in cases of need have not only helped out with seed grain for sewing the fields, but have also lent a hand themselves, but not for the customary interest and peasant's wage, but for half of the crop. . . . Such contracts are cancelled and forbidden, evildoers will be appropriately punished."

The lending out of draught or dairy animals against interest was also widespread. In such cases a lease agreement was concluded. The borrower (lessee) had to pay the annual lease in money or produce. It was considered usury, if a peasant had to pay 14 to 17 guilders per year for a pair of borrowed oxen. Consequently a maximum interest (lease) rate of 10 guilders per year was fixed for a pair of oxen. If the animals died during the term of the lease in the lessee's possession, he was liable to replace them only if "neglect and guilt" could be proved and then only the "reasonable damages for which he is liable according to an honest and upright assessment". If he was not responsible, he need assume no liability.

Contracts of a general nature did not have to be in writing and the manner of concluding them was left to everybody's discretion. In contrast, a written record was mandatory for all credit and loan, purchase and marriage agreements. Such agreements had to be taken down in the "chancellery" and entered in the "Town Register" by the sworn scribe in the presence of two official witnesses, who were mostly councillors. If the distance to the town was too great, such an agreement could also be concluded before the local mayor and two members of the community. The amount of credit and loan contracts in rural areas was limited. In 1723, Rothenburg set the maximum amount at 50 guilders. Where higher amounts were involved, certification by the town court was obligatory. No sales, credit or barter agreements were allowed to be concluded on Sundays and holy days.

Credit and loan transactions were also restricted. Lending to soldiers, officers and students was forbidden. Above all, innkeepers who ignored the ban lost what they lent, other creditors were denied the help of the courts and had to depend on the debtors' good will to honour their claims. To satisfy the need for loans, the towns acted as lenders. From the often very considerable assets of endowments, money was lent out against appropriate security (e.g. houses, mortgages). The interest on the borrowed capital proved a good return on the endowment assets. On the publicly announced "debt days", the debtors had to appear at the town hall and pay the "swollen" (accrued) interest in cash. In the event of default, tower punishments (debtor's prison) and other coercive means could be applied.

In the 15th century, the first public pawnshops appeared, the first in Frankfurt on Main in 1402. Anybody could deposit a "thing of value" there for a specified, agreed time. The pawned objects were valued by a sworn valuer and the estimated value was paid out to the borrower. The interest rate was 5%. If a pawner did not pay his 6- or 12-monthly interest in due time, or if he failed to redeem his pledge at the end of the agreed period, it was sold within a specified period. Any surplus from the sale was paid to the former owner.

Conclusion

The object of this essay was to give the reader an illustrative insight into the ways of life and opportunities open to people in former centuries so that he can draw comparisons with the present day. In conclusion it should be added that town legislation in former times was not the result of deliberate planning, but rather the product of the interplay of living forces within the community, i.e. within the town. The great variety of problems that occurred in communal life resulted in legislation adapted to the given requirements, the vital cornerstone of which comprised the town peace regulations mentioned in the section on "public order police". Those peace codes and the regulations adapted to local conditions and special cases, called police regulations, give a very clear picture of legal, social, economic and cultural conditions in former centuries. They can be fully understood only against the background of those times.

The coffee smeller
Kassel ordinance against the "all too prevalent drinking of coffee", 1766.

Prohibition of smoking
King Frederick William II of Prussia
prohibited tobacco smoking on the street.

In the "Trülle", a rotating pillory.

The Rosary
a church pillory punishment.

Legal Symbolism

Many of our everyday, colloquial expressions harbour memories of the customs of our forefathers. But their full import can be appreciated, only if we know their origin. This is especially true of sayings based on old German legal symbols. Old German law was closely linked with symbolism, but in many respects went far beyond what is generally understood by true symbolism and extended it by numerous emblems and imaginative customs. Their derivation from the realm of religion is unmistakeable and many a legal symbol had its origin in a fetish that banished baneful evil. The conjecture that legal symbolism was deliberately originated by priests is dubious, for the Germanic peoples knew no integral class of priests and any formalism introduced by them could never have induced any strong convictions on the part of the people. Even Jakob Grimm considered it unsatisfactory to regard the symbols merely as empty inventions for judicial forms: "On the contrary, each of them undoubtedly has its dark, holy and historical significance; if that were not so, general belief in it and its traditional comprehensibility would be lacking."

Some symbols, though already known to the Greeks and Romans, developed independently also in the territories of the Germanic peoples; others were taken over in later times through contact with Christianity or were integrated into Christian customs; and others again were forgotten in the train of christianization.

The following compilation of old German legal symbols lays no claim to being complete and is intended merely to give some slight insight into this vast subject. A comprehensive treatment is far beyond the scope of this essay. Since accurate determination of the beginning and duration of their use is possible only in a very few cases, and some symbols were used simultaneously side by side or in different ways by various tribes, no attempt has been made to list them chronologically or in the order of their importance; instead, they are presented in alphabetical order. This will make it easier for the reader to find the various symbols.

Banner

The banner differs in appearance from the flag in that its upper edge is attached to a cross-bar hanging from the staff. The name, derived from the French "banuiere", did not make its appearance until the 14th century under Charles IV, but the banner itself is considerably older; it was the flag of the two Frankish regions. The banner was the insignia of regal rights. Originally, only the territorial sovereign was entitled to fly a banner and thus call up his followers for a military campaign. A red banner was the symbol of "blood justice" and was raised at the site of the court and of execution. When the feudal system was introduced, the right to fly a banner was granted by the king to his major vassals (banner fief), who thus received the higher rank of a banneret in contrast to lower vassals who were only entitled to a flag (flag fief).

Belt/Girdle

The belt signified power and mastery, and in its everyday function served to hold the underclothing together. A man who loosened his belt was left standing in his shirt. This explains its symbolic import in legal acts. A banished person had to remove his shoes and belt and leave house and farm barefooted and in his shirt. As a sign of submission, the defeated had to take off and surrender their belts, i.e. appear in humble dress. When a criminal was delivered up to the court, his belt was taken from him. The great respect for the domestic peace required those conducting a house search to remove their belt and enter in their shirts. A symbol of especially high importance was the bride's girdle; with its removal on the wedding day, the man took full possession of the bride. The girdle with attached bunch of keys was the symbol of the authority of the mistress of the house; if taken from a woman, e.g. on divorce, it signified the surrender of all rights. A widow could discharge herself of her husband's debts by laying her girdle on the bier or grave of her husband (see Cloak).

Blood

The wish of two men who were not related to each other for a close bond between them gave rise to the custom of blood-brotherhood. Blood-brotherhood was the basis of the men's fellowships of antiquity, which were sealed with an oath of loyalty and were already known to the Greeks and Romans. The commitments arising from blood-brotherhood often surpassed the obligations to the family. Blood-brotherhood was always entered into with great ceremony. The two men stepped into a previously dug hollow in the ground, cut or stabbed the palm of the hand or the sole of the foot, and let their blood drip on to the ground so that it mixed. Invoking the gods, they swore to observe the assumed obligations and then stepped out of the hollow together, symbolically emerging newly born as twin brothers from the womb of the earth. In some of the Germanic tribes, oaths were still emphasized with blood at a very late date.

Cloak/Mantle

The cloak is a very old and widespread legal symbol. All custom and usage involving the cloak or mantle conformed to the original purpose of the garment: the attainment and granting of protection and safety.

Pursued or fugitive persons who fled beneath the cloak of a high-ranking person, especially high-born ladies, or touched their cloaks were safe from pursuit or were pardoned. The cloak also played a part in the adoption or legitimation of premarital children. Out of a desire to protect illegitimate children from the disadvantages of a weak legal status, legitimation during the wedding ceremony was customary in Germany from the 13th century onwards. The premarital children took cover under the mother's cloak (see also Veil), and when they emerged from beneath it, this was considered a symbolic new birth as "genuine" children of the now married mother ("cloak children").

The symbolic protective effect of the cloak is also illustrated by the following examples, although they involve the laying aside of the cloak. If a widow placed her cloak on her husband's grave, she was exempted from payment of the debts left by her husband, so her cloak protected her from prosecution by the creditiors. Under Saxon law, judges and assessors were not permitted to wear hats, cloaks or gloves. This uncovered state was intended to demonstrate openness and honesty and thus protect those seeking their rights or defendants from any machinations of the court which might be to their disadvantage.

Cross

The symbol of sovereign and judicial power. A cross set up on the market place with a glove hanging from it represented the person of the king and symbolized the market peace he had ordained. The cross also served as a sign of judicial execution, i.e. it was attached by the plaintiff or a court official to the house or chattel of a condemned debtor as a public notification of distraint.

In the form of a cross of atonement it is also a legal symbol. A person guilty of homicide could agree with the victim's family that, in order to avoid a blood feud and vengeance, he would set up a cross of atonement in addition to assuming other obligations. Isolated specimens of such crosses are still to be found throughout Germany at the site of the crimes, e.g. at the edge of paths or fields. In some cases there are historical records which name the crime, the victim and the criminal. These crosses should not be confused with wayside memorials and shrines.

Fire
Fire was the symbol of purity as demonstrated by the various forms of divine judgment. From time immemorial, fire was considered especially sacred. The lighting and keeping of a fire on a piece of land symbolized the taking of legal possession, a custom that has persisted right up to modern times; on the transfer of a farming estate, the fire on the hearth was extinguished by the previous owner and relighted by the new one. In Friesland, beacon fires were lighted as a signal to assemble and a call to arms when war threatened or rebellion.

Flag
The flag as a legal symbol signifies a variety of things and it has retained its symbolic import right up to the present. First and foremost, it is the symbol of sovereignty. A vassal carried the flag in front of the king. As the insignia of court authority it is likewise a symbol of sovereignty, though it shares this status with the cross, straw whisk, hat and glove. The significance of the flag as the symbol of enfeoffment (flag fief) is also important. The king was handed a flag by the feoffee as a sign of loyalty and the king subsequently gave it back as a symbol of the granting of the fief. This type of enfeoffment was customary up to well into the 15th century. The market flag is the symbol of the market "peace".

Glove
The glove had special significance as a legal symbol. It represented the power-wielding, protecting hand and was thus a personal symbol, the symbol of royal authority. A glove sent by the king was a token of market rights and the market peace. The handing over of the glove signified the delegation of authority to a subordinate. With the glove fiefs were granted and emissaries accredited. It was handed to couriers to identify them and to be passed on to the recipient of the message. Placed on the altar, the glove was a token of symbolic investiture. It signified the granting of protection when it was handed by a subordinate to his lord and the latter accepted it. Thrown before the feet of an enemy it was the renunciation of peace and friendship and a challenge to battle, it was an alternative to the slap on the cheek that was forbidden by the knights' code of honour. The nature of the glove as a symbol of power also explains its significance for the vestments of the princes temporal and spiritual, who always had to wear gloves on ceremonial occasions (see illus. p. 113).

Green Twig
A symbol used when transferring landed property. The previous owner handed the new one a green twig, vesting him with the property rights and making the cession of ownership legally effective.

Hair

A very old legal symbol. The fact that the hair continues to grow for a while after death is probably the reason for the belief that the hair was the seat of magical forces. The symbolic significance of the hair for people of earlier times was probably also derived from this mythical notion. For instance, the growth of the hair and beard was a sign of manhood, i.e. fitness for military service. Hair and beard styles were also marks of one's tribe and estate. Among the Germanic peoples, long hair was the sign of the freemen. Later it was the mark of the nobility and finally of the king. For free girls, long open hair was the sign of their free and unmarried status. A married woman had to bind her hair or wear it under a coif. Bondsmen and the unfree wore short hair.

Friesian men swore an oath by making a symbolic gesture with the right hand, e.g. placing it on a sword, while the left hand touched the hair. Under Bavarian and Swabian law, women swearing an oath had to place the fingers of the right hand on the plait of hair hanging down over their breast. Among the Germanic peoples, the first haircut was linked with the investment with arms. Later on, the cutting of the hair and beard by non-members of the family was the sign of adoption.

The cutting off and handing over of hair was a token of submission. The hair of captured enemies was cut off. The tonsure of monks is likewise a sign of submission to the rules of the order and is attributable to old ritual usage.

Cutting off the hair of the head is an old punishment. Adulteresses had their hair cut off; this punishment has persisted in mob justice right up to the present day. The cutting of men's hair as a punishment was a sign of imposed bondage, for with the hair the badge of the freeman was lost. Even the Sachsenspiegel mentions punishment "to hide and hair", i.e. degrading cutting of the hair coupled with flogging.

Hat

The hat was not merely an article of clothing, but a legal symbol of greatly varying significance. Even among the Romans, it was a mark of freedom and, following that example, in the Middle Ages only the free were allowed to wear a hat; the unfree had to make do with a cap. Removal of the hat indicated submission, and keeping it on was an expression of ruling authority, i.e. it was a symbol of power. Examples are the judge's hat (e.g. in GB the "black cap") still worn on special occasions, such as taking oaths or pronouncing judgment, and the wigs worn by judges, officials, etc. in Great Britain.

As a personal symbol the hat (glove) could represent its owner. When the sovereign donned it, he summoned the people to arms or to the court. The ruler's hat was paid the same respect as the ruler himself (Gessler's hat).

As a personal symbol the hat could be flung into the court or the church to protest against a judgment or marriage banns. By throwing his hat into a place of asylum, a fugitive obtained right of asylum.

When granting fiefs or goods, the hat was also a personal symbol. The donor, liegelord or seller always held a hat into which the donee, vassal or buyer placed his hand or threw a haulm or splinter.

Haulm

The haulm, or stalk, is one of the very oldest legal symbols. It was used chiefly in conveying land by way of donation, sale or pledging. The former owner gave the new one a haulm. And even later, when deeds were drawn up for such legal transactions, the haulm retained its significance as a legal symbol. This is evident from preserved documents which regularly conclude with formulations such as ". . . with haulm and mouth" or "with hand and haulm".

Lily

The lily was the sign of the (legal) peace. In the illuminated manuscripts of the Sachsenspiegel, the king's peace is presented most clearly in the shape of a large yellow lily painted beside the figure of the king (see illus. p. 67 and 68). Broken peace is symbolized by a broken lily.

Rose

The rose was the symbol for the discretion of the court. It has come down to us through the illuminated manuscripts of the old laws, e.g. Sachsenspiegel.

Sceptre

The sceptre, the symbol of the ruler's power, was developed from the staff. Like the crown, sword and imperial apple, it was one of the royal insignia (see Staff).

Spear

According to old sources, the spear was the mark of the man or his tribe. For this reason it was used in the legitimation of an illegitimate son. Like the staff or the flag, the spear was a symbol for the transfer of empire and land by the king to his successor or conqueror (Gunthram to Childebert). Also at investitutres, the king handed a spear to the person appointed to office. As a sign of the declaration of war, the enemy was sent a spear that had been dipped in animal's blood. When war was imminent in Scandinavia, the people were called to arms by sending round a charred stick (symbolical spear).

310

Staff

One of the oldest Germanic legal symbols is the staff. Its simplest form is a stick from a hazel bush. It was ascribed magical defensive powers. Since, according to popular superstition, dangerous spirits could find refuge between the bark and the wood, reverse its powers and bring misfortune to the bearer, the bark had to be removed from the staff. Many knobs and knots enhanced its magical power. As a legal symbol it had a great variety of uses. It was carried to market as an identification mark by servant men and women looking for work. As soon as they had found a new master, they broke the staff. When a debtor was expelled from his home and farm, he had to carry a (beggar's) staff in his hand. If a banished person was allowed out of mercy to remain in the town, he could show himself in public only with a white beggar's staff. A person who capitulated had to go to his conqueror with a white staff as a sign of his surrender. Rebels against the government had to swear to carry the white staff all their life.

The staff had much greater importance as a symbol of power. With the staff, the ruler transferred part of his power. A courier received the courier's staff, a symbolic gesture committing him to carry out his mission. Investiture in office was accompanied by the handing over of the staff of office, which had to be carried by high officials or judges when performing their duties. On withdrawal from office or death, the staff of office had to be returned or broken. The ruler himself used the staff as a sign of power. In the course of time, however, the material of the ruler's staff became ever more costly and its form changed; it became a sceptre, the ornaments of which represented the knobs and knots of wood.

The poses and gestures associated with the staff were as numerous and varied as their significance. The handing over of the staff expressed the transfer of power or property; laying it down, returning it, throwing it away or breaking it meant renunciation of power, office or property.

The judge carried the staff as the symbol of court authority; he had to hold it in his hand as long as he was performing his official duties. By knocking with it he called for order, when he laid the staff aside the court session was adjourned or terminated. Often, the judge's staff had to be touched when swearing an oath.

Lastly, the breaking of the staff by the judge should be mentioned, a symbolic custom practiced in German court proceedings from the 15th century onwards. After pronouncing judgment, the judge broke a staff over the head of a condemned person and threw the pieces before his feet with the words: "Now may God help you, for I cannot help you further"; this bears some similarity to the "expulsion from the family by breaking the staff", wich was customary under the law of the Salian Franks (see also pp. 217–218).

Stirrup-holding

A sign of respect. The man of lower rank helps the higher-ranking person to mount a horse by holding the stirrup. The illuminated manuscript of the Sachsenspiegel shows the emperor holding the pope's stirrup, illustrating that divine power is superior to earthly power (see illus. p. 115).

Stool

A visible sign of the taking of possession of land. The new owner sat on a stool or chair on the acquired land to show that he "besitzt" (OE, besits) or owns it. If a person (insolvent debtor) lost the right to besit his house or land, his "stool was set before the door", i.e. he was turned out.

Straw Whisk

The straw whisk, a bundle of straw fastened to a stick, was originally not a legal symbol, but an instrument of magical power for banishing evil spirits, which also explains its use as a boundary and barring sign for plots of land. But as far back as the early Middle Ages, it was transformed into a legal symbol. For example, it was placed on the house of an insolvent owner when the court decreed its compulsory sale. It was also used as an emblem of the market peace (see Cross, Glove, Flag) or as a sign that goods were on sale (e.g. the "brush", "whisk" or "nosegay" shops in which wine-growers were permitted to sell their own wines, usually only for 3 months in each year).

Sword

The sword always was and still is a symbol of power. In olden times, on special occasions and when held in certain poses, it demonstrated power over life and death. Above all, it was the symbol of court authority. When swearing oaths, the left hand touched the blade or, frequently with the point in the ground, the hilt of the sword. The sending of a sword was an order for execution, its acceptance acknowledgement ot the order.
Great importance attached to the sword in the granting of fiefs. With the handing over of the sword by the king and the acceptance by the feoffee, the latter became the king's vassal.
A defeated man who surrendered unconditionally took off his sword, held it by the tip and extended the hilt to the victor.
At marriage ceremonies, too, the sword was used as a symbol. When taking their bride home, the Friesians carried the sword out in front as a sign that she was henceforth under the husband's control and he had power over her life. For under Friesian law, a woman who could not clear herself of a charge of adultery could be beaten by her husband or beheaded with a sword.
It is also an old custom that a man who slept in the same bed as a woman, but had no intention of touching her, placed a naked sword between himself

and the woman. Numerous sagas confirm this custom (Tristan and Isolde) although there are neither laws nor documents to prove it. In the case of marriage by proxy, a vassal of the king symbolically performed the rite of cohabitation, the act which effectively established a marriage, by placing a sword between himself and the bride.

Thread

The thread was used to mark off the site of the court, i.e. as the symbolic delimitation of the consecrated area. Hazel sticks (see Staff) were planted in the ground and then connected with thin yarn or silk threads. These threads were often dyed red, for among the Germanic peoples red was the colour of law and right; moreover, red thread was believed to have magical power to ward off impure spirits. Much later, the thread enclosure was replaced by solid court bounds. Plots of ground were likewise surrounded by threads which marked the bounds. Thread was also used for the symbolic binding or locking up of prisoners. The door of the room in which the prisoners were kept remained open and could even be closed by them from inside, but a thread was stretched across the doorway. When prisoners were transferred, they were "fettered" with thread. The prisoner was taken to the border and if the bailiff of the receiving court was not there, the prisoner was tied with thread to the boundary stone. Naturally, this was not a reliable safeguard, but for the most part it served its purpose, because the thread harboured a symbolic power that was familiar to all and, in addition, loosening the thread and taking flight made the prisoner liable to severe punishment.

Veil

The veil as a symbol of marriage has not come down from Germanic antiquity, but is one of the customs of church weddings taken over from the Latin southern regions. In Hesse in the Middle Ages, the bridegroom placed his hat and the bride her veil one above the other on the altar during the church wedding to demonstrate that their property belonged to the two jointly and that the community property was to pass entirely and undivided to the survivor on the death of one of the spouses, provided there were no children. The veil or a cloth spread over the bridal couple at the wedding signified premarital children, and if the children stepped beneath it this meant their legitimation.

Water

Water was a symbol of purity as demonstrated by the trial by water, a divine judgment. Springs were considered the refuge of the souls of the dead. The site of the court was often chosen in the vicinity of holy waters, possibly in order to draw the judgment from the water in accordance with some long-forgotten cult rite. The name "Schöffe" or "Schöpfe" (water-drawer) given to the assessors of the court may also be derived from the same source. When oaths were taken, the swearer was wet with water from a holy spring to emphasize the sacredness of the oath and admonish him to speak the truth.

The large council scales

Market
The market master inspects a barrel of salt fish and has it branded with the town coat of arms; the inspectors and gaugers supervise market trading.

Index

317

Glossary

Bambergensis, constitutio criminalis Bambergensis or Bamberg Halsgerichtsordnung; code of criminal law and procedure authored in 1507 by Johann Baron Schwarzenberg and put into force in the bishopric of Bamberg in 1516. It was used as a model for the Carolina.

Barbarossa (Redbeard), 1123 - 1190, Holy Roman Emperor Frederick I, elected March 1, 1152. His reign was marked by revolts and uprisings which he suppressed, bringing order to Germany. He did much to encourage the growth of towns.

capitularies. Legislative and administrative acts of the Merovingian and Carolingian kings, subdivided into chapters (capitula) according to their subject matter. There are no original capitularies extant. Copies were found in a variety of old manuscripts and several collections were made. See p. 8 - 10.

Carolina, the constitutio criminalis Carolina (CCC). The first authoritative criminal code promulgated for the whole of Germany under Charles V in 1532. In contrast to earlier codifications, it was written in German. It incorporated elements of Roman-Italian and old German law and remained in force in some areas until the 19th century. See Bambergensis.

CCC, see Carolina.

centgrave (Germ. Zentgraf). The centgrave, or count of a hundred, was apparently administrative head of a district embracing roughly 100 hamlets and president of the Zentgericht (hundred court), which had jurisdiction over minor offences and in some cases also tried capital crimes.

Charles the Great, Charlemagne (ca. 742 - 814), king of the Franks and from 768 onwards Holy Roman Emperor. He revised the laws of the Salian and Ripurian Franks, and had those of the Saxons, Thuringians and Frisians codified. The capitularies which he promulgated are an excellent source of information and Frankish institutions.

Childebert II (570 - 595) became king of Austrasia after the assassination of his father in 575. His aim to become the king of the Franks was frustrated by his early death.

Clovis (Chlodovech), 466 - 511, king of the Salian Franks by hereditary right and founder of the Frankish monarchy. He was also ruler of other Frankish tribes and of the Gallo-Roman. He had the Lex Salica drawn up, probably between 486 and 507.

c o d i f i c a t i o n   o f   l a w. The early law of the Germanic peoples was unwritten, customary law that was handed down by word of mouth. After the foundation of kingdoms, it became essential to establish written, codified law to ensure more uniformity and greater certainty of the law. The earliest codifications were undertaken at the turn of the 5th and 6th centuries, e. g. the Lex Salica. These leges germanorum were predominantly codifications of criminal law and procedure, comprising partly existing customary law and partly new statutes.

c o n s t i t u t i o   c r i m i n a l i s   B a m b e r g e n s i s, see Bambergensis.

c o n s t i t u t i o   c r i m i n a l i s   C a r o l i n a, see Carolina.

F e h d e. Feud, private warfare between families, clans or tribes.

F e u e r b a c h, Paul Johann Anselm v., (1755 - 1833), German jurist and author of many legal publications. In 1805 he drafted a penal code for Bavaria where, under his influence, torture was abolished in 1806. He is considered an important forerunner of modern comparative law.

f l o r i n. An old gold coin known in German as "Gulden", which had its origin in Florence, Italy. Owing to the good repute of the Florentine florin, similar coins were struck in Germany and other parts of Europe.

H a l s g e r i c h t s o r d n u n g. The name given to codes of criminal law and procedure in Germany in the 15th and 16th century. Such codes were applied by the "Halsgerichte", the superior criminal courts in which capital crimes were tried. See Bambergensis.

h u n d r e d. The German "Zent" or hundred is not precisely definable, but is evidently analgous to the old English hundred, i. e. an administrative district having its own court.

I m p e r i a l   C h a m b e r (Reichskammergericht). The supreme court of the Holy Roman Empire from 1495 - 1806. It was the first court based on an enactment of the imperial diet rather than on the emperor's personal will. Among other things, it dealt with breaches of the public peace, treasury matters, violations of imperial decrees and enactments, and was the court of appeal from many territorial courts.

k i n g' s   p e a c e, see peace.

L a n d r e c h t. The general mediaeval law common to all persons as distinct from the bodies of special law (realms of law). e. g. for towns, royal courts, feudal system. It was purely territorial law, i. e. applicable to all persons within a given territory. The term was later also applied to legal codes such as those of Bavaria and Prussia, the forerunners of the later German Civil Code.

L e x   B a i u v a r i o r u m. The law of the Bavarians, which was compiled probably between 740 and 748, a period of strong Frankish influence in Bavaria. It was derived from the Lex Salica and the law of the Visigoths and Alemanni. For Excerpt see p. 48 - 50.

Lex Ripuaria. The law of the riparian Franks, which was codified in the 7th century. It was based on the Lex Salica and Burgundian folk-law.

Lex Salica, the Salic Law, i.e. the law of the Salian Franks. This Germanic law is a compilation of chapters formulated at different periods. It was primarily a penal code, but included some civil law enactments. See Clovis.

Luther, Martin (1483 - 1546). German religious reformer and founder of the Lutheran (evangelical) church. In consequence of his opposition to the Roman Catholic Church, he was excommunicated in 1521 and subsequently outlawed by the temporal authorities. In 1521 - 22, he translated the Greek New Testament into German.

Munt. Anglo-Saxon: mund, Latin: manus. The sphere of authority of the (male) head of a household, especially a husband's control over his wife.

Nuremberg Reformation, 1479. The oldest, printed code of townlaw. It systematically combined domestic and Roman-Italian, civil and procedural law, and was taken (often by royal command) as the basis for many other town codes.

peace. A state of order and security free from disturbance and, by extension, the sphere of domain in which the security of persons was protected, e.g. the peace of a household or the king's peace, the sovereign domain under the protection of the king.

perpetual peace. A constitutional code for the Holy Roman Empire promulgated by the diet in Worms under Emperor Maximilian I in 1495 to ensure peace and order within the empire, among other things by prohibiting feuds.

pfennig. The basic Frankish currency unit introduced by Charles the Great (see Table p. 52), which was also widely used in other Germanic areas under the name "denar". The pfennig, half-pfennig and quarter-pfennig were practically the sole coins minted between 750 and 1300 in most European countries.

proscription. Exclusion from the community and loss of protection of the law. Proscribed persons were outlaws and could be killed with impunity. See p. 18.

Rachinburgen. Under old Frankish law, the officers of the count's court who enforced judgments and also served as judgment-finders from the 6th century onwards.

Reichskammergericht see Imperial Chamber

Roman Digest. To remedy the confusion in the law of the Roman empire, emperor Justinian I had excerpts made from the writings of classical jurists and arranged by subject matter. The 50 books of the Digest were published and came into force as law in 533.

Sachsenspiegel. The most important and authoritative of the mediaeval "law books", authored by Eike von Repgau between 1220 and 1235. It is a compilation of the customary law of the Saxons, which soon attained statue-like authority even beyond the frontiers of the empire. It was used as a basis for a number of local and regional legal codes and was the model for the Schwabenspiegel.

Schwabenspiegel. The Swabian counterpart of the Sachsenspiegel; a compilation of Swabian tribal law authored in 1275 by an unknown priest.

Sendgericht. A synodal, or episcopal, court to investigate and punish offences committed by the clergy and laymen against the prescribed Christian way of life. Such courts were first set up in Germany in the 9th century, the last of them were abolished in the 19th century.

Thomasius, Christian (1665 - 1728), jurist and philosopher, one of the founders of German journalism and a leading figure in the German Enlightement, co-founder of the university of Halle.

Ungelt, or Umgeld. The oldest European indirect tax. A form of turnover tax levied on bulk goods (e. g. grain, wine) in German towns in the 13th century.

Volksgericht. Folk-courts or people's courts in which the law was administered by the people as opposed to the king's courts in which the sovereign or his representative meted out justice.

wergeld. In Germanic and old English law, the "man-price" or compensation paid in cases of homicide to save the offender from vengeance at the hands of the victim's family.

Willküren. Prior to promulgation of city laws, occasional enactments were collected in "Willkürbücher" (statute books). These Willküren, or statutes, formed the basis for the later, codified laws.